Suzanne Scanlon

COMMITTED

Suzanne Scanlon is the author of two works of fiction, *Promising Young Women* and *Her 37th Year, An Index*. Her writing has appeared in *Granta*, *BOMB Magazine*, *The Iowa Review*, and the *Los Angeles Review of Books*, among other publications. She has taught creative writing at many colleges and universities, most recently the School of the Art Institute of Chicago and Northwestern University, where she is an artist-in-residence.

COMMITTED

COMMITTED

On Meaning and Madwomen

Suzanne Scanlon

VINTAGE BOOKS

A DIVISION OF PENGUIN RANDOM HOUSE LLC

NEW YORK

A portion of this work originally appeared in *Granta*.

Grateful acknowledgment is made to the following for permission to reprint
previously published material: Jane Kenyon, excerpt from "Pardon" from
"Having It Out with Melancholy" from *Collected Poems*. Copyright © 2005 by
The Estate of Jane Kenyon. Reprinted with the permission of The Permissions
Company, LLC, on behalf of Graywolf Press, graywolfpress.org. "From the
House of Yemanja," from *The Collected Poems of Audre Lorde* by Audre Lorde.
Copyright © 1997 by The Audre Lorde Estate. Used by permission of
W. W. Norton & Company, Inc.

Library of Congress Cataloging-in-Publication Data
Names: Scanlon, Suzanne, author.
Title: Committed : on meaning and madwomen / Suzanne Scanlon.
Identifiers: LCCN 2023028089 (print) | LCCN 2023028090 (ebook) |
ISBN 9780593469101 (trade paperback) | ISBN 9780593469118 (ebook)
Subjects: LCSH: Women—Mental health. | Involuntary treatment—
Social aspects. | Mentally ill—Commitment and detention. |
Psychiatric hospitals—Sociological aspects. | Psychiatric hospital patients—
Social conditions. | Mentally ill women—Social conditions.
Classification: LCC RC451.4.W6 S33 2024 (print) |
LCC RC451.4.W6 (ebook) | DDC 616.890082—dc23/eng/20231114
LC record available at https://lccn.loc.gov/2023028089
LC ebook record available at https://lccn.loc.gov/2023028090

Vintage Books Trade Paperback ISBN: 9780593469101
eBook ISBN: 9780593469118

Book design by Nicholas Alguire

vintagebooks.com

Printed in the United States of America
1st Printing

For those who were there

Without something to belong to, we have no stable self, and yet total commitment and attachment to any social unit implies a kind of selflessness. Our sense of being a person can come from being drawn into a wider social unit; our sense of selfhood can arise through the little ways in which we resist the pull. Our status is backed by the solid buildings of the world, while our sense of personal identity often resides in the cracks.

—*Erving Goffman*, Asylums

Contents

AUTHOR'S NOTE   XV

ONE: The Moving Target of Being

Return   3

My Insanities and All the Rest   21

The Vortex Effect   29

A Way of Becoming   32

With Bags   43

DurasSpace, or The Book as a Room (I)   51

At Point Zero   58

Working the Trap   60

The Psychoanalyst   64

Women's Studies   68

Sitting Still   71

The Book as a Room (II)   76

Toward a Theory of My Illness (I)   81

Without Care   84

Stuck in the Story   94

two: I Saw the Figure 5 in Gold

Asylum Architecture (I)   99

The Fifth Floor   100

Too Much   119

Time Passes   131

A Nervous Condition, or What Can One Do?   135

Asylum Architecture (II)   150

Tell Me Who I Am   155

Septimus   157

Hank, a Memoir (I)   159

Melting   168

Interlude, 2022   176

Elena   178

Hank, a Memoir (II)   184

Family Therapy   187

Blossom   199

The Spider's Web   214

Grace   218

Duras Now   220

Then You Will Never Be Happy   222

Off the Couch   235

THREE: Mirror City

Toward a Theory of My Illness (II) 247

The Notebooks 250

Last Days of the Long-Term Ward 253

All of Us Vanishing 258

Toward a Theory of My Illness (III) 273

Good Old Nardil 275

The Shadow Story 283

Angry Women 292

On Recovery (I) 304

The Homelessness of Self 308

The Carceral 319

Q&A 320

Skepticism and Affirmation 321

On Recovery (II) 328

You Seem So Normal 337

ACKNOWLEDGMENTS 345

BIBLIOGRAPHY 347

Author's Note

Names and identifying characteristics in this memoir have been changed to protect individuals' privacy.

Part One

_____

THE MOVING TARGET OF BEING

Return

It was a hot July day, many decades later, that I happened to be in New York. I was house-sitting for a friend, spending a week in her apartment at 145th and Broadway. It was the closest I'd been in years to the hospital that had once been my home. One morning, I decided to walk north. My best days are those that I walk the city, unfettered and directionless, and so it took me a minute to understand where I was going. We are drawn back, aren't we? Even when we don't mean to be and don't want to be. The past is there, waiting for us. I walked the mile or so up Riverside Drive, until I reached my once address: 722 West 168th Street.

Of course nothing in this city remains as it was, and this is no exception: the building, with its grand architecture, is no longer the home of the State Psychiatric Institute. Now it is home to Columbia University's School of Public Health.

This is where I lived, I want to say to someone, as I point up to the fifth floor. But who would care?

In the archway over the entrance, I can read the original name of the building, the Gothic lettering etched in stone: New York State Psychiatric Institute + Hospital. These are the vestiges, for which I am grateful. Another vestige: the two stone benches out front. One etched with the roman numeral MCMXXVII, the year of the building's founding.

Just a year or so after I left for good, the State Psychiatric Institute moved into a new building, larger and grander than the original, with a walkway crossing Riverside Drive toward a second building, which looked out to the Hudson River. By then the program was defunded. No longer would anyone live there as long as we did.

I find the department of records. I ask a woman at the desk about the old building, the state hospital connected with the Presbyterians of Columbia University, the institute referred to as the PI. She looks at me flatly, uninterested. Yes, she says. That's the "old PI."

I tell her I'd like to get copies of my medical records.

Were you an inpatient?

Yes.

When?

A long time ago.

How long ago?

Twenty years ago, I realize as I say it.

She considers, then explains the process of retrieving records. There are forms to fill out, money to pay, permissions for release. Once this is approved, the papers will be copied. You'll receive those copies in the mail.

I fill out the paperwork, pay with my credit card.

It's nearly a year later, I've almost forgotten, when I receive a packet of ten or fifteen pages. A summary of my stay. A stack of narratives, really. Different doctors write different summaries. Each doctor has his or her particular angle. Did I think it would be objective? No, but I hadn't realized how subjective it would be. These character descriptions have much in common with the writing of the students in my creative writing classes. There are consistencies, recurring themes: *Dysthymia* is used over and over again. I was told I had chronic depression, or major depression, or bipolar disorder, but dysthymia is the diagnosis that is repeated throughout the records.

I was disappointed by the stack of papers, which I put away in a drawer. On the one hand, these pages bring up the great shame I feel for the waste of those days, the extent of my abjection. At the same time, I wanted more—daily notes or details that could fill in the gaps in my notebooks, in my memory. I want the details. I don't want the official language, the axis 1 or axis 2, the list of medications and symptoms. What I want is the story of our long, dull days and years in that hospital. Those days, those years. It is the quotidian I want to recover.

I was twenty years old when I arrived. January 1992. New York City: all darkness and disinterest. Who the fuck cared that you arrived? Thousands arrive here every day. The streets around the campus were empty, save for passing traffic, buses, the occasional bodega. Empty Styrofoam cups, plastic tops, straws and McDonald's bags floated in a wet slushy bath of ice. Piles of dog shit half frozen under the ice. A security guard tells me that my dorm is a few blocks away, on the other side of campus. I walk the long blocks, dragging a duffle bag. My room is one in a suite, with a shared kitchen and bathroom. The floors are cold tile; the walls concrete; the only furnishings a metal twin bed, a desk, and a small window with a view of a brick wall.

I dropped my bags, left the suite, and walked to the deli next door.

When I returned, my suitemates were there, a triptych of young womanhood.

Hello, I said, stabbing a baked potato twice before putting it in the microwave.

Is that all you're eating? a small chatty girl asked, giggling. I felt my body flood and knew I'd turned bright red.

Yes, I said. I guess so.

A month later and I haven't made a single friend. You can become strange from loneliness, from days and weeks without speaking to anyone. Occasionally someone from home will call, and I'll pretend everything is fine. In my notebook, I chronicle my despair. Today is Valentine's Day and Leo asks me to meet him downtown.

On the train, I stand across from a stranger. We are close enough to make out, my face in his, but here's the rule: no eye contact. Pretend you are not this close to someone's humanity. Look away or at your feet but never at a face. Get off at Christopher Street, Leo had said. I hold my laminated Streetwise Manhattan map like a prayer card. The train screeches and jerks out of the station. I smell urine and ham, rat shit and perfume. When I close my eyes, I see the chickens, dangling from their feet, moving toward me. I hear a woman cry. The train stops and starts again and again with a jerk, 72nd, 66th, my head against the puke-green doors, red paint splattered across each, as if someone scribbled with a giant Sharpie. A scene from a television movie: *Six Weeks*, the young sick ballerina collapsing on a New York subway, all possibility, all devastation.

Another train passes and I read the graffiti, big white bubble letters jumping out like demented ghosts, the words: ONE IS YOU and IS BACK legible in the splatter. ONE IS YOU: I hear it over and over again, my head softly now against the train door. An announcement for Times Square. From one window, faces speed past and from the other more graffiti. The man next to me is only mildly threatening, in that serial killer way, preferable to the skinheads behind me, one with his groin against my ass. Excuse me, I ask this tall Jeffrey Dahmer.

He turns to look down at me, I see his sharply cut jaw.

Have we passed Christopher Street?

The train stopped so many times. How could I know? He's annoyed. Yes, yes, I am a midwestern idiot. No, I don't know what I am doing here.

Look. He points to the map on the side of the train car. Now he looks me up and down, stopping at my breasts. I pull my coat tight.

Twenty-third Street. A few more to go.

Leo is seated, holding the menu and shaking his leg below the table. Where were you? he hisses. This neighborhood is another world entirely. A few weeks in the city and it's my first time leaving the environs of Barnard's campus, from 116th to 120th, from Riverside Drive to Amsterdam Avenue. There was a darkness to the village, to every street. If the later 1990s brought *Friends* tourism to the city, and the 2000s brought *Sex and the City* tourism; this New York was still resolutely the '80s: the Rotten Apple of that *Time* magazine cover, the squeegee men jumping on your dashboard. Peep shows. This was New York before the real estate investment, before Giuliani decided to sell it, to market it, before Giuliani cleaned up Times Square. Before Times Square became Disneyland. This was AIDS, men were dying all around us, but we didn't know. Alphabet City, which would later reach iconic status via *Rent*, then full of abandoned buildings, garbage floating in the water on the curb. Kathy Acker lived there, though we didn't know. It would be a year or two before I read Acker, before I read the way she channeled madness into artistic practice, and the space she would open for me. *Writing is like suicide*, she wrote, *only you don't have to die.*

Leo didn't get up. I sat and he asked again what took me so long. I was overwhelmed by the gap between what I'd imagined for months, the possibility of a true connection with this man, and how I loved him. And now here he was and here I am and we were as far apart as two people could be. I heard it again: ONE IS YOU. Now Leo is saying something I can't understand; his face floating over the table like a fat balloon. IS BACK. That gauzy feeling, a trap: Everything could get in, no boundary between my body and the rest.

Suzy? The balloon is saying something. What was this city, another planet, a nightmare? I told IS BACK to shut up, I told myself: The balloon is real. This is real, I said. I am in New York. I am with the balloon. I met the balloon a year ago in Los Angeles, a foreign country. Every choice that led me here—to this place, to this moment—was now revealed to be absurd, utterly random. I had told myself it was my choice, but maybe I did just follow Leo here. And now here we were but we weren't here. I couldn't follow him, how stupid to think so.

Sorry, I said. I apologized for everything, that way of young women.

I'm really sorry I'm so late. I had trouble figuring out the train.

I didn't tell him that I'd gotten lost coming out of the Christopher Street stop. Every street became something else, circles into circles. My Streetwise Manhattan didn't help.

Well, let's order. I'm starving! Anyway, why are you so thin? I mean, I'm into it, he added. It's your Jane Austen look. It's nice! It's good, I like it.

I read the menu. I'd never had Indian food.

Do you like daal? We should get naan with mango chutney, okay? You'll love it, I promise. I'll order.

The food arrived: a feast of naan, daal, curries, and biryani; Leo ate quickly, talking while he ate, talking in between large bites, all the while explaining what he was doing at Sarah Lawrence, directing a stage adaptation of Bergman's *Persona*. It wasn't going well. The actors didn't understand *the tone*. It was going to be a failure, he was sure of it.

Why aren't you eating? he finally noticed.

I took a few bites. I tried the chutney on the bread and it was delicious, flavors I'd never tasted.

The waiter came back, asked how it was.

I can't eat this, I said, pointing to the food in front of me.

Why not?

There's oil in it.

Oil?

I leaned toward Leo and whispered: There are things in it. I've read about it.

Leo laughed, then looked at me like I was crazy. The waiter nodded and said he would see what he could do.

You're insane! Who doesn't eat OIL?

I watched Leo eat, samosa after samosa. I listened to his loud smacking noises, watched him shove the food down as if in a competition.

Do you want a beer?

No, I said. I don't drink. I've been reading a lot about all the poisons in food and alcohol. There's a lot you don't know. I'm trying to purify.

The waiter never returned. I would go home hungry that night, but it was better that way. Leo moved to say goodbye, a kiss on the cheek. My hair stayed in my face and I held my arms tight.

On the subway, I opened *As I Lay Dying*. The body as meat. The mother's body is meat. I read the same page over and over again. *That was when I learned that words are no good; that words don't ever fit even what they are trying to say.* I heard voices, saw people, friends and family, my mother. Say it. *My mother is a fish.* Say it, this trap, I see it now, my life.

The next day I went to the student health center, in the basement of campus, winding through tunnels to find the office. I spoke to a nurse. I explained what was happening: my hair, the poisons, the voices, the visions. The nurse said, You need to see the doctor. Dr. Goldberg. The doctor asked me to explain. I don't know what I said. I do remember she was the first to ask me this question, the first person besides Leo to use the words in conversation (it wasn't like now, with the word, the idea, the act itself all over the internet—back then, few people spoke of it), Dr. Goldberg asked me: Do you want to kill yourself? Or did she say, Do you want to hurt yourself? Or do you have thoughts of hurting yourself or someone else? Or do you want to suicide? Was that it?

Whatever it was, I said yes. It was true, and no one but Leo had asked. Yes, I said. I think about it all the time.

It began there, that yes, saying *yes* out loud to a person who seemed to care—and that first yes became an opening, the word a possibility.

The doctor said, I'm going to give you a prescription. I want to see you back here in a week.

I don't think I'd heard of Prozac before, it was still so new. There was nothing like the so-called direct-to-consumer advertising we're so used to now. A few years later there would be books: Peter D. Kramer's *Listening to Prozac* and Elizabeth Wurtzel's *Prozac Nation*. And soon after, those creepy commercials. Ask your doctor if Zoloft might be right for you. Etc.

Yes, that's where it began: that question. That prescription. The next day or two or three days, when I didn't sleep. I could stick with the program. The program enlarged, more to do, more hours of walking through the city, the sense of possibility.

Leo and I spoke by phone, often for hours at a time. We spoke of suicide now as a matter of course. It was what we needed to do. He grew up in the city, he'd been in analysis since high school. He hated the analyst, didn't trust him. He had been through the whole system. All the psychiatrists suck, he told me, never trust them.

Let's just do it, he would say, before hanging up. I'd agree. Of course, I said. We have to. I want to.

When I read the official medical records, I see that this is where the story begins. No matter what, you need a beginning. And this became mine. The narrative over and over again in these pages: the night Leo called me. I was at my desk studying for midterms. Reading my notes. Leo called, he was upset, he said he couldn't take it anymore, it was something about his dad, his play. He was in his car, he said, the college had forced him to see a disgusting psychiatrist and he'd been saving up the pills. He stole a few bottles from his mother's bathroom. He had enough for both of us. You want to do it, right? he asked me. I'm coming to get you now. We'll take all the pills. I had two bottles. We have enough, he said. I wasn't sure. I have to study, I said. Nothing's going to change, he said. You know that, right? It's all the same. It doesn't matter if you study.

I said, No, I can't, maybe tomorrow I'll do it. Not now, I said. He hung up on me.

And the day after that phone call, when I didn't hear from Leo. When he didn't answer the phone, when his roommate said no one had seen him in days, when his mother said he was at school as far as she knew, when I became sure that he was dead.

It began when I left class, and it became clear. The screw. The faces. I knew I was shut out and it would always be this way. I would never be close to anyone and I would live in this trap for the rest of my life. Leo was right.

I went back to my desk that afternoon and took out the pills, two bottles, lining them up in a row, one after another—green-and-orange capsules stamped E 92. It meant something. Yes, I said. The space opened, the Yes.

It was as easy as this, a breaking down of all boundaries. I felt happy.

The desk was long laminated plastic wood with metal legs. My books sat there, a presence. The screw. I couldn't keep up with the program. It was there when I woke, the imperatives: Do this and this then this and this do not stop you suck you will fail you are ugly you have so much to learn you are so far behind you will never succeed you will always be alone your loneliness will never be rocked you will never write the way your heroes do.

I imagined Leo counting the pills and I could do this, too, one after the other, a row or two rows, a line or two lines, counting and it would be enough, I swallowed each row, one and another, stuffing my mouth full, swallowing until I choked. I sipped from my water bottle and lay on my bed: metal frame, thin mattress, one blanket, a crunchy pillow. I waited. I saw the faces on my wall. I could hear one or the other laughing. I heard Leonard Lopate's voice on the radio. The window, the brick wall. I couldn't see out but it all got in: the incessant sounds of that city—an ambulance, birds screeching, garbage trucks, shouting, car horns. I was going to vomit, I was too awake, it was all taking too long. I turned into a fetal position. A loneliness that can be rocked. The great female tragedy. My mother, my love. It was too late. I ate books, I could live here.

The pre-patient's career may be seen in terms of an extrusory model; he starts out with relationships and rights, and ends up, at the beginning of his hospital stay, with hardly any of either. The moral aspects of this career, then, typically begin with the experience of abandonment, disloyalty, and embitterment.

—*Erving Goffman,* Asylums

West 168th Street and Riverside Drive, entrance to New York
State Psychiatric Institute (*Wurts Bros., photographer*)

Through the entranceway. Up the stone stairs. The historic building. I was led onto the elevator by a nurse. The elevator went down,
the front of the building a kind of trick, built on a cliff—you enter
on the tenth floor and from there go down to the patients' wards.
Off the elevator down to the fifth floor. Grilles over the windows
above. There on the wall around the corner: Charles Demuth's *I
Saw the Figure 5 in Gold*.

I was led to an office. This was August 1992. I took off my shoe-
laces and handed over sharps: my eyeliner, pencil sharpener, a
compact mirror, a spiral notebook. I met a doctor. He may or
may not have asked questions. He said it would be six months.
Wasn't it three? I asked. He nodded. We'll see, he said, it usually takes longer than that. I signed papers, I agreed to something.
They were not forcing me to be there, not really, though what else
would I have done? If I say now: That was the moment—I should
have said, No thank you, I should have walked out—it wouldn't
mean anything to the person I was then. She could not imagine
leaving, she could not imagine being anywhere else.

By then, I had been in the hospital for months, since that night
in March. They needed me to get better and instead I got better
at being sick. I got better at being a mental patient. I got better at
planning my death and better at speaking to psychiatrists.
    Others in the short-term ward would come and go, most older

than me. They'll keep you thirty days or until your insurance runs out, one or another would say. Then you're cured.

It was a joke. The system was rigged and they told me so.

Still, I believed in it. It was saving me. I was lucky. I was on student insurance until I dropped out of school, and by then I was in a state hospital. Everything was free. I did not have to leave.

You sit in an office until a nurse comes to tell you, We have a bed. You walk down a hallway, pass a kitchen, a service elevator, more offices. Locked doors, vinyl couches, a television. Now your room, a bed, no door. One window glazed in laminate, unbreakable. A room and a chair. Metal bars behind the plastic. Your room. You have a bag of clothes and a bag of books. You see into the room of the girl across the hall, pink and purple bedding and stuffed animals, a poster from an Anne Rice movie. Clothes on the floor, books. She doesn't look at you, doesn't say hi. It's not like that.

I fall asleep there, thin sheets pulled over me. Sheets marked with a stamp: Property of the New York State Psychiatric Institute. Whatever they gave me—clozapine, thorazine—has made me dizzy and sick. A nurse named Nevada walks down the hall, knocking on the wall where the door would be. Dinner! she repeats over and over, cheery robotic, too loud. It's dark out. I don't know what day it is, and soon enough it will mean little, days and time itself become insignificant. I'm so unsteady I have to hold the wall, walking to the dining area. Dinner trays stacked on the shelves of a silver cart.

Take one! Nevada calls from behind me. We don't serve you here!

I take my tray and walk into the shared dining room. I can feel the cold concrete through my hospital socks. Rows of tables. A view of the Hudson River. At the back corner table I see a woman, older than the rest. She wears a long dress, unlike the others in hospital gowns or scrubs. The dress is lace, a threadbare Laura Ashley dyed black, fishnet tights, and jewelry: bracelets, earrings, long beaded necklaces. When I sit alone at a table, she is the first one to greet me. Hello, she says, my name is Tilda. Hi, I say. She looks at my tray: a scoop of mashed potatoes, slices of beef, green peas, and a roll. A cup of pudding on the side. You don't have to eat it, you know. I wasn't planning to. Well, I get people to bring me food. You can do that, you know? There's a refrigerator here, if you want, my husband can get you something, I'll tell him. Whatever you need. I thanked her. Well. When you're done eating or getting settled in you should come back and see my table. My jewelry table. I see the assortment of beads, stones, jewelry cutters. Now I notice the woman next to Tilda, standing near, walking where she walks, always by her side, close enough to grab her.

Now a nurse named Roxane walks into the room, calls me by my full name: Suzanne. She holds a Dixie Cup full of more pills.

Suzanne? She looks around, then at me.

Are you Suzanne?

I say, No, I'm Suzy.

She replies, It says here your name is Suzanne.

I say, Yes, but no one calls me that.

It's your name, she says flatly. I'm not going to call you Suzy.

She pronounces *Suzy* as if it is the most ridiculous name in the world, and I realize that it is.

That's a cheerleader name, she says scornfully.

The next day she'll call me Suzanne and I won't correct her. I know what your problem is, she'll say, you think you are special. Look around you. She makes a grand sweeping gesture indicating all the sad young women in the dining room. Everyone here thinks she is special.

I make a call back home on the payphone. Get me out of this place, I say to my father, my sister. But of course it is too late. You are not ready, they tell me. You are very sick. It will take time. It gets worse before it gets better.

I lived in that hospital for years. When I think of the other women in the hospital, I don't think of madness, or insanity, I don't even think of mental illness, though of course it was there, it was the story we were told and we were learning to tell about ourselves. Instead, I think of mothers. Some of these women were mothers; some had a mother; some had lost a mother. I watched these women closely, hungry to understand what I did not have.

My Insanities and All the Rest

The word *madness* is literary, philosophical, capacious. We know it can be romantic in literature and wretched in life. Madness was Shakespeare's word in the sixteenth century and Robert Burton's in the seventeenth. For Shakespeare, madness was one with excess; lovers and madmen both have access to a truth only allowed by unreason—their *seething brains,* their *shaping fantasies.* I use the word though I know it can sound at best grandiose, at worst dangerous—because it allows for the extension of a conversation beyond the temporal, beyond the ever-shifting medical or scientific moment. Compared to modern psychiatry, to use the word *madness* is premodern, it avoids the present biomedical moment. Yet the word has not gone away at all, though we know to say something more precise, or so we are told it is more precise to say: a *chemical imbalance.* Bipolar disorder, schizophrenia. Dissociative identity disorder. Anxiety disorder. OCD. Social anxiety disorder. Personality disorder. There are many more and my students inform me of those I've missed. These are all helpful to a point, but when I speak of madness and a life in literature, I am also speaking of something spiritual. I think of what Virginia Woolf wrote in a letter to her friend E. M. Forster:

> *Not that I haven't picked up something from my insanities*
> *and all the rest. Indeed, I suspect they've done instead of*
> *religion.*

And I am also talking about *crazy*—another complicated word. *Crazy* in a pedestrian way. I was crazy when I arrived in New York City in January 1992 and I became crazier in that city. I was crazy in those days, much of the time. Or I was acting crazy—which is what we more often mean by crazy.

I don't act crazy anymore, or I am not crazy. Or I never was crazy. But in many ways back then I just couldn't help it. I think that is part of what we mean by mental illness. What you can't help: starving yourself or bingeing and purging; staying in bed all day or staying up all night or cutting yourself. It is either excess or rigidity and often both. Maybe it was crazy to eat a plain baked potato once a day and nothing else. Though there was a nurse on the ward who ate a package of plain rice cakes every day, and nothing else—yet because she was a nurse, she was not crazy. This same nurse described in my medical charts *my* "bizarre eating habits." It was crazy, how I ate and didn't eat. If I were my own mother, I would have seen that, but that was the point, I think. My mother. Where was she? The best the word *crazy* can do is point to something on the surface, a symptom. It is not the story.

The philosopher Ian Hacking once described the shifting classification of the mentally ill as a "moving target." A disease is recognized and named. A doctor or doctors name and come up with ways to treat the disease. More patients arrive with the symptoms of the named illness. More patients, and more symptoms. Soon enough, there's a cause linked to the illness.

Take, for example, hysteria: the first disease attributable to women, and first defined by Hippocrates in the fifth century. Hysteria was caused, or so the theory went, by the movement of the uterus throughout the body. The word means "wandering uterus." As a modern physical ailment, hysteria was redefined and medicalized in 1880 by a French doctor named Jean-Martin Charcot. Charcot identified symptoms of the disease, naming and defining and classifying it. Soon the number of women in France afflicted with the disease rose exponentially.

The "wastebasket" diagnosis of hysteria remained in the American Psychiatric Association's *Diagnostic and Statistical Manual of Mental Disorders* (*DSM*) until 1980. The removal was a result of feminist activism and the emerging critical perspective on women's health care. (In 1976, the diagnosis of "homosexual" was removed from the *DSM* and replaced by "sexual orientation disturbance." It wasn't until 2013 that sexual orientation as a pathology was completely removed from the *DSM*, the result of years of pressure from activists.)

Hacking is specifically interested in the epidemic of multiple personality disorder, or MPD as it was called when I lived in the hospital. It was Charcot who named and identified the disease in 1880, but it wasn't until the 1970s in the United States that the disease was recognized and treated by the medical establishment. Around that same time, MPD had entered the public imagination. Most powerful among the representations was *Sybil*, the novel and subsequent television film. A "true story" (as the cover of the internationally bestselling book boasted) based on a psychiatric patient named Shirley Mason, *Sybil* helped create the diagnosis of MPD. After the publication and film release, psychiatrists reported a huge spike in cases of multiple personality disorder.

In 2011, a book about Mason, her doctor, and the author of the novel revealed that the diagnosis, and the accounts of abuse Mason had reported, were a fraud. Mason had acted out the personalities, she said, as a way to give her doctor what she wanted. She made up stories of her mother having abused and tortured her. For decades, the disease was seen as attributable to childhood abuse. More and more doctors looked for this cause in presenting patients.

Of course, Mason had been an unstable, troubled young woman. At the same time, the doctor to whom she trusted her care and on whom she became dependent was eager to diagnose and cure this stunning and sensational case of multiple personality disorder. The doctor early on teamed up with the writer who would publish the internationally best-selling book.

The cause of the illness mattered to the narrative structure. In the book, as in life, it was only after the doctor coaxed Mason into remembering her torture that she was cured. After revealing the secret of her mother's abuse, she was able to integrate her sixteen personalities and live a happy life.

After the publication of *Sybil*, there was an exponential increase in cases of MPD throughout the 1970s, '80s, and well into the 1990s. It was only in the year 2000, and rather abruptly, that the disease was eliminated from the *DSM*. The diagnosis had become controversial, with many patients and families reporting that doctors had coached them into revealing "alters."

Here was Hacking's moving target: A patient is suffering, seeks medical help, the symptoms of that suffering are named, noted, and treated, if not cured. (There was usually no expectation of cure in the case of MPD, as with many personality disorders.) The disease is represented in popular culture; more patients (mostly women in the case of MPD) present with these symptoms. Soon patients present with more symptoms, the disease is reclassified. More people who suffer present with these and more symptoms. The parameters of the illness itself adjust and expand.

Many therapists were eager to define and explain a disease. By the 1970s, the presiding theory or explanation was that MPD was caused by an early trauma, most commonly physical or sexual abuse.

When I was in the hospital, the belief in "recovered memories" was at its peak. By the early nineties, more and more patients recovered memories of childhood sexual abuse. Doctors encouraged patients to find these memories. I know that many of the women I lived with in the hospital had been sexually abused, tortured, or raped. I know that many had not been. I don't know who was telling the truth, who was lying, who was creating memory through imagination and expectations. I'm sure we all did some of this.

Whether or not these things happened to anyone, it doesn't take away from the authenticity of anyone's suffering. That was real, even if performed, or especially when performed. As Leslie Jamison put it: *The performance of pain is still pain.* It was our way of being in the world. It was a way to please your doctor, and by extension, to receive care. It was clear enough that if the diagnosis of MPD hadn't existed, many of the women in the hospital wouldn't behave as they did, and wouldn't have those symptoms; but that doesn't mean they wouldn't have other symptoms, other behaviors, other reasons to be there.

I did not "have" MPD, but I do vividly recall meetings with doctors who suggested that I try to remember what I had forgotten or repressed or blocked out of my childhood. What else happened? I was asked repeatedly. Take your time, I was told, day after day. Did someone hurt you? I was asked. What about your brothers? Your father? I recall a young resident in particular pushing me to remember something about the men in my family, something that happened after my mom died. I said no. I was shy, I could not make eye contact. She was gentle, kind. Take your time. I knew if I said yes, she would be pleased. I could give her what she wanted. If I had been traumatized by my mother's death, by the subsequent chaos and neglect of the years that followed, it was not enough. Of course, I knew that I had not been abused, not by my father or my brothers. It scares me now to imagine what would have happened had I said yes, had I created a fantasy trauma to please the doctors. They were, after all, so seductive, and I was so young and susceptible, with complete and naive trust in the authority of the medical establishment, wanting to please them, to give them what they wanted. To say yes would have been another way to perform, to be a person. It was clear that if I'd said yes, if I'd recovered a memory or two, it would have explained everything: my attempts to die, my rage and my self-destruction. If I could make this admission—*Tell us your secrets,* was the motto of the treatment plan. *You are only as sick as your secrets!*—then they could heal me, treat me. A kind of reward.

In the 1890s, Jean-Martin Charcot held open visits to the Salpêtrière Asylum in Paris. Doctors and health professionals, mostly men, came from all over to attend. In these public sessions or performances, Charcot would hypnotize his patients in order to produce their symptoms: tics, fits, and vocal outbursts. Some women became highly sexual, touching themselves or gyrating. The women on display were mostly poor, disenfranchised. They came to Salpêtrière for care and there they learned to perform in order to receive that care. Some of the most famous patients performed over and over again. As Charcot's treatment and methods became popular and celebrated, there was a huge increase in the number of women diagnosed as hysteric.

That Charcot's most famous patient was later revealed to be a "fraud" (as in the *Sybil* case) seems beside the point. She was, rather, performing in a way that would get her care and attention. She was learning how to be in a historically specific time and place.

It would also miss the point for me to call my friend Tilda a fraud. Tilda was there when I arrived and still there when I left. She spent seven years institutionalized. She was diagnosed with MPD and we often witnessed her moving in and out of character. Some of her alters were more entertaining than others. (Jessa Crispin noted somewhere that for patients with MPD, one alter was always a slut. This says at least as much about what it is to be a woman as it does about pathology or madness—what Chris Kraus called *the schizophrenia of being female.*)

It would miss the point, too, to call myself a fraud for cutting myself after I saw other girls doing it, first in college, and then in hospital, and after I saw how the girls in hospital could do it, how intense and extreme it was, how it entered my imagination—they could find a device anywhere, a loose screw or a broken bit of plastic, how then I would imagine new ways to do it, to compete, how we fed on each other that way, how we learned to be patients. I could scream or go mute, I could rage or disappear. There were things we could do and we learned how to do these things and the context made it meaningful. Is this performance theory? Is this why so many people in Germany killed themselves after reading Goethe's *The Sorrows of Young Werther* in 1774? Or why so many people in Sweden filed for divorce after Bergman's *Scenes from a Marriage* appeared on television in the 1970s? Or why so many girls I knew started dieting, restricting, or bingeing and purging after reading a Judy Blume novel or watching an afterschool special or reading *Cosmopolitan* magazine?

I don't want to say (or at least I don't think I want to say) that I was not sick. But I do want to say that nothing is isolated, and especially not what we call pathology; that we exist in context, of the moment and of each other; that we are fragile and fluid. We learn how to be.

The Vortex Effect

Two thousand seventeen. Here I am and here, too, is the past. The days, those months and weeks I keep off to the side and yet return without notice. Today I hear a song and I'm back there. Today I drop my son off at school, I watch him walk into the main entrance, see him swallowed up by schooling, the movement of time. I am far from 1980 but how easily it returns. I tell myself I have left it behind. I live next to it. And that is true, it can be true—and then, I realize as Joan Didion said, how just something slight can move you into the vortex of grief. How life depends on resisting the vortex. I write thinking I have done it, turned shock into words, and then the writing itself undoes me. I will find myself weeping at the kitchen table, which is as close to a desk as I have ever had. I have made those days, those weeks, that period of time into something to write about. Have I become a writer so that I could do something with those days, weeks, months? This book, too, a way to shape the chaos, the formlessness of grief into something else.

This isn't mentioned in the records of my hospital stay, but it is true—the day after Leo called me to suicide, I walked to campus and took my Shakespeare exam. I wrote long essays in blue books, identifying passages from plays. Hamlet as grief-struck. His father has died and his mother has quickly remarried. He is told to get on, to get over it. The very suggestion enrages him. There is nothing to get over from that place of grief. He taunts Ophelia, the woman he loves. He acts out: He puts on a play. Those around him wonder at his mental state. Is he playing at madness? That becomes a question of the play: Is Hamlet mad or is he acting madness? How can anyone know the difference?

In that year before I moved to the city, my relationship with books had changed. Now I read books in a way that felt at once desperate and thrilling. It had become a way to live, or a search for how to live. I suppose it is easy to dismiss a young woman for forming and shaping her identity under the influence of books, of reading—and yet. This was what I had and it was everything. I was called pretentious, weird. This is how you become an artist. You become true to yourself alone. You move away from what you've known, those received opinions and identities of youth.

It was a furnished studio apartment, where I lived those months before moving to New York, with one sofa that pulled out into a bed. From my window, I could see into other people's lives, coming and going. Most were older, husbands and wives, I think. I will always think of that room as the room where I read *The Lover*. The room where I read *Beloved*. The room where I read *Woman at Point Zero*. The room where I began to shut myself off from others completely.

It was the last place I lived before moving into a mental hospital.

In the official records, the word is *stayed*, not *lived*. I *stayed* in a hospital. It wasn't about living.

The months before my stay were the loneliest months of my life—or it was the first time in my life I became acquainted with that particular adult sort of loneliness. A self-imposed loneliness.

In these days, in this room, I would read and I would write passages from the books I read onto note cards and I would tape the note cards onto my wall.

I read *Beloved* just weeks after reading *The Lover*. They were both published in the 1980s, a few years apart. Each title contains the word *love*. Each an exploration of the maternal. The mother to the daughter, the daughter to the mother. The weight of history, the violence of history.

My memory of men is never lit up like my memory of women.

This is one of Marguerite Duras's most famous lines. I agree, and I would add, too:

My memory of a book written by a man is never lit up like my memory of a book written by a woman.

The sofa, the couch, the small lamp, the end of the day, sunset in my window facing north. I remember the edition, the small paperback. I remember the lines, the sentences I remember: *Beloved She is Mine.* I remember, too, reading *The Lover* that first time. *Early in my life it was too late.*

We never have it again, that first time. To read these books was to be held. I hadn't understood that before, what a book was for. I've reread these novels many times since that first time. Each reading matters. As Susan Sontag put it, any book worth reading is worth rereading. Or Italo Calvino: *There is no difference between reading and re-reading.*

A Way of Becoming

Nineteen ninety-two. Down three flights of stairs to a payphone. Glad you made it, my dad said. How is New York? It's fine, I said. It's not like Chicago. I wouldn't think so. Strange, busy. He laughed at this, nervously, in a way that may have meant *of course* or *I'm worried about you*. The things he was unable to say.

Not that I wanted to be back in Illinois; I didn't. But where was I? It was surreal, to call it New York City. How easy, how imprecise.

To communicate, *to be in touch*, meant something else in those days. It was so easy to be *out of touch*. This was the end of an era, though we did not know. An era that had defined and shaped us: what it meant to be human, to be connected, to sit quietly in a room alone. The texture of loneliness was something else in those days. This is not a romantic or nostalgic view of the early nineties; it wasn't better or worse—but it was something else. We speak these days about how fraught and complicated it is to be a young person, to come of age in the era of social media—but it's worth noting, too, how difficult it was to be a person in the pre-internet, pre-networked era. In the midst of despair or loneliness now, a person might post something to social media and receive an instant response, and while these posts surely don't always relieve symptoms, there's some possibility of connection. Sending a text, or an email, couldn't be more different than the experience in those days of making a phone call. Finding a payphone. Hoping the person might be there to answer the phone. Leaving a message. Being available for a return call. It's a profoundly changed world from the one in which I came of age.

At best, the expanded conversation around mental illness has helped reduce stigma, and certainly can explain the next generation's comfort revealing their psychiatric diagnoses and medications. Today you can google your symptoms, from eating disorders to depression, and discover not just a medical diagnosis but also communities and subcultures of people like you. I think there must be comfort there, in a way that wasn't available back in 1992.

But of course the terrible flipside, the current mental health crisis—and social media doesn't help, and it may make it much worse. Just as I read obsessively and wrote in my notebook excessively—my hypergraphia was a kind of desire, a longing for connection—so a young person today might post on social media. But what if no one responds, or worse, someone responds with cruelty? The imagined audience to my notebook, however amorphous, was never cruel and always interested.

Leo was the only person I knew in the city, and he didn't even live in the city. His mom was in Brooklyn, but he was in college a bit north. He came to visit that first week. When he saw me there in my room, he noted how thin I'd become. He saw the microwaved baked potato on my desk. This was what I ate for dinner almost every day, ever since an actress at summer stock told me that there were only 150 calories in a baked potato. *It's really very healthy*, she said. If I ate only that for dinner, and only a bagel for breakfast, my body would stay the same every single day, nothing would change.

I could keep my self in check, my emotions in check. This was the idea.

Leo looked around at the bare walls. This is bleak! he nearly shouted, gesturing toward the undecorated tile floors, the painted brick, the twin bed with a metal frame.

He'd brought a friend. Kristin sat at the end of my bed, looking at the baked potato and then at me, back and forth. She found a yellow legal pad, and was drawing big cartoon faces on each page, silly characters. She'd name each and write a bit of their life story in a caption. She was going quickly, one after the other, flipping page after page.

Leo and I had met a year earlier, when we were both freshmen at the University of Southern California. It was there we'd jointly decided to move to New York City. Los Angeles was not serious, the students were stupid, we wanted to be out east where people read books.

He transferred first, to Sarah Lawrence. I transferred to Barnard. I was following him, though I would not have admitted that at the time. I needed to be in New York, the city that had formed him; I hoped it would form me, too.

Yes, it is bleak, I said. Everything was bleak, but I was trying to pretend otherwise. This was what I wanted. Or at least I thought I wanted.

Still, some part of me wanted Leo to save me from myself. I couldn't say this, of course—I probably couldn't articulate it. I told myself I needed no one, and still all my need went his way.

Kristin ripped her pages off the yellow legal pad, and one by one taped them to my walls.

A few days later and I'm in the bookstore a block south of campus. I'm searching the aisles for my assigned course texts. I'm distracted looking between stacks of books, from one course list to another, so many I want to read, classes I want to take. I have the sense that I am so behind, there is so much I haven't read, so much I need to read. How will I ever understand anything?

I notice a young man following me around the store. We make eye contact and he smiles.

Hi, he offers.

Hi.

What classes are you in?

He gestures to my books. Most are for a seminar on Death and Fiction, I say. I show him: *As I Lay Dying, Beloved, The Diary of a Country Priest.*

Looks great, he says, if a little depressing?

I feel my face flush. Of course it was depressing, I don't say. That's what I want, I don't say.

Well, sure, I say.

He smiles then.

Do you want to grab dinner at Ollie's? I thought for a moment before saying yes. I wasn't sure how I felt about him, but I was desperate for male attention. He was tall, looked down at me.

In the windows of Ollie's were large slabs of beef, whole chickens dangling, turkeys and ducks tied by their feet. The sight made me sick. I looked away and listened as Charlie told me about himself, how he was thinking of being a theater major and how the plays they had to read in the History of Theater sequence were so depressing—*Waiting for Godot,* for example. He couldn't get over how determined people were to be bleak.

I mean, yeah, he said, I get it! We're all out here waiting in this cold parking lot, we're all going to die alone. I get it!

But, you know, he smiled at me, winked, maybe we can just enjoy some hot cocoa together, while we're out here.

I noticed how handsome he was. Thick dark hair to his chin,

parted in the middle, falling into his eyes. He wore a dark sweater, the color of his hair. A smile with dimples. I liked listening to him. I liked disappearing. Especially that. Not really an I.

Back in my room, I write about the date with Charlie. On the pages of my notebooks, I'm beginning to work out my I. The words are there, the details, the rage, the notes and admonitions—a way of teaching myself to speak, I think now. Teaching myself to think.

Joan Didion on note keepers: *Lonely and resistant rearrangers of things, anxious malcontents, children afflicted apparently at birth with some presentiment of loss, the notebooks were a way of noting: This is what it was like to be me.*

My body, the rigidity of my mouth; my face, a shield. Writing longhand—I did not have a laptop then, no one did—one way of becoming, the self channeled through paper and pen. It was something else, bodily. A way to contain some daily struggle against chaos, dissolution. In her magnificent biography of Virginia Woolf, author Hermione Lee notes that *the fear of incomprehensibility links madness and writing.* I think this explains my sense of self in those days, the limits of my ability to communicate, which is why my writing was fueled by desperation, and madness, too. That it would be impossible to explain to anyone, for anyone to understand, the depth of my feeling. This sense of being so far out, this was why I went mad, I think, if that is what I did.

Charlie ordered gobs of food, telling me that he loved to share and hoped I did, too. I covered my mouth with my hand, conscious of the acne on my chin.

And what about you, he asked, what is your major?

I said I liked theater, too, but I'd decided to be an English major. He'd guessed as much, he laughed.

I saw you carrying the *Riverside Shakespeare*: dead giveaway! Anyway, I'm done with English classes, I'm a business major now. It's a more cost-effective major, you know what I mean?

I did not know what he meant, but I thought about that phrase, that way of putting it, for years. *Cost-effective*. Later I would understand. Later I would figure out the perfect response for him, what I should have said. No, it is not cost-effective, I should have said, but it does help you understand what it means to be alive. What it means to be a human being.

The food arrived: potstickers, egg rolls, plates of noodles covered in gloopy sauce. Pork ribs. Charlie put some dumplings and egg rolls on my plate.

What's the matter? he asked when I didn't move.

I'm not hungry.

What?

No, actually—I'm a vegetarian.

Oh, well, why didn't you say so? He looked around for the waiter. They have plenty of vegetables—

No, it's fine, I said. I'm not eating.

I didn't tell him what would happen if I ate, that I would go home and feel out of control, that it would take a day or two of extra exercise to feel better again, to feel thin. It was all so boring, this trap. The scaffolding of a self.

Charlie looked disappointed, then he went ahead. He ate two

spareribs and licked his fingers. Then two egg rolls, and more. I sat in silence while he ate until he couldn't eat any more. When the waiter came around, he asked for a to-go bag.

We sat for a while as he got the check, added a tip, and signed. Before he left, he looked at me, shaking his head.

You seem nice, but I'm going to say good night now. It was nice meeting you. You're very pretty, but the truth is I'm just so tired of women in thrall to the patriarchy, you know?

Then he laughed, winking as he zipped up his coat and walked to the door.

I walked back to my apartment, up Broadway and across the long blocks to reach my new home at 125th and Amsterdam. Things had become blurry; I saw faces and lights but the sharpness had faded. The noises I heard were from the street and somewhere else. Someone came at me, a man laughing, his face close to mine. He sped up, didn't move away. I walked quickly. He stayed just behind me in step, laughed. Are you scared? he taunted me. I ran until I reached the building. A gaggle of students waiting for the elevator. I didn't want to be close to anyone, did not want anyone to see me. I made my way to my room, to my bed, shut the door behind me. The noises began to quiet and I lay there in the dark. I had never felt so alone. It was so stupid, I thought, to suffer like this. There was nothing at all wrong, there was no reason to feel this way. I could not stop crying. This was the beginning of it, I think now, the lights, crying, unable to stop crying. I was crying for my mother. I hated myself for still wanting her, for needing her, for being unable to make a life, or a self, without her.

A few weeks later, in that very History of Theater class, I would read a late Eugène Ionesco play, *Man with Bags*. In an early scene, an Old Woman encounters a Young Woman; she realizes it is her mother. *I think about you all the time. I forget you're gone and then when I remember . . . it breaks my heart!* The Old Woman is in a wheelchair now, at the end of her life. She begs her mother, the Young Woman, never to leave her again. *After you left, Mama, there was such a difference . . . such an empty feeling . . . I could never shake it.* In a later scene, First Man realizes his own mother has been dead for years. *It's hard to imagine my living, without her around.* Everyone in the play is confused, disoriented, living a life that makes no sense. Grief as a permanent problem, what it meant to be a human being.

Aurora, Illinois. 1980. I'm eight years old. My third-grade teacher tells me that she'll be bringing me to the hospital after school. I love third grade: equations and parts of speech, affixes and prefixes. I love Shel Silverstein's "Sick." I love sitting in my own triangle pod with two boys named Eric Twitt and Brian Salerno. I like my teacher, Mrs. Achim, with her smoker's cough and side-eye; I like my distance from her, too. I like that she stands at the front of the classroom and that we sit in seats about the room. I like that I can be one of the crowd, not really an I.

Mrs. Achim is my mom's friend. My mom had many friends, I can see them now, a few months later: the women in the church, rows and rows of nurses in uniform.

I dread staying in the classroom after my classmates go home; I dread getting in the car with my teacher—a violation of some sacred boundary. Teacher and student. It feels wrong to be this familiar with her, to get into her brown Buick, smell her stale cigarette smoke. I look out the window as she drives past Abraham Lincoln Park, past Holy Angels Church, past the old library and then the bridge over the Fox River. We are over there, over the river, another few miles and we pass Phillips Park Zoo, the American Legion headquarters, the Healy Chapel Funeral Home.

This hospital, too, was built in 1888. A Queen Anne Revival with twenty beds. Three decades later, after the Depression, a utility tycoon, politician, and resident of Aurora, Illinois, named Ira Clifton Copley donated two million to its expansion. By the 1970s, it was expanding still, each addition in a different architectural style, side by side, awkward markings of time.

We take the elevator to the second floor. My teacher carries a peace lily.

The room has a window facing west, flooded with afternoon light. There is a table full of flowers, plants, Get Well Soons everywhere. My mother is sitting up with difficulty. A nurse holds her back. She wears a scarf wrapped around her head. As she was bald, she would sometimes wear a wig but now just a scarf. She was no longer beautiful, I think, or not in the way I remembered or needed her to be. The nurse held the straw to her mouth, a Styrofoam cup of ice water. I stayed near the door, watched her struggle to sip. There was a moment, seconds really, before she saw me, and that was when I saw her despair. The despair of the woman in that bed, my mother in great pain, who knew she was dying, was imprinted on me for life.

When she saw me there, she forced a smile, said my name. Everyone left the room, the nurse and my teacher, left me alone to climb into the hospital bed with her, to cry in her arms. With effort she tried to turn back into my mom, to move beyond her suffering, to be there for me. But it was too late: I'd seen her face. I knew she wasn't that person anymore. She was leaving, her body in pain, immense pain that made no sense to me in those days; her body, my origin, was failing and taking her away from me. The mystery of her deep love for me and her simultaneous disappearance shaped my girlhood more than anything else. The early knowledge of love and death as inextricably linked.

A week later was Easter. My dad took us to church and then again to the hospital to visit my mom. When we arrived, the nurses greeted us, told us how pretty we looked in our dresses and bonnets. My dad went in first, and we stood in the doorway. Again, that pain. The horror in her eyes. Something I wasn't supposed to see. My dad hugged her, leaning down, and when he did, she grabbed him, held him and begged, a desperate, rage-filled hiss: *Get me out of this place.*

Witnessing my mother's need that day, her desperation, I surely recognized my own. Her fear was mine. I knew the depths of it, that it would never be fulfilled. I was eight years old, and I was learning that there is no end to need, no cure and no comfort. *Get me out of this place.*

Some weeks later. I've just turned nine years old. I'm sitting on my mother's bed. It is as if she has been told that it will be important to teach me this before she dies. A laundry basket on the floor. Something about how to be a woman. She lifts two socks into her hand. Show me, I say. She can hardly speak, she is so tired. I hate her for giving up. She is trying to fake it. You hold it this way. Fingers at the top, two socks next to each other. I'm ashamed she's my mother, this woman who can barely live. You hold them here, at the cuff, and then you put your thumbs inside. Like this, she says. She holds the cuffs, tries to put her fingers inside. I watch her hands, white and limp. She tries to pull the cuffs over and down, the legs through, to the toes or halfway. I hold my father's black dress socks. I watch carefully. I watch her try: You have to keep the fingers on one hand with pressure against the sock and you have to use your thumbs to fold the top of the socks back over the fingers. You have to do that, that pressure at that moment, two hands, ten fingers working together, you have to do that in order to make the socks into a ball. That pressure at that moment. She can't do it, it's a failure, the whole thing. There's another way, she whispers. She folds one into the other, side by side, but this is not a ball that will remain intact. I do not want to know how to do this, this is obvious. This is not a kind of trick. She lies back now, closes her eyes; it is all too much.

With Bags

Nineteen eighty. When she returns for the last time, I'm just home from school. I have a friend over to play. Our fantasy life is so vibrant; we have created a world where we can live and every day we go to my room to discuss our secret world and then we get a snack and we go outside to the headquarters of the new world. When I open the door for today's adventure, I catch a glimpse of my mom and dad walking up the stairs. She is home, my mom, she is coming home.

No one tells me that she is coming home to die. There are people beside her carrying her bags, her oxygen tanks, holding her up, there are tubes going in and out of her nose. Half human; a cyborg. This is the most disgusting thing I have ever seen in my life. I slam the door shut, push my friend back into my room. I look her in the eyes. Did you see that? I ask. See what? she says. Nothing, I say. Let's stay and play here. I want to show you my Judy Blume book. It's weird! She giggles, picking up *Are You There God? It's Me, Margaret.* I know but you need to read it. I direct her to sit down. And then I want you to tell me about it. After we read for a while, when it's quiet again, I open the door just enough to see if the coast is clear. Let's go, I say to her, come on. I run down the stairs and outside.

I saw this childhood friend some years later, we were in our twenties, but this day of childhood already felt many decades away. Our friendship had been brief, we'd lost touch, but now she is asking me if I remember.

Of course, I say.

You were so weird, she says, laughing.

I'm surprised. Of course, but we both were weird, yes? In the way that children are wonderfully weird. Before we are disciplined, taught to put it away, and get on with the business of adulthood.

No, I mean you, she explains, after your mom died.

Oh. I felt my body flush, my voice faltered.

Do you remember what you said?

No.

You know every day that year those months, every day for weeks, we would get home, drop off our school stuff. I would call you and then walk to your house. We would get a snack and head outside, to the thing, a water heater? Whatever it was, our castle. Headquarters.

Of course, I said.

It was a beautiful memory, the memory of a freedom available to me in that fantasy world, the complete escape of it; we could live there, and she was there, too. It was what I feel now writing, that I can create this object out of the mess of my life and then others can come into it, can live in my world, if only briefly. What is real to me becomes real to them, too.

So, my friend went on, so we did it, you know, that whole week, the people were coming and going, she was in bed. You didn't talk about your mom or let me see her. You didn't go in her room. Our playing was so intense, but I noticed what was going on.

Yes, I said. Well, that was my strategy, I suppose.

I know. But the day she died. That Friday, after school. I got home and I called you, like always, and you answered the phone and this day, like every day, I say, Can you play? And you said, No, I can't play. My mom died.

By weird, she meant that I didn't seem to feel anything. That I ignored my mom's dying, which was right there in front of us, and when I announced her death I felt nothing. I said the words but my friend could see it didn't mean anything. I had learned to separate myself from what was happening.

Grief isn't something you can feel every moment. You can't be sad all the time—life goes on, even if you are nine and your life has been shattered, even if nothing will ever be the same again.

Menstruation, a period, bleeding: It is all mysterious. Somehow I've heard that I'll find answers in *Are You There God? It's Me, Margaret.* My uncle, my mom's younger brother, a teacher and a high school principal, sees the book there in my room. He asks about it; he knows it contains a certain knowledge and he knows I might have questions. Are you reading this with someone? he asks. Or maybe he talks to my mom, or my dad, who doesn't talk about these things. There is something shameful about it, I learn in the silences. The silence around my mother's body wasting, and the silence about my own body becoming.

Among the very limited memories I have of my mother: She watched the performances I would put on at home, she laughed, called me a ham, took me to auditions, took me to see *The Red Shoes*, a movie she'd loved as a girl. The movie was about the drive to make art, to perform, and the often destabilizing compulsion to create. And what if it was my mother who wanted to be an actress, my mother who wanted me to have a life she hadn't had or couldn't have—the freedom to be an actress, not to be a nurse, not only a nurse. I remember her disappointment when I walked out of one audition. *This is what my mother wanted.* I believed that was true.

We do not know why we do the most basic things we are called to do.

We are ultimately unknowable to ourselves.

Even now, telling this story in retrospect, I shift the parameters, I add narrative propulsion where none existed.

I knew so much and had so little experience to make sense of that knowledge.

A week earlier, Leo invited me to campus. Now was finally time for the performance of his adaptation of Bergman's *Persona*. Bergman's 1966 film was about an actress who suffers a breakdown during a performance of Sophocles's *Electra*. After falling into a mute depression, she is cared for by a young nurse, who becomes obsessed with her, a sort of personality diffusion. I watched Leo's play—the college student actresses were of course too young for the film, yet they channeled the despair of Bergman's film. Two blonde women with angled features, sharp looks, I envied how easily they inhabited the gravity of Bergman's aura in ways I never could—my face was too odd, more cartoon character than ingenue. But the desire to play madness in this particular way reached me. This was always it, what actors could do.

Years later in an acting class, I rehearsed a scene from Beth Henley's *Crimes of the Heart*, a popular play about three sisters. The youngest sister, my role, is unstable. She puts her head in the oven, a reference to Plath, though I didn't know it then. Or I did, but I didn't know Plath's genius so much as I knew her story. The scene is funny, a sight gag. We laugh. It strikes me that in these years I was learning about madness, about breakdown and suicide, through the theater. And then in summer stock I played an inmate in *Marat/Sade*. A patient asks: *Who locks us in?* The play within the play is about a revolutionary leader, now staging a play at an insane asylum. The patients are the actors. The actors are patients. The show is put on for the outsiders. The performance for the public is meant to help the prisoners, to show their education. And so it was everywhere: madness. It was the most exciting way to be, onstage, an actor. To play at madness was to become more alive, more authentic. *The freedom of the madwoman*, as Susan Sontag wrote in her journal, both dream and trap.

And maybe I was sick—maybe that story was true. (Why am I so afraid to say so? It is too simple—it cannot be everything—which doesn't mean it wasn't true. I *was* sick. Sick with grief. Sick with the distance between the impossibility of expressing this horror, and sick with a need to shape it into something.)

At some point I learned that there isn't such a thing as a chemical imbalance, and though many doctors didn't use the term back then, that is what others began saying about SSRIs, the phrase gaining popularity. There isn't one chemical that causes depression. This isn't news, but the phrase *chemical imbalance* still gets bandied about in casual conversation, as if we all know what it means, as if it is a shorthand to our disease. Like much about mental health, it presumes that mental illness is an isolated phenomenon. I recall hearing an occupational therapist speaking to a recalcitrant patient, who was objecting to taking medications. If you were a diabetic, the therapist said, you wouldn't object to taking insulin. So, why object to taking X for your depression?

This was so obviously a false equivalency. Even then, I knew how variable the medications were—each did something, but none were a direct cure to my so-called chemical imbalance.

I took SSRIs for stretches of time, over those first two years, among other drugs, and none cured my imbalance. I knew, too, that taking these pills was a gesture, a symbolic ritual necessary to my relationship with my doctor. If I had asked for *something*— help, care, love—this medication was one way to receive it; it was a significant approximation, if not quite the thing.

Before I leave her room that day, she whispers a question. Do I know what happens if I get my period? Menstruation, she calls it. I don't know. It's too soon, anyway, I am still a girl. I won't have a period for another five years. She is running out of time. You will start bleeding, she says. It won't hurt, but you will need to wear a sanitary pad. And you will need to wear a bra soon, she says. You need to ask Daddy and he will take you to get a bra.

Okay?

It is not okay. I will not ask Daddy for that because there is no room there in what I can ask Daddy. And here she is the one who needs to tell me, these secrets. I have heard this is coming: *Are You There God? It's Me, Margaret.* This is how I'll learn what I need to know. This book.

The day before she dies in her bed, I'm on the school bus heading home. An older girl says, My mom told me that your mom is going to die any day now. It is the first time someone has told me. Immediately I know it is true and all my defenses are shattered. I hold my tears until the bus stops, and then I run the two blocks home, up to her bedroom. It is dark, there are two women with her, easing her pain as she dies. I climb into the bed and curl myself next to her, what is left of her body. Are you going to die any day now? Now I cry. She knows me, she still knows me. I will never leave you, she says.

DurasSpace, or The Book as a Room (I)

It might have been any book but it was this book at this time. DurasSpace is how I think of it, the world of *The Lover*, the brief novel by Marguerite Duras which I read that week in 1991, in that room, on that couch. There are books I see or recall and say, Oh, that is a book that meant a lot to me once. There are books like that. And then there are books like *The Lover*. I can say that I do not know who I would be without this book. If I had not read this book at this time in my life. When I first read *The Lover*, I knew nothing of Marguerite Duras's life. I'll never return to that first time. What I had of Duras was her face, once. (*I was so young once*, as the actress in *Hiroshima Mon Amour* declares.) The face on the cover of the book. The face of the young girl. The narrator at fifteen, the age when the story of the novel took place. I opened that book and I read the first lines, the first scene: *A man came up to me in a public place, he said everyone says you were beautiful when you were young. But I prefer your face as it is now. Ravaged.*

The Lover was less shameful than *The Bell Jar* because the author had not destroyed herself, or at least that didn't come first. Her voice came first. The voice of a woman at seventy years old looking back on herself as a young girl. Here was the young girl and here was the woman writer. From this distance, she understood the scope of her life. She could see that this was where her life began. This was not the story of a young American girl like me, growing up in the protected world of a Catholic church and a Catholic school, in a white suburb in a midwestern town. This was the story of a young girl told through the vantage of time—the story was narrated by one who is only now from this distance able to tell the story she needs to tell. Only now able to tell the story of her girlhood.

And Duras herself, the image of her girlhood face on the cover of the novel—the image of her face now, occluded but referenced—*ravaged*—the elegance or gravitas of an elder French author—only heightened the reliability of the voice, the clarity of the voice on the page. Duras showed me the link between grief and sexual awakening. The space of the *Very early in my life it was too late*, the narrator says of this time. Only now, at seventy, is the writer, the author, the narrator able to make sense of this time in her life. Her youth. Then she did not have the words, it was life.

Very early in my life it was too late.

Elizabeth Wurtzel used Duras's line as the epigraph to her memoir *Prozac Nation*. But it rang false. Wurtzel was too young to make such a claim, she was twenty-seven when she wrote her memoir. She'd just graduated from Harvard, it was not too late. (Though as I write this I think of Wurtzel's early death, of breast cancer at fifty-two. How death alters our reception of a text.)

DurasSpace opened to me, too, when I went to see an on-campus screening of *Hiroshima Mon Amour*, the 1959 film written by Marguerite Duras and directed by Alain Resnais. In DurasSpace every love is haunted by what came before—every love is the same love. A man and a woman are in bed, in Hiroshima. He is a Japanese architect, she is a French actress, acting in a film on peace.

They spend the night walking the streets of Hiroshima, into and beyond and through. The city as the site of the trauma, the recent trauma, the horror of the bomb. Images of destruction: the burning, the scars, the children, the adults, the melting of steel. She is acting yet wants to claim her connection to the horror. An actress, she feels it as her own. The man insists that she was not there, that she did not see the hospitals of Hiroshima. The horror. Over the bodies of the lovers, a cloud of debris, ash, the mushroom cloud, the city exploded and fell back to earth. Out of bed, they walk through the streets, seeing the filming of the Peace March. After Hiroshima, there will be nothing but peace. The actress tells him the story of her madness. She had loved a German soldier during the war. She was made the scapegoat of her small town. She was stoned in the village, her hair cut off, she was put in the cellar. The architect wants to know more, the story of her madness, he needs to know more than she can tell. He is something like Charcot with his hysterics—and the actress must perform. Like Charcot, he needs to be the one to hear the secrets—he is thrilled to hear that she hasn't told anyone else. Her secret was now his. DurasSpace offered room for this intensity, a melding of self and other.

I am trying to say something about that sacred relationship between a young woman and a book. I am speaking of my own experience back then, as I moved further from life, untethered, lost, in search of some sustaining framework.

As a sentiment, it too easily becomes saccharine—a book saved me! That is not what I am talking about. I am talking about the reception that is possible when the reader is open, as I was, in need of the voice, of possibility. Reading became a way to actively rewrite my life.

Specificity matters: not any girl but me, who I was then, my specificity: young and full of shame and self-loathing, which I couldn't name or identify—I did not have the language. And my personality then, already closed already shut off defending itself—sure that she will never be known, knowing already the limits of her life. The book a gift, a way to know herself, language for it. It was already there, it was hardening—she will not ever be comfortable being known, her aura of self-protection a measure of her armor and trap, already there, in place.

So I'm sitting on that couch, it is a Saturday morning. Nineteen ninety-one. On the radio a discussion of Anita Hill. I hear Senator Joe Biden asking Hill to repeat the story of a pubic hair on a Coke can. Another senator quotes Clarence Thomas, who used the phrase *large breasts* while speaking to Hill, his intern. More than one senator repeats the phrase there in Congress: *large breasts*. I'm sitting on the sofa. I turn off the radio. I'm holding the slim book. Large breasts. The world is disgusting. I can stop feeling my body as I enter DurasSpace and I want to live there.

There were two worlds—I had begun to see this clearly, and that I could make a choice. It would not be easy, but it was there, a choice; I could make it over and over again, until the first world didn't exactly disappear, but certainly mattered less. There was a world in which men like Joe Biden and Clarence Thomas held authority; and there was the world of literature.

DurasSpace is awareness, the link between youth and old age, between sanity and madness, between the consummation of love and the desire for solitude. The necessity of solitude. I am only now at this point in my life trying to be solitary. I am nineteen and I have had sex with exactly one person. I have never felt loved, never been loved. There was one man, a guest teacher at summer stock. He asked for my number, said, Let's get together in Los Angeles. That was it, and what it meant to him was nothing, another girl, another night, another body. After it happened I told him I was a virgin and he told me my first time should be with my boyfriend. It was too late, I didn't say. Not with someone like me, he didn't say. Someone who doesn't care about you, who would rather not see you again.

It would be years before I would have sex again, and in those years I lived in a hospital, years before I could feel loved again, feel desirable. That early rejection, the violence of it, of being used and dismissed, at nineteen—it provided overwhelming evidence of my worthlessness.

In *The Lover*, Duras tells the story of her first affair—a story she would tell over and over again. The story of an affair between a fifteen-year-old French girl and a twenty-seven-year-old wealthy Chinese man. The setting is French-colonized Indochina, in 1929. For the girl in Indochina, this affair with the older man from Cholon, this early sexual experience is an opening not only to love but desire, the way this desire, the intensity of passion, of sex, would allow her to understand who she was, who she could be. Desire would make her into who she would be. She was a writer, she knew this, and the extremity of this passion, and her awareness of the impossibility built into it, this was the beginning of her story—the story of an artist. The education of a young girl, this portrait of the artist as a young girl in love.

In the opening of the novel, Duras collapses the time between the now and the then, the girl and the woman author and the filmmaker—she collapses that time into the time of the book and the book became the space where I would live—where I could make sense of my life just beginning, the life I never had and wouldn't have—I longed for that desire.

It was longing itself that shaped me.

DurasSpace revealed that the desire had nothing to do with one lover, the lover is a shifting object, and the obvious reading of the title—*The Lover*—is that he is the older man from Cholon. He loves the girl, the love is passionate, but the girl is the lover, too—it is her subjectivity, awakened, aroused. The narrator loves her girlhood friend, Helene Lagonelle, an impossible object of desire. She loves, too, being loved, or she has realized in being loved how impossible it is. To love. To be loved. She doesn't love this man but she loves herself with the man. She is the lover.

The narration wanders through space and time, the space of girlhood and the time of retrospection. In her memory, the scenes of the illicit affair, the freedom of becoming, and of sexual awakening become the story of a life.

A friend read *The Lover* not long ago, in her forties. She found it overwrought. Not for me, she said.

I wonder what it would be like to receive that book now, at this age, in my forties—what it would mean to me. It would not be the same. I would admire it but I would not become it. I know that.

It is a chemical reaction—it is magic, I have always thought—that moment of reception between reader and book. The time must be right. You can't plan it, that vulnerability, that blur between self and text. It is that powerful, it will make and unmake you if you let it.

For years I would've said it could've been no other but Marguerite Duras. But now I think it was who I was at that time.

The Lover is a great book, but it reached me deeply, formatively, because I needed it to.

What the Buddhists say: When the student is ready, the teacher will appear.

At Point Zero

Next I read *Woman at Point Zero* by Nawal El Saadawi. This was in the same class where I first read Marguerite Duras. It was called Minority Discourses. I told Tim, an actor I was hanging out with, about my reading and the book, I told him how disgusting patriarchy was, and that if he read this book, he would hate men, too. Or he would become a feminist. He said it was ridiculous to expect a man to be a feminist. *Woman at Point Zero* is about a young woman named Firdaus who is in prison, about to be put to death, for the murder of her pimp. The novel is framed by the narration by a doctor who visits Firdaus in prison. El Saadawi was an Egyptian doctor, feminist activist, and novelist. As a young doctor, she worked in a woman's prison. It was there she met a woman who became the inspiration for the novel.

The doctor-narrator of the novel is fully invested in hearing Firdaus's story. The story follows Firdaus' life. After her mother and father die, she is then taken to live in Cairo with her uncle and his wife. The uncle was a scholar who promises to give her an education. But when she moves in with him, he is abusive and cruel; eventually he sends her away to be married to a much older man. This older man is disgusting but she gets to go to school and she makes friends. It is her love for school and her education that keeps her connected to life. Throughout the novel, and through-out her life, she sees the eye of her mother over and over again. Her mother's eye is the constant in her life, a touchstone and a haunting; she searches for it everywhere.

Early in the book, Firdaus's friend tells her that she cannot live without love. Firdaus says,

Yet I am living without love.

To which her friend replies,

Then you are either living a lie or not living at all.

I wrote these lines on a notecard and taped them to my wall. An urging. Live this way, I told myself. You need love. I didn't want to live a lie. I wanted love, it was that simple. I got sick, I some-times think, because I needed care, love. And I did not know how to get it, to receive it.

Working the Trap

The idea is that the illness blocks the emergence of the self and so good medication will lift the fog and allow the self to cohere. It is all about finding the right medication. I took notes as I tried each new antidepressant. It may take a week or two weeks to work. So each day, what I noticed or didn't notice. For the rest of my life, I'd be on one or more medications. It occurs to me how unknown I was to myself in those days. So what did it mean to be medicated at that age, before I'd formed a coherent self? With most anti-depressants, I no longer felt unrelenting sadness, but I didn't feel happiness, either.

I think of a recent commercial for a newer SNRI antidepressant, called Cymbalta. In the commercial, the depressed woman has a lever on her back. She is falling, failing, until she takes Cymbalta. Then it is as if someone has wound up the lever on her back—she is working again. She has been turned on (she did not turn herself on, but no matter). Turned on now, she stands up straight, no more slouching, she opens her eyes—oh, look! The sun is shining!

SNRIs turn the lever. Wind you up. If depression is the lack of something, the SNRI is the excess. On SNRIs I needed less sleep, or I woke up ready to go. I could wake up and go for a jog, or at least it felt that way. I could keep my rigid schedule, and yet still I seemed to live on the edge of something. I stopped crying. In the worst days of my illness, I cried often, regularly, without end. I cried as if trying to get to the end of it—the end of something. The SNRI removed that physical response. I couldn't cry. I couldn't have an orgasm. The former is considered a positive effect; the latter an unfortunate (side) effect.

Twenty years later, a relapse of sorts, going through my divorce. In the midst of divorce. The endless tears. This time, the crying seemed an appropriate reaction to the loss, the upheaval and disorientation, the disequilibrium, of my actual life. It was grief, and I did not need to get to the end of it, I did not need to rush the end. By then I knew that everything ends, no matter what.

So it's February now, I'm still there, my first weeks of Barnard, I go to my favorite class: Death in Modern Fiction. I hear a girl say, If you go to the health center, and tell them you're sad or whatever, they'll give you Prozac. If you say you broke up with your boyfriend, they'll give you Prozac. Everyone around her laughed. She was so cool, sophisticated in that raised-in-Manhattan way foreign to me. They hand it out like candy, she said.

She was talking about me. I knew it. Now I knew that it meant nothing; that doctor didn't know me, she knew Prozac. One more poison. I stopped taking the pills.

When Leo said the word—*suicide*—in a very specific, intentional way, it woke me up. It was as if Leo was the first person on the

planet to have this idea. What a genius idea! I thought. I have
never heard of such a brilliant idea!

No matter that suicide as a plot point was right there in front
of me all along. It was in all the great books I was reading, in the
plays, too. As James Baldwin put it, in a passage I read many years
later, *You think your pain and your heartbreak are unprecedented in
the history of the world, but then you read.* I understood this but it
would not heal me back then, when my suffering was so strange
and new and singular, so acute that I could not believe anyone
ever had felt this way before. If they had, they would not survive.
And so neither would I.

I had committed to being an intellectual, I announced this regularly. It was a way, I think now, of making a self. It was being
young. To make such embarrassing pronouncements. When you
are young, you need these sorts of pronouncements. Global,
sweeping, definitive. As you age, you relax. I was trying to work
the trap I was in, as Judith Butler put it. I didn't understand the
trap back then. What young woman does? I understood that. On
some level I knew this. But it did not matter. I had hoped that my
study, that my move to New York, the rigor of my major, would
save me—eighteen credits was a lot, but I felt such shame over
all I did not know, I had such a desire to read everything, to catch
up. The harder I tried, the more impossible it felt. I did not trust
I would get there in time. I had a paralyzing sense of time running out.

A teacher later told me that this is a mark of immaturity, to
consider yourself old prematurely, at twenty or even twenty-
eight. He was right, of course, I see that now that I am in my forties. Preternaturally depressed, an older writer described it this
way. Still, I want to think of this preternatural sense of doom and

despair as a coming into oneself, a fractured coming of age—as it was for Duras, as it was for Sylvia Plath. It was a stage in becoming, an unbecoming. An immature if necessary attempt to avoid committing to life.

Suicide is one way of working the trap, after all. It is always there.

The Psychoanalyst

Nineteen ninety-one. Chicago. Two months before I move to New York, I make an appointment to see an analyst. The Institute for Psychoanalysis. 122 South Michigan Avenue.

How did I find the place? A recommendation from Leo's analyst. I was stupid about analysts. This was not my culture. I grew up fifty miles west of Chicago, which might as well have been another state.

I wear a long brown skirt, a thick wool sweater. I sit in a chair and the analyst sits across the room, far away. The room is larger than my studio apartment. I sit, I don't lie down. The doctor asks about my eating habits, my relationships, my depression.

Why are you here?

My hair is falling out, I say.

A symptom of hysteria, he says.

The final months of 1991: Now my notebook entries become longer, going on for pages, I write in the notebook multiple times a day, narrating my life, every response to every offense: what this man said here, what that family member did. Now I can't relate to this person writing these sentences, these long paragraphs—the amount of time she has, all this time to waste, and the intensity of the detail here. I want to tell her to turn her attention elsewhere. It is as if she believes that writing this all down will get her somewhere. That the writing itself will work out this particular complication, or that irritation.

No, it is not that. It is what is inside of her and the writing of it is this desperate movement, that is clear, to purge it, to set it aside, beyond her. A puzzle. She takes it all too personally. She is too emotional. Anyone can see it, but for her it is just this. This is who she is.

The notebook becomes a place to arrange a self. A testing out—how much can I do with language, what will language contain? My writing traces the extremes of my emotional life: here I am desperately in love, here despairing, alone, lost. I am just beginning to write of my despair and isolation, a development linked to my reading. I write of the thrill of discovering certain writers: Duras and Toni Morrison. Adrienne Rich, Erica Jong, and Alice Walker. I quote passages, I merge these women writers' ideas with my own, an intellectual life I didn't know I could have.

This is the beginning, I think, of making a home. The beginning of creating myself on the page. Thirty years later it still embarrasses me to read, yet I see what I was doing. I was creating myself out of necessity, this removal or renunciation, the move into thirdspace.

There is something else in this notebook, in these months. Occasional but regular mention of screaming, of voices. The circular logic or paranoia of madness. I write of reading and then shift back into the seamlessness of my mindscape. This was DurasSpace and it was a breaking down. A disintegration.

———

Why are you here? he asks again. I am trying to explain something, but I don't know the language, to get from this place to that.
So I say: It has to do with the program. What is the program?
The program requires motion, movement, water, the gym, the
bike, reading, going to work, not talking to anyone as much as
possible, go to work, more walking, home by nine. Avoid that twilight hour, when it begins. Nearing darkness. That time of day, if I
could get through that and get to sleep, I'd be okay.

I began to cry. He stared. He didn't offer tissues. He didn't
move.

So this was psychoanalysis: the unfeeling blank slate. I was waiting for something—care, approbation—something I would find
later, in another institute in another state. Not here. Before I left,
he wrote a note on a prescription pad. A treatment plan. You need
to be in analysis four days a week, for your hysteria, he said again.
I'd taken enough women's studies courses by then to know that
"hysteria" wasn't a legitimate diagnosis. But I only mumbled okay
and took the piece of paper.

Three hundred dollars a week, he said.

It was not covered under my health insurance. I could not ask
my father to pay for it. He didn't even believe in it.

I left that room, and didn't return.

Maybe I knew even then that hysteria meant nothing.

The analyst's indifference felt violent, another blow to a fragile
self.

Whatever hysteria meant to that doctor in that room, a doctor
who spoke to me for twenty minutes, I didn't have it. I had lonely.
I had sad. But if I knew that, or could say that, if it was that simple, if that was enough, I wouldn't have spent years searching for
someone to tell me.

Months later at the New York State Psychiatric Institute, I was told that traditional analysis was dangerous for someone like me. I'd been shattered by the coldness of the analyst. I needed the human response of a caring professional. Something relational. Psychodynamic therapy was what I needed, they said. Days and months and years of it.

Women's Studies

I like to think my mom would've told me the truth—it's stupid to follow the rules of the Church: no sex before marriage, no birth control, no masturbation. And stupid to follow the rules of a doctor like the one at the Institute for Psychoanalysis. She would have tempered the weight of it all, allowed for some perspective. It offers a structure for life, she may have said, but it is not life.

Two weeks after I'm admitted to the long-term ward, a new patient appears in the common area. It is a Tuesday afternoon, which is the only time for new arrivals. Something shifts with each new arrival. This one looks like Madonna, Bridget whispers to Marion. Stella overhears her. I'm better than Madonna, she says, deadpan, not looking at them.

Bridget finds this funny: Will you look at that!

Stacey is staring. It's hard not to. Our days are long and empty. This is an event.

Stella arrives with her mother by her side. Stella's mother's agony is more pronounced than Stella's own. Her mother leans into Stella, her head in her hands, wiping tears. Stella's face stares ahead. She is beautiful: her round blue eyes, defined jaw, full lips.

When they've finished the bureaucracy of the admission, the forms and medications and collection of sharp objects, when the bed is ready, a doctor asks to speak to Stella's mother privately.

I can see Stella there still, frozen on the sofa. Her face remains still in contrast to her mother, who is crying now loudly, wailing, as she grabs her daughter's arm.

It is better for you to go now, I hear a doctor say. It will be better for your daughter.

Her mother again leans into Stella, who doesn't seem to notice. She's frozen.

Her mother, loudly: When can I see her?

We will be in touch, the doctor says. Her mother gathers herself, grips her purse. The elevator is there, waiting for her.

There was one elevator operator, or that is how I remember it. One operator always on duty, always smiling. He sat on a stool and pressed the buttons, making sure the right people were getting on or off. If he was meant to be a guard, it never felt that way. He was a middle-aged man, thinning gray hair. He, too, had a heavy Irish brogue like Bridget, the hospital aide there to greet me at the elevator. It was as if my Irish grandmother were there with me, and her relatives, my lost aunts and uncles, perhaps. Always smiling, making light of it all. Oh, don't worry, the smiles seemed to say, you'll be just fine after all, now, won't you.

I see Stella: her miniskirt, T-shirt cut at the neck and the arms. Her skeletal arms. Her mother calling out for Stella even as she is asked to leave, told that visiting hours are over, assured that her daughter will be safe. We will contact you when Stella is ready, they say. I don't know how it happened, how Stella found her way there, subdued, resigned, signing herself in while her mother begged her not to, pleading that she just come home.

Sitting Still

Who was it who wrote: "All of humanity's problems stem from a man's inability to sit quietly in a room alone"?

I think this is another way to define madness, too—the inability to sit quietly in a room alone. For many years of my life I had trouble sitting still. For most of my life. In the years before my breakdown, I became so afraid of myself. I was terrified of what I felt, of the loneliness that overwhelmed me. I could not sit with a feeling. Neither could I sit with my body—it was a problem, I obsessed over it, how it shifted, grew, and morphed. Instead of sitting with it, in it, I lived as if to control it.

It is a combination of stillness and the single-minded focus that is necessary to write. To sit with a problem quietly in a room alone.

From one medical textbook about the ward, a doctor writes:
   The female patients *have trouble being alone.*
   The female patients *go to great lengths to avoid abandonment.*

———

He does not say, This is one problem with being human. This trouble of sitting alone in a room, having to sit alone in a room, not having a room at all.

A student in my summer workshop, she is older, perhaps in her seventies, she is retired and finally allowing herself the gift of time to write. To tell her story. Every summer for years now I sit with students who have a story to tell. Sometimes I think my job is to help them tell a story. Other times I think my job is to listen to a story. Most times I think my job is to create a space where someone can tell a story to someone else who will listen. Who will care. A way of caring about sentences or craft—about form or content—is another way of saying, *Please listen to my story.* To sit in a circle. To say come sit quietly in this room with us.

The woman was kind and generous to me and to her classmates. She seemed astounded by herself, her ability to write about the thing that had taken up a great space of her life. That thing was food. Or it was not food but it was her body. Or not her body but her body's relationship to food. As I remember now, the woman was recently a widow. Perhaps retired. In any case she had time *to sit quietly in a room alone.* This was late in her life. You may see her on the street and think she is a kind lady, a sweet woman, a gentleness to her. You might imagine her a librarian, maybe she works in a bookstore. A grandma.

But no, she is not a grandma. She did not have children. She is a feminist. She is proud of the gains of second-wave feminism, and she was fully engaged back in the '70s and the '80s, the consciousness-raising groups. She is enraged, to see what's been lost.

But what she wrote about was food. How it began when she was ten or eleven or twelve, and how it intensified throughout her teenage years, into her twenties and through her thirties. And even when it eased off at times, it was still there. Still the preoccupation with her body, the size of it, the weight of it, how many calories had she taken in that day—she kept a list, and now she revisits her diaries and there on many pages, the list of what she ate that day, the estimated number of calories. The weigh-ins. And often the complaints she wrote in so many daily entries—*I feel fat. I feel fat today. I just ate and I feel fat.* The refrain throughout her life. Impossible to have a meal and let it be, not return to the body, the way it has failed, the loss of control. Impossible to sit with that.

What occurred to her now as she hit her seventies—and this wasn't the first time but how profound it felt as she moved into the final decades of her life—what a remarkable waste of time it had been. What if she had been able to think about something else in all those minutes and days and decades. What if she had eaten to be healthy and exercised to be healthy and what if there had not been this constant and whirring engine in her mind's chatter, driving her through her days and nights, filtering her experience.

And assessing her lost husband's life she considers it—the space he had to think about the sixteenth century—his knowledge of the Tudor Dynasty, the writing of Erasmus, Thomas More, and Shakespeare, too. How she loved to hear him discuss Shakespeare, what joy she felt when they attended a performance of *Henry V* one summer in Central Park, how it felt to sit next to him, the breeze there, how she knew she was happy. *This was happiness.* She nearly said it out loud, she knew it was necessary to acknowledge it. Yet even there in that moment, hearing her husband explain how Erasmus's writing on the education of a prince, how his ideas played out in Shakespeare's Henry plays, a kind of thought experiment—she knew her great good luck, this was as good as life could get—and yet still, even there, the problem of her body. The weight of it. How she had failed or would fail that day to eat enough, to stay within the bounds of her forever limits.

And though she had realized decades ago that it was a feminist issue, there was at least one book that argued as much, and that was back in the 1980s; no, it was not a new insight, not a new revelation into what it meant to be an American woman, a relatively privileged American woman. Though she understood the larger context of it—the politics of it—she was not able to make it less important. And that failure, too, made her sad for her life.

After she read her story, there was a long pause, a silence, an inhale and an exhale. A student said, Wow. A few snapped their fingers. We were quiet a bit, in that way that I find comforting after such an experience, but others find awkward. Finally, the woman spoke. She said that this was not what she wanted to write about. She said she would not apologize for it, but it took a lot for her to write this. I had told the group to follow your obsessions, to write into your obsessions. She said that she had tried to locate other obsessions—like her husband, who would be writing about the Henry plays or the chaos of the early seventeenth century, when all was up in the air, the chaos at the end of the long Elizabethan reign. No, her obsession was food, what she ate and didn't eat. Her weight. So she gave in to it. She knew it was privileged and embarrassing, she knew so many people had written about this, how banal. I don't want to write about this, she said.

Why don't you write about someone else, a student suggested. Focus on someone else.

What if, another woman said, it wasn't a waste. What if it was one way of being alive. Yes, maybe you could have been thinking about molecular genetics or quantum physics—but even then, you would be you, you would be trapped in your body, in your life. It is all content, there is always content.

An eating disorder might be the displacement of attention from the body politic to the body personal.

My preoccupation with food made it difficult for me to sit, or it meant there were only days and times of day when I could tolerate sitting in my own body. Many days in the hospital and many days in my life I was overcome—the expression—uncomfortable in my own skin. Yes, that was it.

I'm just saying, that same student continued, that we don't get to choose our obsessions, and really, who says that thinking about Shakespeare or botany or quantum physics is more valuable than thinking about what it means to live in a body.

The Book as a Room (II)

I didn't know what I was doing at the Institute for Psychoanalysis but it made more sense than going to church. For many years, I'd try and fail not to go to church. Something would pull me back, over and over again. I no longer believed, but I wanted to believe. I wanted the home, what it felt like once long ago, that feeling of being held.

Nineteen eighty-six. There was something about being Catholic. It was the water. For years, long after I'd become a decidedly non-practicing Catholic, I swam in it. As familiar as family. I remember the Church or my religion as I remember the school uniform, the texture starchy, stiff, a generic comfort.

One room: I am twelve or thirteen or fourteen or sixteen years old. My body has become a problem to solve. And the solution is a problem. When I cannot sleep, when my body is too much, I touch myself, I find release, peace and calm. It is a discovery. I think it is just me. I know it is just me. No one has mentioned it. It is as if I've discovered a secret, a superpower all my own. I'll find one of my dad's medical textbooks in the basement. I'll find what seems like a definition: a mortal sin. Self-pleasure, self-flagellation. It will stop me from getting into heaven. In 1979 the pope came to Chicago, the pope who served as the head of the Church for nearly thirty years. In 1983, the pope confirmed: Self-gratification is wrong. It is wrong because your sexual life should only exist in the context of marriage, it is selfish to take the power of your body, the potential of your sexual body, and turn inward. Once I figure out what I am doing, once I find the words for it, or read the words, I will know and I will fear it. The pope has said so.

In this room, each day, I will find pleasure, a release, and soon after I feel enormous grief. I can't go on the internet, can't google it. There are no sex-positive feminists to tell me how normal this was, or that my shame existed in the context of a patriarchy that denied women a right to her own body. I could not find a community. The next day, or not long after the calm, I felt tremendous guilt. I was not taught this, what it is, what it means, what my body might want. I know it is wrong. I have been taught that it is a sin. I can last a few days, or a week, and then I give in, I do it again and again. I know it is a mortal or venial sin, I know it will keep me from getting into heaven, and I don't care. Then I say a rosary before sleep, and I go to confession. I stop sitting face-to-face with the priest, I hide behind the screen. *Forgive me, Father, for I have sinned.*

A midcentury-modern–designed school, an open window, sunlight flooded the entrance, four stairs leading to the four glass doors framed in green, one flat buttress overhead and, above that, a second burnt-red slanted roof. To reach the church, you exit through the front of the school. Of course no one called it midcentury modern back then. But I see now, the psychogeography, what we were meant to feel through the space. To see through the entrance to the stairways, the open main office, the American flag, beyond that a door to the gym. We didn't notice the design, it was familiar, ubiquitous: the church, the school, the *Brady Bunch* house.

To get to the church you cross the parking lot, go up one set of stairs and down another. Across the street, you'll see the church. There is simplicity to it, from the outside. Red doors, as high as a large house might be, but nothing like the churches of the past, like my mother's church, St. Vincent De Paul in Lincoln Park with the dramatic entrance, the ornamentation, the imposing structure. The long aisle. In those days, a brief moment between the end of Vatican II and the emergence of a more inclusive nonhierarchical church, a hippie church with a folk choir and pews in a half circle. One of the priests regularly invited the children to the front.

I would go early on a Saturday afternoon, before the 5:30 p.m. Mass. We went each weekend, anytime between Saturday at 5:30 and Sunday at 12:30.

If I go there now, or I see a picture of it, or if I see a picture of me there, what I was doing, why I was doing it—I will say, it was so Catholic. That is Catholic, I will see it now. It will seem (almost) foreign. But that's not how I remember it. What? Some-one will ask me, when I tell him about going to Mass. Your dad made you do that, every weekend? I try to explain, I say: Yes, I say, but it was not like that, though it was like that. I will say, It was more like having to go to Grandma's house for dinner every Sunday.

Is that true? I don't know. I've become more generous over the years, I've come to see that though I long ago left the Church, it hasn't left me. I can say how ridiculous, how corrupt, how misogy-nistic. It began when I sat there, eight or ten or thirteen years old, motherless, telling my secrets to a man in a robe, a man of author-ity. Secrets about my body. He blessed me. It began in a room where the contract was clear: If I confessed my sin and my shame, I would be redeemed.

It had something to do with the beauty of that emaciated, wounded body hanging there every Sunday over me, above me, a body to worship and honor. Was that part of my desire for annihilation, oblivion, a holy anorexia? I can say, too, that it shaped me, formed me, that I was loved there, that it held me.

So today I'm here for confession, a sacrament I took in second grade in preparation for my third-grade Communion. Confession took place to the right of the altar, an offstage area through small doors next to the priest and altar boys' quarters.

First time in this room, I sit behind the screen.

Forgive me, Father, for I have sinned. It has been three weeks since my last confession.

Since then, I have fought with my brother, I have lied, I have talked behind a friend's back, I have drunk too much alcohol, and (I would save this for the end of the list) touched myself impurely.

Later: I was touched impurely. (Worse.)

My religion teacher told me how to say it, how to put it. These were the words. The language of it, of my body.

I wish I knew what the priest was doing there behind the screen. Was he bored, was he daydreaming, was he getting off on it, a young girl speaking of masturbating? The likely answer to each question is yes. And then he blessed me. And then he assigned me the requisite rosaries, Our Fathers, Hail Marys. Be nicer to your brother. Obey your parents. Go and sin no more.

I would go home absolved, relieved. I may go to heaven now, I would tell myself. If I die right now, I'll go to heaven. The pleasure of that knowledge. Sitting there, in that moment, the moment just after I was forgiven. I would say my rosary, I would go in peace to sin no more—but I would sin more. And I would return, then again, later I would return to be absolved. It would go on this way, for months, for years—until one day, I didn't know it, but it was the last day, the last time, there was no more to confess, or there was no more to forgive, there was no going in peace, no sin no more.

April 1992. Still the beginning of my moral career. It's a few weeks before I get to the long-term place, I'm still here in the space of the liminal, or the preliminal, I have moved from pre-patient to inpatient. This is the beginning of my moral career. Here the lights are always bright, there is always the noise of someone coming and going, there is an intercom, there are nurses chatting, patients making noise. There is a man, a Holocaust survivor, seated on the sofa. He will not speak of the Holocaust (how do I know this? The patients talk, sometimes a nurse or a social worker talks). His children and grandchildren visit. A patient is screaming. I can see the face of the girl in the next bed, she must be sixteen, I can't move. I see a man walking by, wearing Orthodox garb, I've met him, his name is Shlomo, he pauses near the door to our room. He looks in. I call to him, Please turn off the light. He has stopped in the doorway now. Please, I say again, only now I see he is shaking his head furiously. I cannot, he doesn't say, just continues to shake his head, moving back now. It is the Sabbath, he says, walks away, shuffles down the hall. I'm moved by his devotion. I think I understand it. We all have our rules, our ways of being. In here we are the selves we were out there, more or less.

Toward a Theory of My Illness (I)

1. A mark of being young—you have so much knowledge, and no experience with which to make sense of the knowledge.

2. Many years passed before I saw myself, my experience, in a larger context.

3. Over time I realized that everybody was depressed. I mean, everybody my age was depressed, or everybody the age that I had been when I became depressed was also depressed. It turned out that many other people become depressed at that age.

4. By everybody, I don't mean everybody at all. I mean artists and writers and actors and, in general, these were the people I spent time around.

5. Or I mean *the melancholy of being human*.

6. I discovered that Dr. Triel was right—there were as many sick people outside of the hospital as there were inside.

7. This wasn't necessarily a comfort. If it were true, if I was one of many, then my long hospitalization seemed more shameful. If so many people were like this, deep down, yet were living lives, however compromised, well, then there was no point

in me being in the hospital that long. I wondered if the nurse
Roxane may have been right—I was there because I thought
I was special, that my suffering was worse than anyone else's
suffering, that I needed more help, more care than the normal
depressed person who was everywhere.

8.   The Buddhists call this the second arrow of suffering—
blaming yourself for your suffering. Freud differentiated between
mourning and melancholia. While mourning is a normal
reaction to loss, a transitory process, melancholia is the result of
turning the loss inward, directing it toward the self. Unable to
face the pain of the loss, we turn against ourselves.

9.   Is it possible, if I had known that so many others were
suffering as I was, that I would've felt less alone? I think I did
know that many others were suffering. I just didn't know what
that suffering looked like, or what mine should look like. Or I
thought it was my fault (self-reviling).

10.   Still, to follow this inquiry would lead me to ask why
everybody who said they were depressed hadn't also found
themselves in that place. I knew they all had their reasons, but
it didn't seem reason enough, and if we all were feeling this, why
was I the only one who'd been there?

11.   As often is the case, the problem is language. There is
language to speak of depression, and over the past thirty years
there is more language, and more deployment of language
with which to describe mental illnesses like depression. This
is meant to decrease stigma, which is very real, which I myself
internalized and might still project onto others, if I am being
honest, but the solution to this problem—the increase in
language around mental illness—like everything else flattens
language, makes vague words like depression even more vague
and meaningless, so that you might be depressed because it is

a cloudy day and you might be depressed because, like Sylvia Plath or her son, Nicholas, many people in your family have been depressed. There is the depressed you can talk about, as Leo often would and still does, and the depressed that is Julia Kristeva's melancholic, with her turning inward, this inability to use language. The manifestation of depression, too, is wildly variable—it may be suicide, not leaving the house, not sleeping or eating. What is called clinical depression is a depression that has become a problem. As Dr. Triel told me thirty years ago, welcoming me to the long-term hospital—and this before he knew my story at all—my depression was classic: not eating, not sleeping, feeling worse in the morning, not speaking, giving up on relationships, low self-esteem, losing faith in communication or language at all.

12.   It was so clear, the way he put it. I did want help. I didn't believe I could get better—I understood what I felt as the end of things, as what I would feel forever: some defining part of me. Unchangeable.

13.   To believe Dr. Triel, to enter this world, this institution, was to take a leap of faith not unlike what I'd learned as a Catholic. Give yourself over. You will be saved. Let go of your need to understand. You were born this way—original sin; mental illness.

14.   To be there, to sign myself in, to stay there for years—this became further evidence of my illness.

Without Care

We lived in a newly developed subdivision of Aurora, Illinois, called Sans Souci. My mother had grown up in Chicago in a two-bedroom, one-bath, third-floor walkup with her parents and her three siblings, in Lincoln Park. The artist Henry Darger lived in a boardinghouse just down the street. He went to Mass three times a day at the church my mother saw from her window, St. Vincent De Paul. When they discovered the massive trove of artwork in Darger's apartment after his death, they also found, among hoards of documents, a stack of missives from the Catholic Mass at St. Vincent's. Each day Mass attendees would get a missive, it would list the day of the year of Our Lord, the gospel verse that day, it would list those who needed prayers.

The home in Sans Souci, the life of a doctor's wife, in a home with four bathrooms, four bedrooms, a wet bar in that '70s way, a huge backyard—was this her dream?

As an adult, I look at suburban subdivisions with minor horror. I could never live in one, which feels like death.

———

But as a kid, as a girl, in that Edenic time, I was so happy. Happy to have a backyard that extended all the way into my best friend's backyard. Happy to go outside after school nearly to dusk, with friends. Happy to play Colored Eggs or Bloody Murder around our house or someone else's house. Happy to get on my bike and ride to the pile of rubble around the block, the rubble where Astrid and Benita's house was being built before they moved in. And it sat there the rubble, all fall and all winter, a pile of rock and stones and whatever else, we didn't care, we climbed the mountain of it, hid in it, a place to go after school, a secret. Even happier in the winter when the rock was covered with snow, and the mountain was larger, more exciting, a new land.

Aurora was a vast expanse of cornfield in those days. Our subdivision had been a cornfield. When we drove to the grocery store, the west side of the road was cornfields. The corn was high and then cut and it gave me a girlhood sense of possibility. Our cousins said we lived in the boonies, but when we went to their homes in the North Shore, we recoiled from the congestion of it, the old houses close together, the smug contentment of a perfectly contained and designed space for the wealthy to live just far enough north of the city.

The yard behind our house seemed to extend for miles and the blue sky never ended. From there we could see stars, a joy or comfort I took for granted, as all children do. I rarely see the stars in my adult city life.

Patient: "I guess I haven't been happy since I was six years old."

I read this line in my chart and I don't believe my younger self. Or I understand her now, what she was doing. She'd read *The Bell Jar*, she read Esther Greenwood's line: *I haven't been happy since I was nine years old.* Esther's father had died when she was a girl. Her unhappiness was located exactly here, demarcated by the blunt violence of loss. This is what Plath offered me: a narrative frame for my grief.

That made sense to me. That my mom's death was the end of my life, my happiness. But it wasn't entirely true. Sylvia Plath helped me explain my suffering. It was language that I would use to get help.

For a long time I felt shame over this, finding my self, my words in a novel by Sylvia Plath. But now I think that it was the only way I knew how to explain what I felt.

My mom drove a blue station wagon, and on the bumper were many stickers, including her favorite, a PSA, also on a button on her kitchen cork board: HAVE YOU HUGGED YOUR KID TODAY? It was a movement in the 1970s; I didn't know if her parents had not hugged her? I think they were formal and repressed, and perhaps had not grown up in a culture or a world or a time where people believed that children needed to be hugged. Her parents had come from Ireland as teenagers, without a high school education, and maybe they hadn't been hugged at all. They grew up in County Down, which is in Northern Ireland, and when they left, it was the early 1900s and if you know Irish history, you know that Irish independence from British rule did not come until 1922. Which is not that long ago. And when it came, it came with a price—the price was that six counties in Northern Ireland would still belong to the British.

And in those counties, there would not be stability, not for a long time, and the Protestants and the Catholics (my family) would live separately, would walk on separate sides of the street. The Catholics would not own property, would never progress. So that is the world they left, my mother's parents, one first to the Midwest, Nebraska, finally to Chicago, and my grandmother to her sister in New York and then Chicago. They were part of what Fintan O'Toole calls *the vanishing Irish*. When my grandmother arrived, she was married. She was old to be married, in her thirties, and then came four children in a row, over forty, unusual back then.

HAVE YOU HUGGED YOUR KID TODAY? Why did this 1976 PSA slogan appeal to my mom? I remember the red font, the big letters, the hug bug who looked like the Kool-Aid Man. Only later did I wonder about it. It's not quite saying, *Don't beat your kid today*. Which is maybe why it worked, if you can measure a thing. Innocuous enough, no one can disagree. Yes! you would answer. Or you would look for your kid, the closest one, and hug him. Yes, you would answer. I hugged my kid today!

I was happy to have my mom there after school, though she could be awful, too. A Friday, a half day at school. No lunch. I am in second grade, my brothers in fourth and fifth. My little sister is in preschool, so already home. My mom has stopped to get us lunch at the bakery. Ham salad sandwiches. We are sitting in our kitchen, full of light, a dream kitchen of the 1970s, a separate eat-in kitchen, a wooden table, brown curtains around the windows. Only I am still there when everyone leaves. I have to sit there until I finish the sandwich, which I will not eat. It is disgusting, I will vomit if I eat it. Okay then, she says. You won't get dessert. She has dessert for us, also from the German bakery. When you are done, you can come join us. I sat there. I studied the curtains, the dark brown background with a flower print, winding vines and yellow flowers. There were valances up top and short curtains on the windows. From the Sears catalog, which she adored: a swag topper, a valance, matching canopies. I can see the backyard, which extends until it reaches the backyard of my friend's house. I won't eat, I won't go outside. I'll become the curtains, the floral print.

I will always live in an apartment, I think. The work of a house scares me. What a job that would be. I think of Anne Sexton:

Some women marry houses.

But it wasn't tidy, not the way it would be when we moved into our new house a year later. Never, ever a thing out of place. Our new mom was so angry at the mess, angry at anyone who made a mess, anything out of place, how it undid her, how she cleaned all day long and still it was never clean enough and mostly because there were so many children there and those children had stuff and they left the stuff everywhere.

You had to walk on eggshells in her presence, how scary she was, her explosive temper, her moods; you never knew.

My mom had a poster hanging in my brother's bedroom, a quote by Carl Jung: *Creative minds are rarely tidy.*

We lived in the Sans Souci house until my mom died in the house, in her bedroom, the large king-size bed with her own large bathroom and her double vanity. That bathroom where I first saw her dye her gray hair, where she put on her Wind Song perfume, lipstick. Where I watched her.

———

On the wall, a photographic portrait of her in her wedding dress. A bookshelf: Herman Wouk, *The Winds of War*. Another book with an exciting title: *We Don't Want Nobody Nobody Sent*—this title I went over and over in my head for years, I was hailed by this title as much as I had been by *Shyness* or by Erma Bombeck's *If Life Is a Bowl of Cherries, What Am I Doing in the Pits?* Or *The Grass Is Always Greener Over the Septic Tank.*

There was equilibrium in these titles, each a valve to another world.

I knew this then, but I didn't need it yet. I still had the calm, the peace, the equilibrium of Aurora.

I was six, seven, eight—the years when life is concrete, reliable, before the cracks begin to show.

I remember that year after her death in that house as a beautiful time, but only because it was brief, and it was like living in the aftermath of an explosion, everything settled but destroyed, the quiet of it, nothing to do but play.

That year was just the five of us: my dad, two older brothers, younger sister and me. The gap of my mother. The absence. This configuration never came again and never would again. It was before the chaos of the new family, after the horror of her dying. It was a liminal moment, the five of us. Often someone would come to help, an aunt or an uncle. A babysitter. A nanny named Shirley for a while, and another named Marilyn, who I made a point of torturing.

The house was a haunted house after her death, her clothes still in the closet, her perfume, her favorite things. That Christmas in a tall cabinet we found a box of Christmas presents she'd ordered from her favorite Christmas store—named, To Erin, Love, Mom. To Suzy, Love, Santa.

Did she put them there knowing she was dying or did she put them there and forget or did she put them there to be ready for that Christmas that she wouldn't live to see?

That Christmas Day my dad invited every single relative we had, on his side and on my mom's side of the family, to our house for the day. I remember it as the day when I felt most loved, it was the most Christmas Christmas. It was our *Fanny and Alexander* Christmas, all love, festivity, and sadness. So much love and so much sadness.

I think for some people Sans Souci was the site of a happy childhood. A subdivision of the 1960s and 1970s, single-family homes. Sans Souci was the name of a palace in Haiti. A French name from a French word, for the palace of a Haitian king. Without care—*sans souci*—without worry. Carefree.

We lived on a street called Wyckwood.

A month after my mother died, the same neighbor girl who told me that my mom was going to die was at my house. We were sitting outside around the porch table. The girl asked me if I knew that the word *wyck* meant "death."

I did not.

Strange, isn't it, she said knowingly.

————

She had the authority of the older girl, the teenager among nine-year-olds.

It wasn't true (I looked it up later), but that didn't matter. Everything meant death in those days.

How do you not measure your life in a before and after? Does anyone not do this?

Maybe there are people for whom the after doesn't come until very late in life. There are lucky people, blessed people, but most people on the planet aren't lucky this way.

The before is solidified, demarcated early on. The after is the rest.

Flannery O'Connor: *Anybody who has survived his childhood has enough information about life to last him the rest of his days.*

My dad found a book I wrote in that year after my mother's death. It was a book about a character named Action E, who was my little sister. I made my sister be the protagonist of my first novel. It was a book with photographs. I wrote an outline: the life of Action E. She does this and this and this. She is a happy girl, a busy girl. I used my dad's camera to take a picture of E for each scene—he brings the film to the film store, he has it developed, picks up the prints, and brings it home. On each page I taped a photograph and written text. On the cover, the title, and on the back, my photograph. I am standing next to the refrigerator, I am holding the handle. I wear my short-shorts and roller skates. Roller skates in the house. It was a free-for-all, those weeks after her death, before the new family; my dad worked so hard to make us happy, to play games. He was playful by default, social and sweet, gentle. His mom did play, hugged, giggled, did not seem waylaid by sadness. So my dad, how he kept those days so light, despite the nightmare it must have been for him, and who knows, I never imagined what it was like for him, a young doctor, to see his wife get sick, to take her to other doctors, to understand what those doctors meant when they said words I only overheard but did not understand: words like *malignant* and *remission. In remission. Inoperable tumor. Mastectomy. Metastasized.* What it was like for him, that he could not save her, that all his medical training meant nothing when it came to this. And for her—she'd married a doctor, for a girl of her generation that meant stability and hope, that meant a good life, a safe life—but how quickly all of that fell away, her cancer, to have to sit her children down, the day after Christmas, the tree still there, decorated, our presents under the tree, to have to tell them that she would be going into the hospital after the New Year, they needed to do some tests. She may be in a few days, she explained. Okay, I said, and went back to my Barbies. Did it mean anything then? Did she know she would not live to the next Christmas? The next summer? She was a nurse, after all, and those words meant something to her, too—this was the second time, the cancer in remission was now back, and her daughters were five and eight, her sons ten and twelve.

When my dad gives me this book, I realize that I have been a writer, that it's not true that I never wanted to be a writer. My author's note ends: *This is her first book.* And there I am in my roller skates. My long hair knotted, my dad had no idea how to do our hair, I stopped combing it, stopped brushing it. My little sister stopped wearing underwear. Our clothes are now mismatched. On the floor-to-ceiling cork board next to the refrigerator, vestiges of my mom everywhere—messy paintings, our drawings, pictures, the mess she wanted us to live with; *creative minds are rarely tidy.*

This is her first book. I sit here writing this, and as often happens when I write of my mom, I'm crying, I'm in tears. It seems like something I shouldn't admit, as if these pages arrive from some secure and demarcated cerebral space, that I shouldn't admit that this is what I've chosen to do with my life, to stay here in her room, in that kitchen in my roller skates, in her bed, in that backyard, writing my book. About the author. *This is her first book.* Of course, it is so obvious now, or for me, that I had to write this story, that the only way to live with her death there with the end of that first life was to write about it forever, over and over again, and sometimes that means falling apart on the page, crying into sentences. I am here trying to get to the space, to get back to it, to make it work, to help her understand it, that it was brief and beautiful, that it was the rest of her life right there, holding the refrigerator wearing her roller skates.

Stuck in the Story

I turned twenty-one in the hospital. Someone sent flowers. As the reminder of or an urging from the outside, I was offended.

If I could explain my madness, it would be the persistence of a certain feeling—I remember the feeling but I can no longer feel it—the memory of it is vivid, and enough. It came over me around twilight. The intensity of a great, irrevocable loss would wash over me and with it, the absolute certainty that I would not survive it.

Strange you can remember the texture of a feeling without feeling it. With this as measure, I know I got better. But I also grew up, and *no feeling is final,* and I came to understand the waves of feeling, to know *this too shall pass.*

Every once in a while I'll feel a sadness or a loneliness that will remind me of the mad feeling, but it is nowhere as strong, and more importantly, it is never concomitant with the belief that it will last forever.

It gets worse before it gets better. I think of this phrase, which has become a meaningless cliché. It was new to me back then, but how false it feels now. I certainly got worse in those years, but it did not get better. I got so much worse that it was nearly impossible to reacclimate to the life of a functioning civilian. In the context of the institution, the effects of talk therapy are undermined. The power dynamic becomes everything. Tell me your feelings, talk to me about your problems, and I will decide if you are well enough to leave or if you must remain here. It was a sport. I came to love my doctor and so no, I was not well enough. So I must make things worse than they are, I must leave out the ways in which I am okay. It was a negotiation: they wanted to cure me and I wanted their attention, which offered me love and care.

Not long after I left the hospital, I worked part-time as an assistant to a former ballerina. She hired me to spend time with her mother, who lived in a nursing home near the Cathedral Church of St. John the Divine at 120th Street and Amsterdam Avenue. I was still unstable, in and out of hospitals.

One day, walking with the ballerina, she explained to me that in order to see New York, to truly take it in, you must look above the first floor.

I've thought of her advice often. In some ways it is an apt metaphor to explain how I suffered in those days. I could not see above the first floor. Above the first floor, the original architecture, the testaments to history, the reminder that we are all always living in history.

New York in those days was the first floor. My eyes on the first floor.

The first floor was my skull, a trap—the *get me out of this place*. Before long, it was a psychiatric ward, a mental hospital, a doctor and a nurse telling me how to be.

New York was the beginning and the end of possibility for me, all within a few months.

Or, to paraphrase Georgia O'Keeffe:

You cannot paint New York as it is, you must paint it as you are.

Part Two

———

I SAW THE FIGURE 5 IN GOLD

Asylum Architecture (I)

I'm there a few days and already the geography of the place is familiar. The desert of time, the rhythm of days, nights, weekends. I don't know how soon I became used to it, how long it took for me to belong. But it happened—it became my home, and it was never my home.

I'm not sure when I began saying that I lived there. I was in the hospital. I was hospitalized. But after some years or decades, it shifted. *I lived there*, I would say. I lived there for years, two or three, I couldn't remember. I'd go back and check my journals, and the records: 1992–1996. It didn't seem wrong to say I lived there.

Stayed. As if in a hotel. It was a *stay*. Perhaps this is why I'm drawn to hotels, the freedom there, the way they always, no matter what, move me toward an edge of despair. Like psych wards, hotels are non-spaces. No places. The liminal. You stay but you don't live in a hotel, just as you don't live in a hospital. No one lives there. But a stay is also a possibility, a way to get away, to be away . . . to renounce all that binds you to home, to identity.

The Fifth Floor

Let's call it an E. An E facing the river to the west. The windows face west. There are windows facing east but they are not visible from here in this ward on the fifth floor. If I drew a picture of the long stem of the E, the top line would jut west: this is the women's dorm. The bottom line of the E is the men's dorm. There are only a few rooms in the men's dorm; the hall is mostly empty offices. The rooms in the men's dorm have doors. The offices are hidden there to the north. There is always less action there, in that direction. In the middle of the floor, the midline of the E, you'll find the community room. This room has the best view of the Hudson River. Near the window a television sits atop a wheeled cart. To the side, a stationary bicycle against the wall. It was a gesture. How strange, I think now, how undervalued diet and exercise were. We were served bland institutional food. We didn't leave the floor, or the building, didn't take walks. There were no yoga classes. We led sedentary lives.

In *A Room of One's Own*, Virginia Woolf describes her experience eating lunch at the women's college of Cambridge; the meal is unsatisfactory in comparison to what is served at the men's college. She reflects upon how such a meal dampens one's spirit, how our moods and intellectual energies are altered by a bad meal. *One cannot think well, love well, sleep well, if one has not dined well,* she writes.

The grandeur of the New York State Psychiatric Institute's 1895 exterior—the ornamentation, patterns, flowers, lions; the Corinthian pilasters on the archway; the scrolling about the Romanesque lettering—none of this plays out from the interior, the space of the fifth floor, the setting for our lives. From here, you can't imagine the exterior's declaration. What were they thinking, etching the name in stone? Was it a feat, the building in 1888, the creation of a space for the lunatics and imbeciles?

An elevator no longer up to code, the manual scissor gate, a birdcage, opened and shut by an operator. Five floors are patient wards; the others classrooms, offices, labs. I didn't know. I didn't know until years later that the institute was built on a cliff, something you can't see from the entrance on 168th Street. Across from the elevator, a door to a stairwell.

The elevator stopped at the fifth floor. The floors are simple and sterile, worn down in the way of an imaginary mental hospital, what you knew it looked like already, we've all seen it on television or in movies, we've read about it in novels or memoirs.

So let's say you are a visitor. There was a protocol for visitors to the fifth floor in the fall of 1992. Let's say you are a friend of a patient, a family member. You are restricted to areas of the hospital, to certain hours. First, you stop at the front desk, sign in, and receive a visitor's pass. You show your pass to the operator, who will take you to the assigned floor. The doors open onto the fifth floor, and you step right into a common area. You see one or two patients. You have a view not unlike that of a medical student on rounds, on a rotation: from the hallway, as you walk with the supervising doctors, you see the patients sitting in the dining room, at tables, smoking, playing cards. A patient on a sofa, talking to a nurse. You walk into a conference room. The door is locked. Dr. Triel explains what you will see, a patient with a severe attachment disorder, abandoned by his mother and abused by his father, a Romanian immigrant. The doctor unlocks the door, invites a patient inside.

The medical students arrived in packs, accompanied by a superior. They looked shocked or curious or disturbed. They did not know how to hide it, how to normalize the space, us. The context.

Some patients look just as you've always imagined mental patients. This one has come from a state hospital called Creedmoor. She wears makeup as if she's a child who just discovered it in her mother's powder room. She rocks. Another looks hip, a college student. She speaks in a forthright manner. She is saying something about Austen Riggs, another hospital. A private hospital, she explains, where there are fireplaces in the bedrooms. She's offended by *this* hospital, where she was transferred. They kicked her out, she said, because she needed her methadone three times a day. They wouldn't do it. This is her story, anyway.

You see a patient curled up in a chair, sitting across from a formal-looking man and woman on a sofa against the wall. They are dressed the way you remember your Irish grandparents, always a suit, a dress, a hat, and soft white curls. Cat-eye glasses. Unlike your grandparents, they are not smiling, not looking to the young woman with love. They stare straight ahead, and the girl doesn't look at them, either. She is shaking. They sit as if they are forced to sit there, that way, the enforcing of a skeletal nuclear arrangement.

Maybe these were Rose's grandparents, not her parents. She didn't speak of them. After they left, she found new ways to mutilate herself, and then it seemed that the man and woman never came again.

To the right of the elevator, sparsely populated bookshelves. Next to these a row of vinyl sofas, some pink and some green. One sofa faces the elevator, and across, two chairs of coral-shaded vinyl. This is faux living room furniture, but no one relaxes here. What is a living room if no one lives here?

The design of it reminds you of, or indicates that this is something like home, a gesture toward home and comfort—a hollow signifier. It is not possible to be comfortable on these couches. Everything is incomplete.

This is the long-term ward. This is a space of the past, in disrepair. These were the last years of it, though we didn't know. Like many old buildings, it needed updates, or it had been updated—but there is only so much you can do with nineteenth-century asylum architecture.

If you were a visitor to the floor, you would turn left and walk all the way down the hallway (you wouldn't be allowed, but let's pretend). First you would pass the dining room and the kitchen. Down the hall you would encounter the locus of the panopticon. This room is in the center of the hallway. You must walk by this room in order to get to the women's dorm. This room is covered in glass. They could see us and we could see them. They are inside and we are outside. Their room was soundproof. They had the keys and we had couches. In between the couches, a place for vitals—every day they took our blood pressure, pulse, temperature, and weight.

————

So the office was glass, in the center of the fifth floor. You could walk on all sides, they could see you from each side, you could see them in there talking, laughing, doing the crossword puzzle.

It seems like I'm making it up when I say that the office was glass, that they sat in there talking about us, that we sat on the couches, that we saw in and there on the wall was a photographic portrait of Sigmund Freud. One day a man came to the floor, just for a week, and he spent his week at a table in the dining room reading *Civilization and Its Discontents*. Was he even a patient? Or was this a conceptual art piece? He didn't speak to anyone. He would not become part of us. It was an effective strategy. Maybe it worked, maybe he didn't belong there.

There was another woman, only briefly a patient, who spoke regularly of the child she cared for. She was given afternoon passes to attend to her responsibilities. She was also given daily passes to attend AA meetings in the adjacent hospital building.

I remember her as the only one to speak openly about the absurdity of the place. She saved particular scorn for Dr. Triel. She told us that he accused her of overvaluing her sobriety. Dr. Triel had told her that she used AA as a crutch.

Is it real that the image of Freud hung over and above us, in the middle of that fifth floor? *That's so Foucault*, a friend will say, because it is too obvious, because I won't tell anyone this detail. Freud there floating overhead. (Freud's theory behind psychoanalysis, beyond the talking cure, greatly informed the treatment I received in those years. This moment marked the end of the dominant psychoanalytic model, soon to be eclipsed by the biomedical. However meaningful years of talking about my problems to a doctor were, it is also true that these insights—about my mother, my grief, my sadness, and fears—did not lead to change. There is a great gulf between an awareness of a problem and an ability to change.)

Down the hall, past the dining area, a door to a room that is always locked. Only staff members have a key. On the door a printed schedule of our daily activities. Not every day has an activity but I've always liked a schedule and so there I am at the long table, Monday at 2:00. IT'S DEBATABLE! Matt Riccio stands at the whiteboard, writing in all caps. Today's topic up for debate: THE DEATH PENALTY! YES? OR NO? Pick a side, he will direct us, the unlucky few who've landed here. I point to the No. Duh. Okay! Matt elicits responses from the others. Patricia plays with her buttons. Stacey sucks her fingers. Stella's pulling her hair, then darts out of the room without explanation. Molly shakes her legs, rubbing her palms hard against her thighs. Soon enough she leaves, too. Now it's just me and Hank, so Hank says, Okay, I'll play. Matt's thrilled. Great, Henry! What's your side? Hank's all my side? No. No way. Of course not, what the fuck.

Tuesday in that same room, another group, led by a woman named Cherise. She's gentle, smiles, carries a book. She doesn't care that we are in here and she is out there. She begins each group reading, a story. One day it is Sandra Cisneros, another day Raymond Carver, today a poem by Ntozake Shange,

I survive on intimacy / and tomorrow

Cherise passes paper and pens around the room, asks us to choose one line from the reading, write that line at the top of the page, and go from there. What do we write? someone asks. Whatever you want, Cherise replies. She sets a timer. Behind us the late-afternoon sun hits the window, blurring our view of the river.

One group wasn't on the schedule. It was a secret. I was there two or three weeks before Stacey told me about it. Literature Group, she said, led by the night nurses, Roxane and Elsie. This month they were reading *Mrs. Dalloway*. I was excited, eager, I wanted to read everything by Virginia Woolf. I felt some hope for the place. I asked if I could join. I had much to say. It is a feminist book club, Stacey said, but don't tell the doctors about it. It's just a night thing, Roxane and Elsie's thing.

The first and only night I attended, Roxane was talking about the orgasm scene in *Mrs. Dalloway*. She read a passage aloud, Clarissa Dalloway recalling her girlhood friend Sally Seton. I found the page and read along. I was confused. Where's the orgasm? I asked. I don't see an orgasm! I thought I was a good reader. Roxane looked at me as if I was daft. She rolled her eyes, then looked at Elsie, who smirked. Well, I sure see the orgasm, Roxane said. Don't you see it, Elsie? Elsie's long red hair fell to one side. She was pretty, a heavy Scottish accent. I never not once saw her smile. Of course, Elsie whispered, looking at Roxane, as if to say, Don't bother with her; with me, this *naif-imbecile*.

There is an orgasm in *Mrs. Dalloway*, but it would be a decade or so before I could see it there. How little I knew myself. No wonder I wanted someone to tell me a story.

Of course, you can't read the story until the book is in you, until you already know what the book says. Clarissa is fifty-two, her life is memory now, most of it behind her—there'll be *no more marriages, no more having of children*—

I read *A Room of One's Own* there, in that single bed against the cement wall. My room of my own without a door in the psychiatric ward in Washington Heights. I read about the necessity of the room and the income necessary to be a woman writer. My room was paid for, but it had nothing to do with liberation. It had little to do with independence or artistic flourishing. The room was a place of confinement, discipline, containment. A knock on the wall, the fifteen-minute checks. To be sure we were still there? To be sure we were alive. I still don't know. The person had a clipboard. Rarely said hello, I was a body for a checkmark, a yes or a no. The next day, if I stayed in my room of my own, if I stayed there too long, looking at the walls, dissociating, I was warned against isolating. Isolating was unhealthy. Isolating meant I could lose privileges. A privilege meant I could go on the apple-picking trip to Nyack.

Woolf's book-length essay began as a lecture she was asked to give for the women's colleges of Cambridge. Early on she describes a meal she has at the men's college,

> It is part of the novelist's convention not to mention soup and salmon and ducklings, as if soup and salmon and ducklings were of no importance whatsoever, as if nobody ever smoked a cigar or drank a glass of wine.

The women, Woolf notes, do not receive salmon or ducklings; the women are served *plain gravy soup*, and

beef with its attendant greens and potatoes—a homely
trinity, suggesting the rumps of cattle in a muddy market,
and sprouts curled and yellowed at the edge, and bargaining
and cheapening, and women with string bags on Monday
morning.

Each morning I walked down the long hall from the women's dorm, and saw Rose and Stella there, awake before everyone, up in time to get a Styrofoam coffee cup or two from the breakfast trays. There were always extra trays and Rose and Stella always took more than the one cup we were meant to take. Stella and Rose sat on the vinyl chairs next to Marion and Bridget, each holding a cigarette, fingers shaking so much it was hard to get the cigarette to the mouth. Hard to hold a Styrofoam cup without spilling coffee. It's called tardive dyskinesia, a common side effect of antipsychotic drugs.

So her name is Rose, the one you saw there with her parents, the formal and stern unhappy man and woman you could never imagine as her parents, but then what more did you need to say. She spends her days here, curled up in a chair, animal-like. She was a model, someone tells me, until they couldn't cover all the scars on her arms. She modeled hats for a while. The way her hands shake is most noticeable when she's holding a cigarette, and she's always holding a cigarette. You can smoke in this room, which is not a room but the midway point between the length of the fifth floor, across from the kitchen and dining room, next to the service elevator. From this point you can see into the dining room, which is where patients and staff are allowed to smoke. There's an ashtray on each table.

No one believes me when I tell them that you could smoke in that hospital. When a chain-smoker was admitted to the ward (which was often) they weren't encouraged to quit. The philosophy seemed to be that that would only make things worse.

Nobody mentioned secondhand smoke back then. Also: There were no open windows on the entire fifth floor. It was a sealed chamber.

Across from the staff room, there's an open dining room, where Richard and Reg and other staff smoke through their shifts. Rose and Stella, Patricia, Happy, Audrey. Sometimes I would smoke, too. Stella or Richard offer me a cigarette and a light. Each one a nail in your coffin, Richard would say, laughing through his cough.

This was poison, too, of course—but I was too young to care, each cigarette a nice death, a way there, and each time I finished I saw my mom on the toilet, the day I walked in on her smoking in the bathroom. She'd flush the butts. She didn't explain, sprayed the room with aerosol disinfectant. Don't tell your dad. She'd been a nurse. That's what nurses do, she told me. It's how you get through. Only now do I understand it, or imagine what it was for her, to be a young nurse in Chicago in those years. What she saw, the suffering and pain, unprocessed. Empathic *to a fault*, she took it all in, she was unable to separate it from herself. She carried it with her, absorbed it. Those cigarettes were my first clue that my mother contained another world.

I'm sure you've seen it in the movies. It is like that, or it was like that, and I can't add much by writing it. Yes, some things in the movies are just that way in life. This room had a thick door, sound-proof, and every side of the room, top to bottom, the floor and the ceiling was padded. You couldn't just go in that room, you had to be put in that room, and they'd put you in, or me in, after they'd injected thorazine into my veins. The cushions everywhere, it was too much, so much like the movies, and how stupid it felt. It was Roxane who put me there and now I think there was something thrilling about it, too, that my desire for Roxane was impossible, how she terrified me and disgusted me and how I wanted her, all at once. I wanted her to take me, to hold me, and she did, this was how she did it, directing two large men to grab my arms, to lift me up, to hold me down while she put the needle in my arm, and soon I was gone, she locked the door. I'm still turned on by it, the memory of it, how it was to be with her, in her presence, to be overcome. Through the small rectangular glass I saw her face, her concern, her voice calm now, now she liked me, all I could think was that I'd finally made her love me.

It occurs to me now that in all those years I rarely looked in a mirror. The mirrors in the bathroom were made of bent metal—my face a distortion. I saw what I knew was my face, but it was distorted and vague. Every month around my period, I broke out with horrible acne which embarrassed me. How funny, I think now. Of all the places not to care. When I complain about it, a doctor adds tetracycline to my long list of drugs. This clears my acne but permanently stains my teeth. Not long after discharge, I saw a dentist who was astounded by my mouthful of cavities. Reviewing my chart of listed medications, he asks, Why did they put you on Nardil?

In this room you have to believe that you are special. That no one can understand you. That there is no way you could possibly turn your suffering into words. No way to communicate the depth of it. In this room a nurse will ask you: X? and you will say: X (I can't use language) and the two of you will sit in that space of silence for a long time. The nurse will say, finally: I'm sorry, my dear, but this is all we have. Words. This is our medium.

One day my brother called the payphone. There are seven of us siblings, and over my years there, two will visit. This brother is the next oldest to me, the second oldest. The payphone is across from the dining area. Next to the geometric lines, the red and gold, the echoing Figure Fives. Someone will answer the phone and call your name, leaving the receiver there hanging from the cord. You can walk into the phone booth; you can close the door, the folded glass; you can say hello and your brother will say hello. What are you doing? he will say. And you will say something. And he will say, Do you think you are the only one who suffers?

I didn't answer my brother. Years later, when we were in our thirties, he confided in me: I think of Mom every day. We had never said such things to each other. In the rooms of our childhood, in our new mother's house, the new family house, we wouldn't speak of it, of her, of that other family. After her death, the five of us—my father, me, and my three siblings—had come to an unspoken agreement. Our grief was so enormous, we turned inward, and inwardly we turned on one another. We saw each other's faces and there we saw our own loss or desperation, the pathos of it. We recoiled. The agreement was reached swiftly, settled silently: We would not speak of her, of the mother who left.

Now I want to tell my brother what I could not say. I want to tell him that maybe the story wasn't about me or my suffering, it wasn't a story of how unique or special that suffering was. Maybe that room, the phone booth, the glass doors, the quiet room— maybe those are the rooms of everyone's suffering. Maybe the psych ward was just that, one possible stop on the pathway to becoming human.

Too Much

It is the summer of 2020. Her name is Ece, and she's come with my friend. She is twenty years younger than me. Turkish. This is our first gathering out of quarantine. Ece notices Sylvia Plath on my bookshelf. She tells me something of her teenage years, back when I killed myself. The construction surprises me. A mistranslation or not. I understand. When I killed myself.

Sylvia Plath writes a note in her diary. She must write an asylum story. She needs the money. I'd be a fool not to, she writes. There is an increasing market for mental-hospital material, she encourages herself. In the diary, she considers many names for her protagonist, settling on Esther Greenwood. The book opens in Esther's voice. She tells us the story of her summer in New York. Esther's story of when I killed myself.

The cover of the Bantam Books $1.25 paperback edition of The Bell Jar features a wilted black rose. The three words of the title in black calligraphy, a Gothic font. It was 1990 when I discovered the book on a sidewalk in L.A., displayed on a blanket among other one-dollar paperbacks. I buy The Bell Jar and I buy Erica

Jong's *Fear of Flying*. I've heard these titles but I don't know what they mean. I stay up all night reading.

For my young friend, to read the novel and to know the story of the novel is to read the novel. I try to remember what it was to read Plath beyond the knowledge of her death, of the novel's reception, the second life, the death of the author, the posthumous fame, the complicated legacy. For my young friend, too, it is the grotesquerie of Plath's suicide, the abjection, obsession, all of it. Did I read with or without the story of the writer running ahead or alongside the book? I read with hunger, I was looking for something, the bottom of it. It was a devouring. There is no control group for how a young woman receives a book, how she reads it, how it enters her, and who she might become (Maggie Nelson). Esther's disgust was my disgust. Her alienation, hope, despair—that was mine, too. Plath's book became part of me, a place to live.

Esther attends a luncheon for the *Ladies' Day* magazine interns. She is the only young woman who eats ravenously. The other girls are trying to *reduce*. The banquet table is full of *yellow-green avocado pear halves stuffed with crabmeat and mayonnaise, and platters of rare roast beef and cold chicken, and every so often a cut-glass bowl heaped with black caviar.*

Esther's hunger—her desire—for food and sex. Her appetite. The other side of her death drive. Esther Greenwood eats. We understand her appetite as an extension of her ambition, her desire. Impossible for a young woman in 1950s America and yet. *I loved food more than just about anything else.*

I was almost twenty years old when I read *The Bell Jar.* I have read books and passed tests about the books. I have written essays about the books. But I don't think I understood the point of a book before that year, when I read *The Lover* and *Beloved* and now *The Bell Jar*. I did not know that a book is about communication. Or if I knew, it didn't matter before now. A book is a way to speak to someone, across time and space. This book was telling me something about how to live. Other ways to live.

Now I am the teacher and I read the book with my students. I read passages aloud. I ask questions. I like this book too much, one or another will say. Everyone has something to say. I identify with her, a girl says, and I'm not sure I'm supposed to. She is unreliable, another will say. She's shitty to her friends, a student points out. This wasn't something I'd paid much attention to, but okay. Very shitty. Now I can focus on the craft, yes, Esther is unreliable. I am not the person I was when I read this book at nineteen. That book is not this book. Yes, yes, I say to my student. This evidence of Esther's cruelty, her disregard for the women around her. I would never do that, my students say. I'd never leave my friend drunk or passed out at some guy's apartment. That's so shitty. Why does she abandon her friend? they ask.

I stopped returning phone calls, letters. I'd moved to New York to be someone else and the rest would get in the way. It was a gradual and then complete distancing, removing myself from the intimacy of girl friendships, like Grace's, which had once been so essential to my sense of self. Like Esther I had decided good grades, my achievements, and coursework would save me. I felt competitive with the women around me, envying them everything, afraid of their judgment. It was easier to keep distance. It was a way of controlling my emotional life; I was sensitive in a way that was considered pathological, the people around me crossing some boundary of identity I was still creating.

In a compulsory visit to the state hospital, my father was asked to describe my mom. She was *empathic to a fault,* he said. Empathy can be *too much,* shyness can be *too much.* Our sensitivity to the world around us, to the suffering of others, can be *too much.*

My mother was of the Sylvia Plath generation. My mother was alive when Plath killed herself. My mother was twenty-seven that year. She was still single, she didn't yet have children. What was my mother doing? Did she hear the news? Did she read the poet, had she read *The Bell Jar?*

No, she didn't know of Plath's death because it wasn't news. There were few obituaries. Plath was not famous when she died.

Can a writer—a person—ever have too much empathy? I think Henry James was right when he wrote that those without empathy make our lives hell. Or Marguerite Duras: *The only true democracy is that we all live the loss of the world.* And Virginia Woolf, who noted the dangers, the dissolution possible if we had not this skill *for shutting people off from our sympathies.*

So Doreen takes Esther to a party at Lenny's. When Lenny and Doreen start making out, Esther leaves. She leaves Doreen at Lenny's place and walks the forty-eight blocks back to the hotel. Later that night, Doreen returns to the hotel, knocking on the door and waking Esther. She pukes on Esther and Esther decides to leave her there on the floor outside her hotel room. The next day the interns all attend a *Ladies' Day* magazine luncheon, and that night, Esther and Doreen puke. All the girls have been food poisoned. For Esther, the puking is a purging. She wasn't bulimic, yet the symbolic weight of that scene is clear. Puking as an attempt at purity. Esther takes a bath, another attempt at cleansing, at purity.

The world sickens her, femininity sickens her. The 1950s sicken her. The 1980s sickened me.

Dr. Triel explains to me why it is that a woman might starve herself or diet or exercise excessively. It is about attachment, he explains. A secure attachment means that your needs were met as a child. The trauma of a parent's death for a child can create an insecure attachment. A dismissive attachment, he clarifies, your need to guard yourself, always.

(I think that is too simple. I think there was something spiritual in it—a search, seeking. I wouldn't have said that, but I don't think anorexia is so simple, or one thing.)

We don't always get to pick our influences. However impossible and insistent her influence, to be a white depressive woman writer obsessed with Sylvia Plath is redundant. For a long time, I dismissed her. I ignored the book, what it had done to me. It wasn't like with Duras, a book I would hold in place of a self. It was too obvious, even then I knew. I read Plath and I knew she was mine and not mine at once. How could I explain the influence, how her death aligned with that influence, how her death was a part of it.

After her transformational summer in New York City, Esther returns to her mother's home in the suburbs, to the news that she hasn't been accepted into a summer writing program. She enters her bell jar: stays in bed, doesn't shower or change her clothes. For seven nights, she doesn't sleep. Her mother finally takes her to a psychiatrist. Esther notices the pictures on his desk, the perfect family. She knows Dr. Gordon cannot help her. He asks her about her college, and remembers being there: *My, weren't the girls pretty*. Esther hates him and tells her mother she's never going there again. Her mother is pleased, relieved: *I knew my daughter wasn't like those people.*

So it was a few years after my mom's death, when I transferred my suffering onto my body. What was called an eating disorder, though I couldn't recognize it as that then. It was a natural shift, it offered some fleeting sense of control, and it would consume me for many years. My days expanded and contracted in connection to the shape of my body, what I ate, what I didn't eat. This was my site of control: I was not Esther; I tended toward the ascetic. My refusal was a refusal of vulnerability, of need. Intellectually, I knew this, but I could not stop. The thinner I was, the less I needed. In these times of transition, when all felt out of control, with the ground shifting beneath me, I needed to be thin. I got up early each day. I rode an exercise bike in a sad basement gym. I ate alone: one plain bagel for lunch, and vegetables for dinner. I wouldn't eat oil or fat. I wouldn't eat protein.

The young friend of my friend, visiting that summer evening, asks me, Did you identify so much—feel such recognition—that it was uncanny, that your connection overwhelmed you, that you felt closer to this novel, to the consciousness of this novel, than you'd ever felt to another human being? And you didn't want others to know it as you did. And what to do with that, that thrill and that intimacy. To speak of it was impossible. To mention Plath and *The Bell Jar* was to encounter eye rolls, notes of disapproval. If the person had read *The Bell Jar,* or the *Ariel* poems, they looked at you with concern. If they hadn't read her, they'd certainly heard about Sylvia Plath. They said, Oh, god, or sighed or looked for the nearest exit.

I read knowing that I should not be reading it. There was a Judy Blume book, popular in my school: *Tiger Eyes.* We passed it around in junior high. We weren't supposed to be reading it. We knew that it was about sex. The warnings made it more exciting, of course.

Reading Sylvia Plath that first time was nothing like reading Marguerite Duras. There was something closed off about Plath—but I think I feared what I wanted, the contagion that is quite alive in *The Bell Jar*. You can't deny it. The way the book and the consciousness of it pulls you in—Julia Kristeva's *spiderweb of the text*. Kristeva on the death-saturated books that *domesticate the malady of death, they fuse with it, are on the same level with it, without either distance or perspective*. That was the power of it. When I read the book again years later, I was not susceptible in the way I had been. I was no longer what Kristeva called *a fragile reader*.

For Kristeva, Duras does not write *about* madness; rather, she brings the reader *toward* madness. I read Duras when I was nineteen and fragile. I wanted to be led *toward* madness. I stayed home that night, alone in my furnished studio apartment, reading *The Lover*. Even after my failed attempt, my hospitalization, *The Bell Jar* was not on my mind. I had resisted it so completely (or so I told myself). My life was something all its own, or so I wanted it to be. As with reading Shakespeare—*Romeo and Juliet, Hamlet*—I told myself that the script of my madness was mine alone. These were my plot points.

No one would advise identifying with Esther Greenwood, but I'd read *The Bell Jar* that year before moving to New York, and if I didn't identify with it, the book did open up imaginative space. I wasn't going to kill myself, but I was going to study, to read, to improve myself in a way that would make me immune to suffering. I would be the best student, a great writer; this would save me from loneliness and unhappiness. The more I could achieve, the less need I would have for human connection.

I ask everyone: How old were you when you first read *The Bell Jar*? Do you remember where you were, who you were? One friend explains that he first read it in a class at community college; it was the first time he understood how a novel allowed for the revelation of consciousness. Someone else read it at summer camp; she was sixteen. Another friend explains that she read it in seventh grade. I was too young! she says now. I didn't know about it in seventh grade, but I was also too young for the extremity of emotion, the intensity of Esther's consciousness.

Feminist literary critic Jane Marcus on *The Bell Jar: Esther and her creator are so blurred that the reader is not sure what to think of an author who speaks through so self-pitying a narrator. Confessional whining in the novel makes one squirm.*

She was a problem long before I found her in 1989, when I was nineteen years old. It was a problem to identify with Sylvia Plath. Fair enough for Marcus and other feminists to reject Plath's solution, both in the novel and in life. No one can say if the novel caused any young women or men to commit suicide. I can't say, but I suspect that it helped me open that door, imagine that possibility in that particular time of my life. I was susceptible. I was searching for mothers. This is why the discovery of women's studies classes was so thrilling. I wanted to know how to live. For Esther, how to live was to reject life, to reach the limits of it, to imagine a way out.

Six years after Plath's suicide, Ted Hughes's girlfriend, Assia Wevill, killed herself and her daughter in the same way Plath had died. In 2009, Plath's son, who had been a baby when she died, killed himself. From his *New York Times* obituary: *Nicholas Hughes, the son of the poets Sylvia Plath and Ted Hughes, killed himself on March 16 at his home in Alaska, four decades after his mother and father's lover took their own lives. He was 47.*

It is hard to imagine a more comprehensive and devastating pair of sentences to summarize a life and death. Of course, we know that suicide is contagious—we know that depression runs in families. We know that the loss of a parent in childhood increases the likelihood of adult depression.

So why am I shocked by Marcus's pronouncement: *These* Ariel *poems are both unignorable and morally repugnant.* Or Elizabeth Hardwick, writing of *The Bell Jar* in 1971: *In Sylvia Plath's work and in her life the elements of pathology are so deeply rooted and so little resisted that one is disinclined to hope for general principles, sure origins, applications, or lessons. Her fate and her themes are hardly separate and both are singularly terrible. Her work is brutal, like the smash of a fist; and sometimes it is also mean in its feeling.*

These aesthetic refusals are marked by an unexamined fear of contagion. *And so little resisted.*

Plath's rage in her final *Ariel* poems was infectious and dangerous, a virus you needed protection from. In the movies I saw in those years, movies from *Annie Hall* to *Heathers*, *Ariel* was a punch line and a joke. It was wildly popular among young women, and therefore it could not be taken seriously. The rage of Plath in "Lady Lazarus" or "Daddy" was Plath at the height of her powers.

It is an idea easy to dismiss, that we can be altered by books—don't read too much, they tell young girls—but it is also a very serious idea. This was the advice of the ancients: it matters what a young person reads; it shapes a personality. I had to change my life. I knew that much. It feels too simple or too obvious to say that I was there in New York because of Plath, among others, these women writers who led me to this city, whose characters led me to that city. But it is true I read that book months before moving. I read *Fear of Flying*, too. The electric intensity of recognition. It is very likely that I chose to attend Barnard College because I'd read *Fear of Flying*, whose main character is at Barnard College having a lot of sex.

I didn't know that Kathy Acker had been sending up Erica Jong in her "Hello, I'm Erica Jong" prose poem, which later became part of *Blood and Guts in High School*, Acker's signature rejection of Jong's realist-conventional fictive universe. No, this was, however, another singular chemical reaction—a recognition that offered hope. And what was the zipless fuck? I didn't know, but I wanted it.

If I wanted death that year, I also wanted sex. I did not know what to do with all that twenty-year-old want—and who ever does?

Not long ago, I attended a dinner party where I was the only writer. One man, a doctor, asked me what my book was about. When I said I was writing about women and madness, women like Sylvia Plath and Janet Frame (I did not include myself in this list), he seemed annoyed. Why write about *women with such messed-up lives?*

(*And so little resisted.*)

I know by now what not to say, how not to answer the question. I don't say: I am writing about how I lost my mind. I am writing about how I was institutionalized for many years. I am writing about that space the writer occupies, that balance between sanity and insanity.

Still, whatever I said it was too much, I had given away too much. And now I was forced to answer for it. How ashamed I felt, even as I knew it was his problem, his assumptions. Even as I knew this attitude—that women with "messed-up lives" weren't worth consideration—was part of the problem I wanted to solve.

A few months later, I was asked a similar question by a woman in Ireland, who works in hospitality. This time I brought up Marguerite Duras and Virginia Woolf. The word *Woolf* was barely out of my mouth when she shuddered, said with alarm, Oh, so depressing, no? Everyone laughed. Again, I felt like I should apologize, my instinct was to be ashamed to see myself as everyone there saw me—as someone who has chosen a very depressing life. Who chooses to spend time thinking about these depressing women writers with their messed-up depressing lives?

I am not witty or quippy, I don't have a quick response to such annoying remarks—remarks that reveal such a gap between the interlocutor and me that it is not worth a reply. I don't say anything about that, which would seem harsh, antisocial; nor do I say that thinking about or writing about these writers makes me happy. It would be worth explaining but, in each case, there was little room for explanation. These sort of parties, where a life's work becomes a sort of currency one must share, must reduce, make digestible—there is little to do but get through, to avoid the topic of one's self, one's passion.

I don't say that I've come to see the corpse of Plath's genius and the hope of her spectacular death. *She blew herself up so we could live,* I won't ever, ever say to the man at the dinner party. Her death, like Madame Pontellier's in *The Awakening,* like Emma Bovary's—her death was *a liberatory practice,* I don't say. And I won't say to him, though it is true—it is because we love ghost stories. And we love her for dying of our sins, all the girls with the ugly feelings, the rage and the disgust and all the rest.

I won't say that I find so much hope in the lives of Woolf, or Frame, or Shulamith Firestone—what they accomplished despite these madnesses. How each was able to offer to me a truth, a vision, a guiding light. Where would I be without these women with messed-up lives? I don't ask the man at the dinner party, or the woman in the hotel.

Time Passes

Now it is November. A recreational therapist gathers a group for an afternoon outing to Nyack. Apple picking. I'm not allowed to leave the hospital grounds yet, it is too soon. There are steps, stages before a patient receives privileges.

Three days a week I meet with a doctor. Every four months, a new doctor. These are residents, and unlike the head doctors, these doctors are young women. On rotation. They are just out of medical school. They take notes, write down everything I say. They write as if it all matters, these trivial concerns of mine, the daily annoyances of life on the ward. Because that is now the material for this therapy. How do you feel about this person or that person. We become inhabitants of this foreign country, and the doctors are there as translators, ethnographers.

Today I meet with Dr. Smith, she is tall, striking. I'm intimidated by her authority, her elegance. She asks me the questions I've been asked many times. I find new ways to answer. Reading through the medical records, Dr. Smith's notes stand out. Her writing is literary, detailed character descriptions that remind me of a Brontë novel. She writes of me as if describing a novel's heroine.

———

After the introductory questions, the regular assessment—there seems to be one every six months—I am asked about life on the ward.

What happened last night?

She knows what happened, of course.

Monday evening, that long gap after the dinner trays are carried away, after Bridget and Marion go home, Roxane and Elsie take over the ward. They've been away since Thursday, and that has caused dis-ease among certain patients. I sit across from the dining room. I have a book, though I read intermittently, half-focused. Life on the ward takes up the space of my interest now, my concern, my study. From here I see Molly at the far end of the E's long spine. When I arrived a few months earlier, Molly was preparing for discharge. A date had been set. She'd been in the hospital nearly four years. Through other patients, I learned that she'd been in the military until she was hospitalized in the VA after a psychotic break. From there she'd been transferred to the state hospital.

Molly is sitting across from Elsie on a small vinyl couch. Elsie's long red hair falls to the left; her face hidden. It seems that only Molly is speaking, or that Elsie whispers, in between long silences. As often happens, sooner or later, Molly charges up from where she sits with a start, often yelling or shouting, first at Elsie and then to the air as she walks down the hall, this way or that, punching a door or a wall. Today Elsie waits, sits on the chair. On occasion, Molly will have her tantrum and then return to the sofa, where Elsie waits. Tonight she does not return, she rages down one hall and another. The support staff stand up, walk to Molly. She won't stop, they must restrain her. Now everyone has gathered, the spectacle. Over the intercom across the hospital now: PSYCH EMERGENCY, FIFTH FLOOR. Soon others arrive from the elevator and staircase. Doctors, nurses, support staff I've never seen. They go to Molly or where she is held. Before long, many of them walk back toward the stairs; they are relaxed, she's been subdued.

How did it make you feel? Dr. Smith asks. It must have been upsetting.

It was interesting, I don't say. It gave some shape to the evening, I don't say.

How did you feel about all of the attention going to Molly?

It was spectacle.

It is negative attention, Dr. Smith explains, this is what Molly wanted. Negative attention is still attention. Is this what you want? Do you want more attention from the nurses?

These were the questions, the ways we were taught to be subjects. This was the material and our progress or lack of progress depended on our response.

I didn't have that sort of relationship with Elsie or Roxane. I couldn't explain this to the doctor: She couldn't understand the night-shift society. We lived in another world at night, there were other rules, ways of being. Some parameters were clear: Elsie was there for Molly. Elsie was terrifying and few of us spoke to her anyway. We knew better. She never smiled and she seemed annoyed to be asked a question. She only engaged with other patients at 9:00 p.m., when she returned to the office and opened the window. Dixie Cups of water. We lined up, received our medicine, swallowed with water. An hour later we were meant to be in our rooms, in bed. Lights out.

It didn't occur to me to ask why Molly was like this, after so many years in the hospital. I did not ask why she seemed worse than the patients who had arrived a week or two ago, three months or six months. There was the story of progress, and we were meant to follow that storyline. *It gets worse before it gets better:* This can mean so many things, including the possibility of getting so much worse that you won't get better. There was that. There were so many who did not get better.

It is so strange to me now, but in the hospital I took it for granted—the idea that we somehow needed to get worse. They would break us apart and then put us back together again. Was that the idea?

A Nervous Condition, or What Can One Do?

Another summer, 1993 or 1994. Let's say you're back, visiting the ward, and this time you notice the sparsely populated bookshelf. It's there to your right as you get off the elevator. The book you'll see, small with a yellow cover, sits next to a biography of Greta Garbo. *The Yellow Wallpaper and Other Stories* by Charlotte Perkins Gilman.

I only recently remembered it was there. Like the other stories, everywhere, like *The Bell Jar*, it was too much in those days. It was received knowledge—about myself, about women, about madness, about the history of mental health care—that I was trying to resist, even as I lived it. Especially as I lived it.

I returned to Gilman's book years later, when enough time had passed for me to become interested in my experience, and these writers offered me a way to return, to figure it out, to stop time, to understand that girl in that hospital. What was she doing there? What had seemed like blind fate might have been something else. If I could just figure it out—this book, too, an attempt to answer that question.

———

But in 1993, these questions were far away—I was acting out the madness—so to read these stories would not have been enough. I needed to believe I was special, that my suffering was unique, and this story, like so many, might shatter that illusion.

Or maybe I couldn't relate to this woman who lived a century earlier. Maybe her story was insignificant. Her book had not been assigned in my college classes and therefore it must not matter the way other stories, other books, other writers mattered. I was so attached to my education, to the authority of it, that it limited my reading.

Or maybe I found Charlotte Perkins Gilman's famous short story, "The Yellow Wallpaper," to be boring, dull. As a teacher, I am often reminded how difficult it can be to make even the most obvious connections between literature and life. Or rather, while a good reader, a good student can find the connections, it is something else entirely to feel the connection. To be able to make meaning of it and apply the meaning to one's life—this is something else altogether. It is closer to Method acting than what we call literary analysis. For me, it began with feeling. As Hilton Als put it, *If I can't feel it, I can't write it.*

And so it was that the next time I read the book, I'd been out of the hospital for many years. This time I felt it. This time, the recognition stunned me. It was still too close, too real: I didn't want this story any longer, I was trying to shake it. But there it was, getting to the truth of something in me. Now Gilman's story illuminated my own. By then, I was newly married and trying to put these years behind me. Though I didn't believe it possible, not really. Six years, eight years, even a decade after that last discharge, that final hospitalization, and I still feel scared to see it, to say it. I couldn't tell anyone where I'd been, and for how long.

Two thousand eight. My son was a baby the next time I read "The Yellow Wallpaper," which I'd assigned in a class on women's literature. Finally, I could read the story as if it were someone else's story. It had something to do with becoming a mother, my body at that extreme, and the peace I felt, too. One day before class, before we will discuss the story, I go into a bathroom, close the stall, and use a small breast pump to expel milk. I have a baby at home; this is my first time teaching since his birth. One class, one day a week. My breasts fill up, painfully so, I must pump them every hour, just for relief.

When I'm finally back home it is 6:00 p.m., the baby is there waiting, ready to nurse endlessly; he has not taken milk all day, he waited, and so will be up most of the night, making up for lost time. I'm in an apartment on the third floor with a man who loves the baby as much as I do, our love is enormous and impossible. We are nothing like the couple in "The Yellow Wallpaper"—and I am nothing like the narrator who has a baby she barely mentions—I can't *stop* thinking about the baby!—and he is nothing like John, who condescends to his wife. And yet this man, my husband, cannot comprehend the anxiety or terror that arises in me now, or throughout the long and occasionally frightening pregnancy. He cannot understand how it has transformed me.

I am an adjunct, ancillary and contingent, precarious—but I don't teach that way. I have a few weeks to prepare the syllabus. The recommended anthology contains the story whose title I remember seeing on that bookshelf. The story is about a woman prescribed by her doctor to take a rest cure. This is 1899. The narrator of the story has just had a baby, though the baby does not appear in the story. The narrator refers to her problem as *a nervous condition*.

She wants to write but her doctor has told her it is not a good idea for her to write. What she needs is rest, seclusion, no more writing or reading.

The narrator doesn't think the doctor's idea is a good one but so it goes. (How many times, in all those years on the ward, did I think, This is not a good idea.) That gap between what we know and our ability to change, to resist authority. Or the time it takes, if you are lucky, to get there.

She cannot leave her room. There are bars on the windows in the room where she's been confined by her doctor and her husband, also a doctor. She is staying in the nursery at the top of the large Victorian manse, a country estate her husband, John, has rented for the summer. A nursery, with bars on the windows—so the children won't fall out? Or is it that they can't escape? Always this tension within childhood. This is the narrator's tension. They have taken her newborn away, and she becomes the baby. Like the doctor, her husband knows what is best. Or so she tells herself. He knows more than she does. He knows what is right for her. Yet the narrator's equivocation comes through in each sentence: *I think this, but John says this, I must be wrong. What can one do?* She asks her reader and her diary over and over again—*What can one do?*—but of course she knows what she can do. She can write. She does write.

Now I read the helplessness at the heart of the story—a learned helplessness—that I knew too well. The desire to be told who you are, what you need.

If you know the short story, you might know Charlotte Perkins Gilman's story. In the early part of the twentieth century, Gilman, an author and activist for women's rights, had, as she wrote later, *a*

*severe and continuous nervous breakdown tending to melancholia—
and beyond.* This was a struggle of "many years." She reached out
to Dr. Silas Weir Mitchell, famous for treating mental and emotional illnesses in women, ranging from PMS to pregnancy to
menopause. It is unsurprising that these varied life stages were
lumped together, given the lack of any specific focus on women's
health care.

Thanks to 1970s feminism and the role of feminist scholars in
reshaping and reimagining the canon, Gilman's work, generally
ignored until the 1980s, now helps us understand how misguided
and historically contingent women's health care has been. Suffering from melancholia, Gilman solicited Mitchell's advice (from
"Why I Wrote the Yellow Wallpaper," 1913):

> *This wise man put me to bed and applied the rest cure, to
> which a still good physique responded so promptly that he
> concluded there was nothing much the matter with me, and
> sent me home with solemn advice to "live as domestic a life as
> far as possible," to "have but two hours' intellectual life a day,"
> and "never to touch pen, brush or pencil again as long as I
> lived." This was in 1887.*

The popularity of Weir Mitchell's treatment coincided with what
was called "the woman problem" in the popular American press
of the time. Many educated women did not want to stay home
as housewives and mothers. As Elaine Showalter writes in *The
Female Malady*, part of the appeal of becoming the madwoman,
or the hysteric, was that she would be relieved of her domestic
responsibilities. Weir Mitchell's "rest cure" was wildly popular in
the late-nineteenth and early-twentieth century; Virginia Woolf,
too, was prescribed a version of the rest cure—by the doctors she
satirizes in *Mrs. Dalloway*.

———

Weir Mitchell's rest cure was considered best practice for treating all sorts of nervous illness and "hysteria." The rest cure involved staying in bed most of the day. Intellectual activity like reading or writing was verboten. Of course this was disastrous for many women, especially so for writers like Gilman and Woolf.

> *I went home and obeyed those directions for some three months,*
> *and came so near to the border line of utter mental ruin that*
> *I could see over. Then, using the remnants of intelligence*
> *that remained, and helped by a wise friend, I cast the noted*
> *specialist's advice to the winds and went to work again—work,*
> *the normal life of every human being; work, in which is joy*
> *and growth and service, without which one is a pauper and a*
> *parasite; ultimately recovering some measure of power.*

Now I noticed something loose and sloppy in the first-person narration of "The Yellow Wallpaper," meant to evoke the voice of a secret journal writer, a note keeper—Didion's *lonely and resistant rearrangers of things, anxious malcontents.* The narrator reminds herself that she shouldn't be writing—her husband and her caretakers have warned her of the dangers of mental stimulation.

> *John laughs at me, of course, but one expects that in marriage.*
> *You see he does not believe I am sick!*
> *And what can one do!*

The story is full of exclamations like this—rhetorical questions, objections on the page:

> *Personally, I disagree with their ideas.*
> *Personally, I believe that congenial work, with excitement*
> *and change, would do me good.*

As with Offred's secret writing in Margaret Atwood's *The Handmaid's Tale*, the narration takes on an urgency against this prohibition. When I read the book that first time, I surely read for this urgency—the voice powering me through those pages. The desperation of it. If you write into the madness, it becomes something else, something you can reshape. I didn't yet know how to do that, but as with the work of so many writers, it was a beacon.

You can read the story, too, as a kind of pleasure or play. The writer here is clearly happy to be writing this madness. It is infectious. The patient was infected and she wants you infected. Over the days of her seclusion in the nursery, the narrator becomes obsessed with the room's wallpaper. "The Yellow Wallpaper" is a ghost story, a horror story, or that is one way to read the ending (paranoid): the narrator on all fours. She is creeping along, she has ripped off the wallpaper. It is not clear what is happening— she is the unreliable narrator ne plus ultra.

"The Yellow Wallpaper" is widely taught in high schools and colleges; it is read and reread and analyzed—the ur text for those wishing to discuss patriarchy and how it plays out in the medical establishment. Occasionally, I have students who arrive in my classroom with confident knowledge of the story. They explain the history of it, of the author's experience. Since the book was included by Sandra M. Gilbert and Susan Gubar in the 1985 *Norton Anthology of Literature by Women*, there have been a range of scholarly readings. The "calling out the patriarchy" reading is the most commonly reproduced. The portrayal of a woman's descent into madness. Her world becomes small, as small as the nursery. Some scholars (and students) confidently diagnose the narrator. She is psychotic or schizophrenic. She has postpartum depression. Sometimes she is writing as a resistance. She has triumphed in her madness. Going mad is her way to subvert the patriarchy. In this reading, she is like the heroines of *Thelma and Louise*, driving off the cliff as the police close in—or like Edna Pontellier in Kate Chopin's *The Awakening*—swimming out to freedom. Suicide as salvation.

We don't see *Thelma and Louise* crash, just as we don't see Edna die. The stories end in a moment of release. Refusing the spectacle of destruction. The ambiguous ending.

Here's another way to read the story: The narrator is living up to the diagnosis she asked for. She has become the perfect patient. So much for the husband who has insisted that nothing is wrong with her. Well, very well then, I will show you that there is something the matter with me. She is crawling around, an infant at last, triumphant in her identification with madness. The ongoing tension of the mental patient, the relief of commitment, and the danger of it, too.

In "The Moral Career of the Mental Patient," sociologist Erving Goffman wrote of the effects of institutionalization, describing in detail the self-fulfilling quality of diagnosis: The patient desires a diagnosis, a parent, a healer. When she receives it, she needs to inhabit it, to make it her own. And the staff is there to confirm this, in a long-term hospitalization; it becomes an endless loop of solicitation and confirmation: *The hospital staff will be in great need of a rationale for the hardships they are sponsoring—evidence that they are still in the trade they were trained for. Their problems are eased—by the case-history construction that is placed on the patient's past life, this having the effect of demonstrating that all along he had become very sick, and that if he had not been hospitalized, much worse things would have happened to him.*

"The Yellow Wallpaper" seemed to me now to be the story of what can happen when you listen to a doctor—when you buy into your "case-history construction." When you don't listen to yourself, when you place your trust and authority elsewhere. The narrator loses her mind completely, becomes the madwoman, the identity they've given her. The "rationale" for their treatment of her is now confirmed; she is sick, indeed. This is what can happen: You are seen as mad, you begin acting mad.

Many of my students have been taught to declare it a feminist tragedy—the woman goes mad because she has been oppressed by her husband, they say. I understand this reading. I have said or taught that this story will save lives, and maybe that is true. This is what Gilman said about her story, this is why she wrote it. But I think you must want your life to be saved. We don't always understand why we do what we do. Or what we want. What does our narrator want? Like me, she wanted the womb, the return to childhood. The helplessness, the comfort that comes with believing that someone knows you better than you know yourself. *Tell me who I am.* What we all wish to believe of our parents, and especially our mothers—at least for a while. Gilman's narrator was writing her story, but was that enough? The acting out is the real story. The getting worse.

It's difficult for me to imagine being told not to read or write—an activity that provided me a way to live long before I could admit that I wanted to live. I spent a good portion of my many long days in the hospital reading and writing. I wasn't told explicitly not to read and write, but I was often told to come out of my room, out of my head. You are isolating, I was told many times. Don't isolate. You are making yourself worse by isolating. If you isolate so much, no wonder you feel lonely or sad. But a life of reading and writing is a life of necessary isolation. This is what writers do.

When I taught the story for the first time that semester, leaky in my own post-partum body, I said to my students: This is what the story is about. It is about trusting yourself. A doctor may tell you what is wrong with you or tell you what you need. And you may know that is not it at all. I don't tell them that I know what I am talking about—that I was in the hospital, or that this was my experience, too. *What can one do?* I shrugged. I might have been the woman in "The Yellow Wallpaper," I don't tell them. I don't tell them that I first found this book on a shelf in a hospital where I lived for years.

I don't tell them that I had no idea what was best for me back then, or that I wanted my mom to tell me, and no one else. Without her, I was lost, and certain I'd always be lost. I hated her for abandoning me, and turned that rage back onto myself: I should be dead. I shouldn't have lived. How could I imagine life with this body, which had become my mother's, a body I associated with illness and death?

What happened in the hospital, in the almost daily intensive therapy, was an unearthing of my cataclysmic loss and grief. My learned passivity and now complete helplessness. What I'd repressed for so long, since I'd decided, as children in trauma must, to defend myself from my mother's death, now was released, transferred repeatedly, as I was encouraged to do, on therapist after therapist, on all the caretakers. On the place itself. A kind of womb. And that is how I got worse—because I did get worse. This unearthing did not, in fact, help me to heal or get better. In a hospital setting, getting worse just means getting worse.

Not long ago I heard a social worker discuss the history of humanities-based treatments in psychiatric settings. I hadn't thought of my hospital that way, the ways in which it was trying to be a humanities-based hospital. Listening to her, I try to see it as a positive moment in health care, an attempt to merge the humanities with medicine. The remaining legacy of psychoanalysis as key to self-knowledge. The groups we attended nodded to that effort: Emotional Identification, Debate Group, Creative Writing, Literature Group.

Still, the importance/relevance of these groups was largely undermined by the focus on the new drugs, the influence of the pharmaceutical industry—not just antidepressants, but also antipsychotics, mood stabilizers, sleeping pills, and much else.

I began noticing it then, something that is manifest now: the increasing distance between the humanities—the study of literature—and science or medical training. I'm sure that very few doctors have read "The Yellow Wallpaper." Or if they did read it, as I did, they were immune to the iconoclastic power of it. It was a book on a shelf.

I wonder now what Gilman's book was doing in a psychiatric institution. We were not in prison, what we read or wrote was not examined, though it was mentioned in our charts. We were asked to share our writing in sessions with doctors. We were meant to be in touch with a larger world of ideas, literature and art significantly. Was that book their way of saying, Look how far we've come? We even allow you to read literature that critiques this institution.

In the same way, I remember conversations about the movie *One Flew Over the Cuckoo's Nest*, for example—and how this 1975 movie would be referenced and then dismissed, or invoked only as a negative comparison, a way to say that we weren't so bad off—that ha ha, it couldn't be that bad!

I remember a day very early in my mental patient career, sitting around a table with other patients. A social worker named Joe, always busy, overworked, in and out of the ward. He was warm, likable. A girl named Reina complained to him, Look at what they are doing, they are making me take this and it's making me fat. Reina, Joe scolded her, this isn't like *One Flew Over the Cuckoo's Nest!*

But it was like that, at least sometimes it was. The homophobia, the misogyny that Ken Kesey wrote about—it hadn't all disappeared. That declaration from our caretakers—that this was *nothing like* that movie—was its own kind of gaslighting. Kesey's book and the more famous movie show patients infantilized in thin hospital gowns, patients and staff separated by the hierarchy of the *total institution.*

Most of us had never seen the movie, or at least I had not. But we knew it had something to say about what we were doing there. What was Joe trying to say? Books and movies don't matter, don't mean anything, don't provide us with information about what it means to be alive in a shifting historical moment? Or was he saying that the biomedical approach had figured it all out, and so it wasn't like that anymore, back when they gave lobotomies and so on?

When I finally read the book years later, I discovered the misogyny in the character of Nurse Ratched, one of the ugliest depictions of the "castrating mother" I'd ever encountered in a celebrated novel. Nurse Ratched a stand-in for all disgusting hag wenches. A scapegoat for a larger patriarchal system of discipline and control. Nurse Ratched is a symbol of the larger system—the system Erving Goffman describes in *Asylums*—to which a patient must submit, relinquishing individuality.

Yes, our experiences in 1995 were unlike the experiences in the novel of 1962, but structurally, much hadn't changed. Asylum architecture. The hierarchical system. Reward and punishment. Overmedicated, dependent, passive patients. We weren't in a nursery, but there *were* bars on the windows.

Asylum Architecture (II)

It is easy to find photographs online that show the front of the old building. It seems normal enough, it might be anything—a classroom, an office. It is only when you are in the ward that you realize that those windows facing west are not visible from here. The windows to the north, south, and west are secured.

On the website of a private security firm, I find a photo of the old building. The photo shows the building as viewed from the Henry Hudson Parkway, bars on the windows marking it as a carceral space.

This is notably not a photograph used by the state hospital system, not one that Columbia University will use on its websites, or in promotional material for the hospital. From the internet, there are few traces of this history. The architects of the new building were careful to create a space that did not look like the original state hospital. It is only from the highway that you'd have the view shown in the image.

So when we looked out, we were reminded that we were locked in. This wasn't always awful. That was the problem. There was comfort there. It has always been one of my great dilemmas, as a girl as a person as a writer—how to protect my inner life. I was so ill-equipped to create or adjust to the demands of the outer life. My entire existence in those days, in that hospital, was the cultivation of an inner life. This is the *reparative reading* of my experience. I am thinking of literary critic Eve Kosofsky Sedgwick's conception of reading as either paranoid or reparative. A reparative reading searches for the positive in even a deeply flawed work.

You could say that by living in a psychiatric institution, by signing ourselves in voluntarily, by asking for help, over and over again—this was evidence. We wanted our lives to be saved. We wanted to die, or we wanted something in between life and death. This was as close as we could get.

Years after I was discharged, I found a photograph on the internet. It is a photograph of Allen Ginsberg from 1950, standing in front of that old building at 722 West 168th Street, near Riverside Drive. He's been a patient there for one year. In the photo, he stands next to Marilyn Monroe, who stands next to Arthur Miller.

I don't know why I have such a clear memory of this photograph. I look for it now but can't find it. No matter, I still see it: Marilyn Monroe leans into Arthur Miller, and looks away from the camera. Allen Ginsberg stares straight into the camera's lens; a doctor stands on the other side of Marilyn Monroe.

And one more trick of memory, I see now that the man standing next to Marilyn Monroe is Joe DiMaggio, not Arthur Miller. How I recognize him as DiMaggio I'm not certain, but I know that it is a husband who escorts her; I also know that it doesn't matter much who—either one is viable in this photograph.

Anyway, I don't want to talk about Allen Ginsberg, though he did dedicate "Howl" to Carl Solomon, the friend he met in that hospital. A friend who got shocks and a straitjacket. The way he and Carl tried to decide if they were crazy or the doctors were crazy.

And he said something about leaving the hospital, about the self-rejection, the way you've internalized all that you've been told is wrong with you; how you bring that out into the world with you. How he walked the streets after discharge, seeking validation everywhere, not finding it. How he had to get out of New York.

And if I say anything about Ginsberg and madness, I should say something about his mother, Naomi Ginsberg, whose story didn't just begin in an institution but ended there, too. Naomi Ginsberg who was institutionalized, who was lobotomized, who died in Pilgrim State Hospital, in New Jersey, after a long career as a mental patient, a life in and out of asylums. If her son was the exception, the young man whose eight months inside led to the richness of a long life in literature, then she was the rule.

Tell Me Who I Am

Two thousand eight. Now the baby is a year old. For reasons I don't understand, I call Dr. Triel. On the phone he is nice. Charming. Happy to hear from me, he said.

Maybe he was a kind of Weir Mitchell, in that I hoped for— I admired him or was drawn to something in him and for that reason I wanted to see what he could offer. Even if I knew that his treatment was flawed. I knew—I wanted something from him. It had been over a decade since I'd allowed him to make any pronouncement about me. In one of our last conversations, by phone, he had said: *I didn't know you were still sick.*

It had been so unsettling, I was thrown back into my role, the trap.

So why would I return to him now?

We don't always know why we do the things we do.

I made an appointment to see him. I went to his office. It was near Museum Mile, on the Upper East Side. I had my baby with me. I was thirty-seven, old, I said, to have a baby. He said the women here, on the Upper East Side, only begin thinking about it at that age. He laughed, and said, There is nothing like having a baby to stop you from being self-centered.

It was true for me. Though I know it is not always true. There are plenty of mothers who remain self-centered, reject the role, use the child as a narcissistic extension.

Why did I go to see him? It was the one and only time after I'd left the world of mental hospitals. Did I want his approval, still? Was I testing something out? Did I want him to say this, what he did say, that I was cured?

Or was I there because I wanted help?

Even then, I see it now, the doctor was asking me for a narrative. The narrative imperative was still there ten years, twelve years after my last hospitalization: I was better. I was married. I had a baby. These were markers of progress. Of stability. I went along with this because, yes, I saw it, of course, this grounded me.

Still, it was flawed. I had many years ahead of me. Life isn't a clear progression. What did he know? No, I would not be there again, in that hospital at that time, but it isn't true that it all led quite neatly to this moment. His was the narrative of therapy, of effective therapy. The expectation or hope of the treatment we received. It was not a guarantee, never a fait accompli.

When time passed, when I was in a new life—I discovered the pleasure of writing about these lost years, and it was not unlike the narrator's secret writing, that urgency and thrill. It was similar to the pleasure I felt writing about my mom—I think I became a writer so that I could spend the rest of my life writing these two stories which are really one story: the story of my mom's death and the story of my institutionalizations.

This was a new movement, an attempt as I aged, as my child grew, at stopping time, of returning to those years, attempting to sort the material of my life in writing, and understanding that my writing was never separate from my life.

Septimus

For Virginia Woolf, being told to leave the intellectual and sensory stimulation of London was devastating. She skewered the medical establishment most notably in her greatest novel, *Mrs. Dalloway*, through the character of Septimus Smith, the shell-shocked World War I veteran. Septimus is disconnected from his life, his marriage, and deeply haunted by the death of his friend Evans. He saw Evans die, and this grief has made him mad. Home from the war, the rigidity and formality of British life appear absurd. Septimus's madness is an untethering—he is both unable to feel and yet too porous; he has a growing sense that the world is sending him messages. His interiority is incommunicable to everyone, especially his wife and his doctor. Woolf understood both the protective quality—a numbing of feeling—and the great danger of madness: to be so far out with no way back, and to lose all means of communicating that gap. A famous poem by Woolf's lesser-known contemporary, British poet Stevie Smith, comes to mind: *I was much further out than you thought / and not waving but drowning.*

How often has a doctor—or a friend—diagnosed a person as waving, when she is indeed drowning?

Through Septimus's treatment, *Mrs. Dalloway* offers a vivid indictment of the profound limitations of medical authority. Sep-timus despises his two doctors, with good reason. The first, Dr. Holmes, a general practitioner who believes that there is noth-ing wrong with Smith, suggests the patient live a normal life. Play golf! he advises. The other more formidable and pompous doctor, Sir William Bradshaw, is a rigid specialist with a grating theory of Proportion. This is the key to mental health, Bradshaw declares, his condescending upper-class approach to madness. Septimus's mental instability is a personal failure, a failure of discipline and self-control.

You almost have the sense that Septimus's final act of suicide is a rejection of these prescriptions, the invalidation of the world. His suicide an *I'll show you*. His suicide a way of getting worse, if not better. It is similar to the narrator in "The Yellow Wallpaper," whose husband tells her that there is nothing the matter with her. She just needs to rest, take her phosphites, and get over it. She, too, will show him—her physician husband—her move into madness a rejection of his assessment. You don't think I'm mad? Well, I'll show you. It is not enough—not for the narrator, not for Septimus—to tell the story of their madness; they must act it out.

Hank, a Memoir (I)

One

He wears front-pleated jeans, belted at the waist. A pink T-shirt and a beige Members Only jacket. Over his shoulder, a LeSport-sac bag.

He gets on the elevator. A Sunday afternoon. It is 1992 or 1993 or 1994.

I didn't realize that a patient could come and go.

When he returns, a few hours later, he sees me looking at him. He nods.

For a while, it's like that. We are just here and we see each other.

I become used to the pattern of his coming and going, every other Sunday afternoon. Something to count on.

Now it's a Monday in November.

———

Today Hank stops when he walks by me. He nods, says hi. Hi. He looks down before he says it, doesn't exactly make eye contact. But it's okay. There are other ways at intimacy. He sits on the next sofa, on the other side of the aides' station.

William tries a joke. But today Hank doesn't smile, he's serious, focused.

Now Dr. Triel comes by, stops, says, Hello, Henry.
    Dr. Triel sees me, nods. Back to Hank.
    Henry, are you ready?
    Hank gets up, doesn't look at the doctor, follows him down the hall toward the offices on the north side of the building.

Two

The next day Hank comes and sits almost next to me on the sofa. In between us, there's room for another person, but still.

We sit there for a while. I understand something of this gesture. The doctors have told us to talk to each other. Our peers. Make friends. This is part of the experiment, to have intense transitory relationships, not just with the doctors, nurses, staff, but with our peers, too.

A peer is a wildly variable thing. I can talk to Stella and Rose every day, but I'll never feel close to them. Are they my peers? We were all born in the 1970s, and we all live together now. Is that enough to make a peer?

With Hank, I can already tell, there's more to it.

———

For one thing, he is functional. In a way. That he comes and goes somewhere. He has a responsibility, unlike the other patients here. Unlike me. What do I have to do ever? Nothing, just sit here and feel sad. Read my books. Cry. Try new medicines. Complain. Put on my Walkman and listen to my audiocassettes, Tori Amos and the Indigo Girls.

Three

The sun sets earlier and it's dark when I wake up. Another Sunday. I'm on a new medication now and I can't sleep in. It's quiet here on the weekend and they don't turn all the awful lights on. Institutional lighting.

Oona is in the station, crossword puzzle in front of her. She's almost finished. She leaves it there when she sees me at the door, turns to find my doctor's orders, comes back with a Dixie Cup. Oona wasn't mean, but she definitely didn't care about any of us. She did her job, which didn't include emotional labor, as it might be called now.

Here's what you have today.
    What are these?
    It was often changing.
    She reads from a prescription sheet, quickly, dares me to object.
    I swallow and she goes back to her crossword puzzle.

Later she returns the magazine to the table in the main area, next to the rest of the newspaper.

Eventually I noticed that *The New York Times* book review was always missing from the paper. Every Sunday. The paper would be there in full, Oona's magazine returned, but no book review.

Eventually I noticed it was Hank.

Hank was always up early, he would find the newspaper before anyone touched it, somehow he would get there first, every Sunday. And somehow he would remove the book review so that it looked like nothing had been removed. Once I was cognizant and less than fully drugged-out I wanted to read the newspaper. So that's when I noticed that it was gone. The book review. I'd have to find him on a vinyl couch or wait for him to come out of the toilet (which was in the main hall, next to the women's toilet, even though the men's dorm was way on the other side of the building). The toilets were all together, and we had to be observed in the toilet. There were mirrors in the bathroom but they were made of sheet metal, so in all those years I rarely saw my face.

So I'd wait and eventually Hank came out of the toilet, I'd have to listen to him make the most disgusting farting noises. He'd spend like an hour in there, at least, and it was all I could do to stay anywhere near. He explained that he could only take a shit after he got all the gas out, and that took a while.

I suppose I never really shared a bathroom with a man before this. Not even my brothers, or not after they were old and gross like this.

I mean, girls were gross, too, but it was a familiar gross, bloody pads and menstrual blood. It was gross for a few days, for a week, some girls would sit there all day on the toilet, bleeding and shitting. I didn't care. Or it was me. They never connected our moods to our periods back then, but all it took was a simple observation to see how it was connected. How insane nearly every girl became before her period, myself included, more crying, more screaming.

And then the quiet, the peace that came as soon as the bleeding began. Even with the cramps.

Anyway, I'd wait for Hank to appear with the book review, and if he was coming from the toilet, of course I no longer wanted to read it. No. He'd have it still in his hands, folded into the style of a magazine.

He read it from beginning to end as if it were a novel or a book and it made sense to read it that way.

What's it like reading it that way, start to finish?
    He looks at me. That's how you're supposed to read.
    A book, yeah.
    No, you should read everything this way.
    Do you read magazines this way?
    I had learned from another patient that Hank was an art director at *The New York Times*.
    Of course.
    We are laughing, or smiling at least, I guess this is flirting, that's what it was. We were young, in a psych ward, why not.

Are you going out today?
    Yes.
    What time?
    After lunch.
    Where do you go?
    He looks at me, mockingly: I go to the zoo.
    The zoo?
    Yeah, the zoo.
    Wow.

You're pretty gullible, huh?

I don't know.

A long pause.

I go to my aunt's.

He pronounces *aunt* the way I've heard my cousins in Cape Cod pronounce it, with an *aw*.

Back in Aurora, my aunt is my ant, like a bug.

Where does your aunt live?

In the Bronx.

Oh. Is that where you grew up?

No.

She needs my help.

Oh.

My cousin—she raises my sister's kid. But my aunt is elderly, it's too much for her. She's not entirely healthy, either.

Right.

I visit. I take my niece out, you know, we do something fun. Or I just have supper. Today it's just Sunday supper.

That's nice?

I should be doing more, but I'm here, you know? He looks around, a what-the-fuck look. We start laughing again and we don't stop until Oona comes in to call out, *Henry, I have your pass.*

The hospital itself was never going to be funny or a place for lots of laughs. There was a solemnity and that above all makes it hard for me to believe that I lived there so long. Did I really not laugh for three years? No, it's not true. I did laugh, it was so absurd, I laughed more than I'd laughed in years.

Hank and I don't have another conversation for some weeks. Still, we say hi regularly now, and with intent, we will be friends, but for the most part we're too busy suffering in our own corners. It takes a lot of work. This is what everyone does here, or at least much of the time, you work in your corner and you work on your story. The story is about your suffering and the story creates your suffering, too.

Hank was at *The New York Times* until his suicide attempt. He'd gathered up everything in his studio—drawings and paintings, sketches and nearly complete compositions—carried it all to the George Washington Bridge. One piece after another, threw it away, over, watched it fly up by the wind and then down to the water. Some floated for a while, most of it sank. A passerby cursed him for littering. Yes, it was just that, so much litter.

And he would go, too, over that bridge, suspended over the Hudson River, spanning Manhattan to New Jersey. He found the pedestrian walkway. It was nighttime, someone saw him, this time the stranger asked what he was doing. Was he okay? Or the stranger didn't ask. But something in Hank, as he told me later, heard a voice—someone somewhere asking him, Are you okay? Can I help you? That voice was what made him walk away. Walk home. Walk himself to an emergency room. A jumper. That's what they call them now. Jumpers. There are so many more jumpers now, on that bridge and others, than there were in 1992.

Melting

I'm up too early for a Sunday. I hear doors opening and closing, a loud voice. A room without a door doesn't help. What I took last night: Depakote, Zoloft, Mellaril, Halcion. The days are getting shorter, it's still dark.

Hank and the others stayed up last night to watch *Saturday Night Live*. This—watching television, and especially watching television in a group, and especially watching television in a group of mental patients—was almost always the last thing I wanted to do. Though I made friends on the ward, I resisted these connections. I didn't want to be a member of this club that would have me, and so tried regularly to position myself as not-as-sick as these others. The time to read and write in my room was more important to me than ever, it was how I got through, sorted myself out. It was a forced meditation, too, to have to sit with a book, to pay attention. If my loneliness had become terrifying before I entered the hospital, now I was able to balance my need for solitude with the awareness of people, care, and belonging just down the hall. If I resented the surveillance, I think now that it allowed me to cultivate an intellectual life.

—#—

There is a new woman in the room two doors down from mine. Pam. She had attempted suicide and was diagnosed, or so her sister told me skeptically, with gender dysphoria.

Pam was skinny, androgynous, thick glasses and curly short hair. She didn't speak but always smiled at me when we passed. Anna, her older sister, visited every evening. Anna talked a lot. They looked like twins, but Anna was confident, at ease in the world. It was as if she'd received so much of some crucial element of personality and there was none left over for Pam. Nothing you could identify exactly, but essential to getting by. Without it, you could slip utterly, lose your place, end up here. You could melt into another person, or melt into a place like this. There was nothing secure, for some of us, no glue. Anna had that glue.

Other people would call this mental illness, or this was a way to think about it on that ward. But I experience this in life still, and I'm not the only one. I see it everywhere. Stephen King called it "the shining." Others call it sensitivity, insecurity, shyness. Fragility. My son does not have this quality, and that is a relief to me.

(I know it is dangerous to define my son this way, or to set him down in writing at all. Every time I do, I think of one passage in Didion's "On Keeping a Notebook." Just before identifying herself as part of a group of anxious malcontents, Didion expresses relief over her daughter, who she assumes will never be this way— *Although I have felt compelled to write things down since I was five years old, I doubt that my daughter ever will, for she is a singularly blessed and accepting child, delighted with life exactly as life presents itself to her, unafraid to go to sleep and unafraid to wake up.*

I've reread that line for some years now with the knowledge of her daughter's life story, the tragedy of her early death; Didion's assessment of her seems almost a curse in retrospect, wishful thinking at least.)

—*//*—

Not that Hank was an extrovert; he wasn't. Only the rare patient could be described that way.

But Hank was better than I was at being with people. He was accommodating, he could *make allowances*. And he took seriously the admonition from the doctors to be social. Don't isolate! I was quite content to isolate, and was often warned against it.

To not isolate in a hospital setting, as Erving Goffman notes, is to become part of your assigned class, the class of inpatient as inscribed by the organization of the ward—that happened to me, of course, but some part of me knew that the only way to survive, to get out of there, would be to resist total identification. Like many mental patients, I wanted to see myself as not-so-bad. This is not unlike what writers do, a distancing from experience, a desire to stand apart. It is a long-standing trope in the literature of psych wards, from Plath's Esther Greenwood to Susanna Kaysen's *Girl, Interrupted* to Bette Howland's *W-3*. I am here but I am better than the rest of you, I'm special, I'm not that bad— a thin survival strategy, since, like Esther Greenwood and Susanna Kaysen, I was that bad. I was there.

More and more patients are up, coming in for breakfast. They all smoke before they eat. That first cigarette. Not Hank. We were the only patients who didn't smoke.

Soon I hear him—he is talking about Sinéad O'Connor.

Something about the pope.

William is laughing, and says, Crazy bitch.

Bridget is shaking her head. Irish Bridget. She won't believe it. Right there on live television. Jesus, Mary, and Joseph. She makes the sign of the cross.

I find the newspaper. On today's cover: an article about the Clintons, another about plastics. Nothing about Sinéad. I think of the cover of my cassette tape, Sinéad O'Connor's *I Do Not Want*

What I Haven't Got. The cover her face floating against a black background.

(Growing up Irish-American, we were taught to be proud of our heritage, and we understood being Irish as magical, charming, innocent. My mother romanticized the country her parents fled. As a young woman, she traveled to Ireland. She told me about kissing the Blarney Stone, how it gave you the gift of the gab, how I, too, had *the gift of the gab*. It's funny how *the gift of the gab* didn't mean that you would be a writer. It implied, rather, that you talked too much, at least it did if you were a girl, or a woman. Too much gab. Men, too, had the gift of the gab, but there it was charming, to hear them tell stories, punctuated by laughter and tears.

It's still like this in Ireland, the Irish. They have the gauzy shining thing. The sadness or terror so near the surface. Aside from other writers, they are as a group the meltiest people I've ever known.)

In childhood I wasn't told much about the reality of Ireland. Or the Ireland of the 1980s. I received hints through music—through U2, and Bono, but most forcefully through Sinéad O'Connor. Her voice, her sensibility. The wail of history in her. She taught me the truth of the Irish famine. In the United States, as in Ireland, our education erased the true narrative. So we didn't know. It was not a famine. Sinéad explained that the so-called famine was the result of British colonial rule—meat, fish, vegetables were shipped out of Ireland to England, and so the Irish people starved, left with little more than potatoes.

But long before this, we knew the floating head of the music videos. Her voice wailing: "Nothing Compares 2 U," the breakup song—Prince's song—that spoke to my bones long before I'd broken up with anyone. Sinéad was melting, shining. I felt it immediately—this quality of a great artist. Why was the head disembodied? She was so beautiful, yet it made it strange to see her later, with her body, that head's body. It didn't fit somehow. It was not fair to her body, which was beautiful as bodies go—but it seemed unnecessary, as we'd learned to love her face and that head she had shaved, rejecting beauty standards, rejecting femininity.

She was celebrated, for a time. Until they called her crazy, which happened soon enough.

She was Cassandra, calling out the abuses of the Church.

I can't find it in the newspaper but now I hear someone explaining what happened on *Saturday Night Live*. Maybe it is Hank. Sinéad sang and ended her song declaring, FIGHT THE REAL ENEMY. She took out a picture of Pope John Paul II and held it to the camera. She ripped the photo into four pieces. She was like a child, daring the audience, the viewers. Fuck you to patriarchy. She was like one of us there in the hospital. Only her protest meant something. FIGHT THE REAL ENEMY.

Jesus, Mary, and Joseph, Bridget says again.

You used to hold my hand when the plane took off. Sinéad was channeling something that belonged to all of us, and it reached me, before I had the experience of love—I had lost my mother and it was already clear that every loss to follow would echo that first loss, the devastation would be the same. This was part of my illness, I was told: that I misread it, that I felt too much, that the mindfuck of my mom's deterioration and death would return to me over and over again for the rest of my life. Sinéad made this illness of mine into art. Sinéad's head opened and the truth spilled out like so many jewels. She was defiant. The artists who mattered most to me in those days were like Sinéad, always on the edge of disintegration. The best artist willing to fall into that space just beyond control.

In those years art became a light—it showed me that there was a space for that wail, that longing—there was something to be done with this living on the edge, or just over the edge, I had the sense that if I could turn my own melting into something the way Sinéad did—the way Audre Lorde did, the way Virginia Woolf did—it would mean something. All my suffering, my stupid life, would mean something. The urgency and compulsion, the way Jean Rhys, a melty woman writer, felt: *I knew that if I could get to the end of what I was feeling it would be the truth about myself and about the world and about everything that one puzzles and pains about all the time.*

So a bunch of mental patients and workers sitting around talking about Sinéad O'Connor. We might have been discussing another patient. Was she crazy? Wasn't she actually speaking the truth? I didn't say much, but I listened. I rarely spoke; I found it excruciating to enter a conversation with a thought, an opinion. So I listened, and later wrote in my notebook what I might have said, had I dared, had I known. *I don't know what I think until I read what I say,* as Flannery O'Connor put it.

Though I wasn't a superfan, I felt protective of Sinéad, as if they were talking about my sister, or me. Later I learned that in her protest that night, she was referring to the extensive, hidden child abuse by the Catholic Church. This was 1992 and it would be some years before this was confirmed in a more extensive and darker way than even she could have known back then. But I wouldn't say she was ever vindicated—her life was very hard, and she came to identify as bipolar, instead of radical.

(Some weeks after I turned in the final draft of this book, Sinéad O'Connor died. She was fifty-six. As I return here now, to update this chapter, her funeral is being held in Wicklow, where my family lives. It takes my breath away to see images from the funeral, just as it took my breath away, in the car last week, driving on the highway, to hear the news of her death: *Fans around the world are celebrating the life of Sinéad O'Connor*—how I knew where the sentence was going, how I held my breath as if to forestall or avert its dreadful conclusion—*who died today at the age of fifty-six.*)

Two weeks later, Hank told me what he saw on the nightly news. Sinéad went onstage at Madison Square Garden for a Bob Dylan tribute concert, her first performance since *Saturday Night Live*. She walked out on the stage in her blue outfit with her bald head—she was so thin and tall and fragile looking—and before she could open her mouth many in the audience booed her. I find it on the internet now. The surprise, the vulnerability in her face, and, quickly, the acceptance and awareness of what she'd done: These were the consequences. She gathered herself, sang Bob Marley's "War" again, as she had done on *Saturday Night Live*, this time screaming the words into the microphone as the audience continued to boo. I remember understanding then that the Catholic Church had not only been so powerful and dominant in my own life, in my very sense of myself as a young woman, but it was dominant and powerful globally, and it would use that power to shame this beautiful young woman artist. With such wealth, such power, did the pope, the Vatican, really have such fragile feelings that they were threatened by Sinéad O'Connor, a twenty-six-year-old pop star?

She was the perfect scapegoat. Who would take her seriously, after all?

Interlude, 2022

(Q: *Why does it bother you, that Sinéad identified as bipolar?*

I meet a painter at an artists' residency. She asks about my book. What is it about? I never quite know how I will answer this question. I have less control over the answer than I've imagined. I may decide or have the instinct to be guarded, and then I will hear myself say, It is about being a career mental patient. Or I will say something about a woman writer, about my own illness and hospitalization, about coming of age. Whatever I say, it is not right, it is never right. So today I surprise myself by saying, It is about mental illness and women writers.

Oh! She is interested.
    Are you looking for more material?
    Oh, well, I say. (Not really.)
    (I am not looking for it but it is looking for me.)
    My daughter, well, she's a writer. And she's bipolar. I don't know if she identifies as bipolar.
    Oh, I say.
    I appreciate how she puts it—that it is her daughter's choice whether or not *to identify*.

A: That is my problem with Sinéad. That she did not choose how to identify. That the identity—the designated patient, the scapegoat—chose her. That she was trapped. What if she knew herself as I know her—radical, iconoclastic, an artist? And if she was indeed bipolar, if the diagnosis helped her, then what if she'd led with all the rest? What if bipolar—so large and vague and often meaningless—didn't dwarf the rest, didn't become the dominant read on a person? This is what bothers me, the way people (and NAMI, the National Alliance on Mental Illness, doesn't help) embrace diagnostic identities—for themselves or their family members. However useful it may be, it is often another way to get stuck in a limiting story, someone else's story.)

Elena

It was a Tuesday in October when Elena arrived on the ward. There is nothing better than fall in New York, though I could not say that back then. I could see it, though, the trees, the colors changing. The end of the day, just before sunset, the light that makes me cry these days. Simple and profound. Seasons and time. Some of the patients were like me, far from home, but many were local. The Bronx, Brooklyn, Connecticut, New Jersey. Harlem. Park Slope. Queens. Elena was from Queens. She was the second person I'd ever met from Queens. The first was Barbara, the nurse who cared for me those first days after my half-hearted suicide attempt, my first weeks in the acute unit. Unlike the doctors, who always seemed to be seeking a grand narrative, certain nurses didn't have time for that. Which could be a relief. Or rather, they chose to see me as I was, a young woman, not a mental patient, not crazy, not even sick. A troubled woman whom circumstances had landed in a place like this. Barbara, like Pam, had a no-nonsense way of responding to my quiet angst. On a morning when I was sad, as was often the case, she saw me take a small container of Rice Krispies off my tray. I wouldn't use milk, I was against milk, it was poison. I poured water into the little cereal box and ate it that way. She laughed at this, but she wasn't mean. It was something a girlfriend might do, laugh at you, how weird you are and funny, too.

It is as if you live in a house with a fence, the nurse Pam is trying to explain something to me. When a friend or family member or anyone at all comes over, you open the fence. You let them in. Sometimes you enjoy seeing the person. I have seen you enjoy people, she said, of course you do. You don't really want to eliminate people. But your problem, Pam says, your problem as I see it, is that when the person leaves, you have trouble latching the fence. You can't secure it. The person leaves and there you are with the fence swung open. They've left but to you they are still there and so you can't go back inside your house and sit still and think how happy you are to have a friend. How lucky you are. Instead, you are bereft, lost, the fence is open and what to do? You can't live with your fence open like that, everything gets in, she explains. You feel unsettled until you can shut it.

I think of Lauren Berlant's posthumous book, the evocatively titled *On the Inconvenience of Other People* (other people are inconvenient, if you are lucky, she writes) or Woolf's Clarissa Dalloway, who leaves her friends and experiences that subtle, sharp, and complicated return to the self, with all its comfort and limitations: *And they went further and further from her, being attached to her by a thin thread (since they had lunched with her) which would stretch and stretch, get thinner and thinner as they walked across London; as if one's friends were attached to one's body, after lunching with them, by a thin thread, which (as she dozed there) became hazy with the sound of bells, striking the hour or ringing to service, as a single*

spider's thread is blotted with raindrops, and, burdened, sags down. So she slept.

For Neville in Woolf's most experimental novel, *The Waves*, this self-other identity is fraught; Neville's fence won't latch. After leaving his friend Bernard, he reflects: *How curiously one is changed by the addition, even at a distance, of a friend. How useful an office one's friends perform when they recall us. Yet how painful to be recalled, to be mitigated, to have one's self adulterated, mixed up, become part of another.*

Elena wasn't dramatic. She was sad, the shut-off quality of being. She was a nurse. She arrived to the hospital with her husband. The two of them, not yet thirty, newlyweds. They seemed like a small couple playing at adulthood. Twenty-four or twenty-five or twenty-six. Elena didn't speak to anyone for a day or two and then slowly, she adjusted. For the first few weeks she was required to have an aide by her side at all times. Marion or Bridget in the day shift, and Roger at night.

She quickly renounced her profession. It was as if she had nursed enough and now she was ready to be nursed. Like the mothers wishing to become children, so the nurse wished to be a patient.

Her husband brought her to the ward. He stood next to her, though she wouldn't look at him. Wouldn't speak. After a week, he was allowed to come to the hospital for visiting hours. I remembered him arriving on the ward in his trench coat, looking very much like an adolescent dressed up as a grown-up. An attorney. I remember how he looked at us, we were strange to him, he could not relate to us. You could always tell when someone could relate and when someone would not.

Anyone could relate, but you have to stop yourself, we all do, that's part of staying sane—*going sane*, as psychotherapist Adam Phillips calls the other side of it, the place we want to stay.

On one or two occasions Elena and her husband met with the doctors. I saw them come out of these sessions, Elena distraught, her husband swiftly moving to the elevator, serious, not hiding his exasperation. By then, Elena was speaking. She would break out in an enormous laugh, that is what I remember of her, the laugh that came out of her anger or despair or depression. It is never one thing, we laugh through it all or some of us do. And it always seemed to me that this was Elena's gift, this laughter, the way it filled the halls, reminded everyone of life. I would say that we all laughed but no one laughed like Elena, and in Marion and Bridget she found her people, the ones who would listen to her jokes, shaking with laughter, near tears. When the doctors came to get Elena for a meeting or something else, that was when she stopped laughing. Or when she came out of her sessions. That was it—she was either laughing wildly or not at all. There was no in between.

One day, a month or two into her stay, she told us what was happening. Her husband's anger, his disappointment. By now she'd lost her job. It was a good job, her nursing job. He thought she loved her job, or at least liked it. None of this was in the plan. Worst of all, the husband told her, there was nothing wrong with her. She was doing this on purpose. Now she was here having a good time, and didn't want to leave. It was not supposed to be this way, they were just married, why did this happen, only months after their honeymoon, it had been such a joyous time, after all. She agreed, it had been. Now she was giving up, he said, on their life together.

One day, after he left, Elena told us that he'd asked for a divorce. She had already gained weight, and would continue to. He couldn't put up with this. He wanted another wife, she said. She wasn't crying, she wasn't laughing, just sitting there, matter-of-fact. She couldn't explain. She had found a place here and it made more sense to her than her marriage ever had. It wasn't her fault. He came one more time, with divorce papers. That was the last time we saw him.

Now it was just Elena's mother and father who visited every day. They were there when visiting hours began, and left only when they had to. Her mother was middle-aged, probably in her forties, with dark hair and blue eyes. Elena was Italian but her adoptive parents were from Ireland. Like Bridget, they lived in Queens, in Sunnyside, around other Irish immigrants. They sat there staring at the floor or the table, rarely speaking, smiling, nodding. What was there to say? They waited for Elena to change and to get better and when she didn't they waited still. What happens if your child is in pain and they can't tell you what's wrong and you can't make it right? It is my worst nightmare, now that I am a mother, what I couldn't have known back then. How life shifts as my child's life shifts, how I try to maintain stasis or equanimity and how impossible it is. *You will only be as happy as your unhappiest child.* That bit of folktale wisdom—or curse.

Elena's mother was unusual among the mothers. Her sadness attended a kindness. She and her husband could not have their own children and so they'd adopted Elena and her sister when they were babies. Elena's mother was not needy of her daughter. She was present. Was that enough? It had to be enough. There was Jonathan's father, a gymnast who leered at us, the young women. Irene's mother or Stella's mother always in tears, worse than a patient. The many mothers indistinguishable from the patients. And then the many mothers who did not show up or were not allowed to show up.

And so Elena's mother stood out, that must be it. The way she and Elena's father arrived and stayed for the evening visiting hour each weekday and the two afternoon hours each weekend. That's all they did, arrive and stay, until they had to leave. Elena occasionally sat with them, but often they sat apart or alone, patient for something, which would never come, but no matter. It was the waiting that mattered.

Hank, a Memoir (II)

One

Time passes.

Today Hank appears with a copy of the newspaper, folded open. He has circled two listings with a black Sharpie. One is a chamber concert on the Upper West Side, the other is a Sophie Calle exhibition at the Met. Taxidermy, he explains. He's read about it. Do you want to go? He's serious this time.

How can we go? I say.
    I'll ask my doctor, you ask yours.
    Okay.
    If mine says yes, it should be okay. It's culture. Right?

My doctor asks if I'm ready for this.
    Ready for what? Leaving?
    Yes.
    I don't know, I said, and I didn't. I'd been there so long the idea of leaving on my own, or with Hank, was terrifying. What would

happen to us? I tried to imagine it, the two of us, out in the city, on our own. No doctors, nurses. Nothing.

Well, do you feel like you can be safe?

Maybe.

Why don't we have you write a contract?

What's the contract?

Dr. Triel found a piece of paper. I'm going to write this out for you and I'm going to have you sign it and then I'm going to have Hank sign it. Now. If one of you on the way out or while you're out, or while you're at the museum, or in Central Park—if one of you decides that you want to run away from the hospital, never come back—or alternately, one of you decides again to kill yourself while you're out there—well, then, the other of you will need immediately to find a phone and call us back here at the hospital. Or call 911.

We signed our contracts.

This time we mean to leave. We have our passes. We have Dixie cups of medications in Ziploc baggies, just in case we are out past the next meds lineup.

—#—

End of Act Two:
 Estragon: Well? Shall we go?
 Vladimir: Yes, let's go.

[*They do not move.*]

Two

Hank got better before I did. But that's not really true. He just had to leave before I had to leave. His time ran out.

They said he had gotten better. He told me they were wrong, and he hadn't gotten better.

We went on dates like this, to the Angelika movie theater in the Village, to the Upper East Side museums, to Shakespeare in Central Park.

The more dates we went on, he said, the more convinced they were that he was better. He was being a leader, taking me out, helping me get better that way.

But you don't have to leave, he said.
    I'll have to leave someday.
    Yeah. Hope so.
    Yeah. I mean.
    We can't stay here forever.
    That's true.
    But.
    Yeah.
    Change. You get used to things, it sucks to leave. Or it's just change that sucks.
    All of it.
    Sucks.

[*They do not move.*]

Family Therapy

So it was a year into my stay when I was called to a meeting with the two head doctors. Dr. Triel and the playwright Dr. Prince. The handsome playwright. He was something like the vice president of the ward, second to Triel's presidential status. A quiet, calming force, but often invisible.

Except that he wasn't invisible because he was so good-looking, particularly in contrast to Dr. Triel, who was overweight, with sweat stains visible through his suit, a belly nearly bursting the buttons. Dr. Triel leaned forward as he walked, in his brown leather heavy orthopedic shoes, always wearing suits in colors and fabrics that were out of season. Square glasses, but not hip. Curly hair, receding hairline. Always smiling, always making eye contact. An intense hello, leaning forward. Nothing evasive about him, as there was with the handsome Prince.

Dr. Prince rarely made eye contact, and when he did, he seemed to have to make a point of it. His long hair fell over his eyes, he pushed it back, smiled.

————

When he walked by, the girls ogled him, Rose and Stella sticking out their tongues, mouthing *hubba hubba* and fainting, as if they were construction workers or Beatles fans, a hey, baby kind of thing. Bridget would slap Stella's hand playfully: Cut it out.

Tilda spent the most time with Dr. Prince. She was his specialty. Or he was a specialist in whatever she had. Which was multiple personality disorder.

Erving Goffman writes of the vocabulary unique to the mental hospital. For example, to elope. *Eloped* was a word I'd associated, as most people do, with running away to get married. But in the context of the hospital, of inpatient psychiatry, eloped means something else. It means a patient runs away. I remember at least two occasions when Tilda eloped. Each time she was found by the police and returned to the hospital. The first time she showed up at the home of one of the nurses. The second time, she made her way to Dr. Prince's home near Eighty-first and Central Park West. This was before the internet, before smartphones, so how she found Dr. Prince's address was impressive. Later she bragged about it, his home, it was a prewar co-op, she said, as if that meant anything to me, in a building called The Beresford. Lots of famous people lived there, she said. Right near the museum.

I only remember the name of it, The Beresford, because a year later another woman arrived on the ward for shock therapy. She was catatonic for a week or two, but then became very chatty. She, too, lived in The Beresford. Her ex-husband had been a famous television producer.

Eloping was just one stage in a larger event, which I only understood days later, after other patients filled me in.

———

So today I'm in Dr. Triel's office, suddenly everything is official again, formal, according to the rules. A minute ago I was in the hall hearing Bridget tell a story, and Elena's coyote laugh.

Luka took a pack of gum and chewed it one stick after another, chewing one until the flavor ran out and then another. Luka was always smiling, always talking about her close-knit Italian family. Her father owned a restaurant in Queens.

This was called gum bingeing, she explained.
    Was that a thing? I'd never heard of it.
    I'm oral, she said.

A few days into her stay, Luka started scratching herself with her fingernails. She had come to admire Rose and Stella, Happy and Patricia, the master cutters.

Rose, who didn't react to much at all, found this attempt amusing and disdainful, too. Baby cat scratcher, she would say, mocking Luka.

So Luka is laughing at Bridget, Elena, too. It turns out all of them—Luka, Elena, and Bridget—live in Queens, first generation, Italian and Irish, and they all have the same sense of humor. I found it hard to laugh with Luka and her gum bingeing. It felt like my little sister had showed up, a tagalong in a serious place. Plus Luka's mother was always there. Why would you bother being there if you had a mother? A mother who was your best friend?

So I walk from this gathering to my office appointment. We live in a timeless nowhere nospace, but every once in a while we are told we have to attend a "meeting." Nurse Margie suggests I get dressed. I am dressed, I say. Sweatpants, a sweatshirt. Why not jeans at least? And shoes.

So I get dressed and I wait outside of the office, down in the hall-way near the men's dorm.

I wait and soon the doctors show up, walking, smiling, as if they've just shared an amusing story, something benign. Just a moment, we'll be right with you, Dr. Triel says.

After some time, Dr. Prince opens the door to invite me in.
　　How are you feeling?
　　Not great.
　　Do you enjoy spending time with Marion Smith and Bridget?
　　Sure.
　　That's good. You are connecting with people. Elena?
　　She's okay.
　　Yes, well, maybe you will learn to connect with your peers, too.
　　Okay.

Do you know why we are having this meeting?
　　No.
　　We've been discussing this as a team, your team.
　　I'd gathered by then that my team meant Roxane, Nurse Mar-gie, Marion Smith, whichever rotating resident doctor I'd been assigned.

Okay.

We have a sense, based on all you've said, based on your father's visit, our meetings with him, we have a good sense of the family dynamic at home.

————

Okay.

Have you heard of the concept of a scapegoat?

Maybe.

Well, we like to talk about the family scapegoat. And here on this ward, we sometimes call this person the designated patient.

Okay.

Do you think of yourself as the designated patient in your family?

It's something like thinking you are special, I don't say.

It's clear to us. Your father and stepmother remarried too quickly, but of course it was necessary, or it was all your father could imagine doing, with four young children, his job, he needed labor. He loves your stepmother, but in practical terms what else could he do? And then there is the Catholic thing.

Nineteen eighty. A memory. It's the day after my mom's wake or funeral. Sitting in the back of the station wagon with my friends, our neighbors, my cousins. One or another asking, Do you think you'll have a new mom? Don't you think your dad is going to get married again? My mom, a cousin said, told me that your mom told your dad to get married again. She gave him permission. She said it before she died.

Everyone nodded, as if this was the most logical thing in the world.

I was horrified by the idea. But more importantly, I knew it was a lie. I knew my mother would never have said that. Or if she had, it was an abstract idea, it was not a real plan that she would approve when it came down to it.

And what does that mean anyway, when you are almost dead; what does it matter what you say? Wouldn't a person say anything when she was dead, or almost dead? I knew enough that my mother as she lay dying was not the mother who saw me and put me first and cared about me and my life. They were speaking of someone else: the benevolent newly sainted mother who offered absolution for all sorts of ill-advised plans.

Dr. Triel continued, Our sense is that the remarriage, however helpful it was, and full of love, was also full of conflict and further loss, for you. And your father, whom you love, did not deal with that conflict. He ignored it. You can't criticize him, you never could, because he was all you had left. With your mother gone, it was your greatest fear, to lose him. But he didn't help you, not in the way you needed. And so it played out between you and your stepmother, all of you, the hostility and jealousy and competition. You bore the brunt of this. Maybe it was your closeness to your mom, the age you were when she died.

I stopped hearing Dr. Triel. I was peeling at my nail polish, looking at my fingers, at my Doc Martens. On the wall a poster reproduction of a Matisse painting, one that seemed unfamiliar. A woman who looked very interested in something, but apprehensive. She had dark hair gathered on her head in a topknot. I squinted and saw that the painting was really just blocks of color. The woman's face, her raised eyebrows, her skeptical look, faded away or fell into the background, and now it was all color—green and pink and red—and the color became the woman—the green stripe down her face, or the color was her face, her dress, too, was the red or the pink. And now her face came back into focus, and I saw that the green stripe separated one half of her face from the other, each side of her face a different color.

Does this make sense to you?

I suppose so, I said.

We think the best way to help you with this, with the fact that you've become the designated patient of your family—

That you are the one carrying your mother's ghost on your back, Dr. Prince added, out of nowhere, making my situation poetic.

Yes, and because of that, because you are the one who can't adjust to the complicated and fraught new family configuration—you've become the patient. We call it *designated* because, well, we see the entire family as sick. You are here, but you are not the only one who is sick. Your sickness is a family sickness. It is always this way, everyone you see here. If we can treat the sick family, it's something like removing a tumor, not just a Band-Aid.

Make sense?

I examined Matisse's woman. What was her family sickness? What was her designation? Why was she in this painting?

As you see it, your father betrayed you, replaced your mom with a caregiver who did not like you very much, who did not want the best for you.

———————

It seemed so simple the way he said it. Well, I suppose that was it. No, she didn't want the best for me, now did she. And of course she didn't like me.

And so, Dr. Triel added, Dr. Prince and I are going to invite your family to the ward. Not as visitors, outsiders, but as patients themselves.

What does that mean?

Dr. Prince smiled, added gently, What he means is that we will speak to them as we speak to you. We want to get to know who they are.

Are you going to tell them what you just told me?

Not necessarily. We want to hear their stories.

This seemed like a terrible idea. Still, Dr. Prince seemed confident we would get somewhere with this. But where were we getting? I didn't want to work things out with my stepmother or my father. I wanted to get away from all of it. That's why I was here, after all, in this city, in this hospital.

Every Wednesday evening, just before Literature Group, Irene's mother, father, and sister came for their family therapy sessions. Irene was tall and blonde, Scandinavian, she was always whining, such an Eeyore, she had no edge like Hank or Stella or even Luka—no ability to make light of it, this place, the absurdity, what a joke. No. Irene was a persistent complainchick.

———————

We watched Irene and her family march into therapy together, with the saddest looks on their faces, and when they left, Irene was inconsolable.

Well, we all complained. That was part of what we did there. Complaining to people who were paid to listen to us. It was some years later, I was working as an intern with a small publishing company, when a guy I met there observed how much I complained. He sort of stopped one day, we were in the middle of some tedious task—boring, but not difficult—when he said, You really complain a lot, don't you?

Did I? Well, yes I did. It hadn't occurred to me how debilitating it was, not to mention how unattractive, to complain about every little thing. How I amplified my misery when it was really just a part of life? *Coping with life's challenges,* a friend described it lately, the thing that she finds young people (i.e., those in the generation after ours) unable to do, or at least not without making a scene about it.

But the truth is, I *was* ill-equipped to cope with life's challenges when I was that age, and even older. I think I was a patient in part because I couldn't cope with many tiny daily boring things, all crucial to getting through a day—I couldn't ask for help, or keep a friend, or tell myself it would be okay. I couldn't get over myself.

Anyway, watching Irene's family come and go, as if heading into a criminal trial, and then leaving as if they'd just received the worst possible news, left me with no hope for the benefit of family therapy.

(We did go, Hank and I, once or twice. It was Hank who told me about the upcoming memorial for Audre Lorde. I asked my doctors if I could leave the hospital on a pass to attend Lorde's memorial at the Cathedral Church of St. John the Divine. In order to receive this *privilege*, as certain freedoms are called in the context of the asylum, I had to be accompanied by another patient, someone deemed stable. Hank agreed.

It was a cold January day when we rode the subway from 168th to 110th, feeling like runaways, excited by our escape and nervous for the freedom. We made our way into the crowded cathedral. Hank led me to a pew, we squeezed in on the end. Episcopal priests and altar boys proceeded up the aisle next to us. A drum circle followed. Angela Davis spoke. Barbara Smith, with whom Lorde had begun the feminist Kitchen Table Press, spoke. When it was her turn, Angela Davis instructed the crowd that they need not follow the Episcopalian ways. Feel free to call and respond, she offered—soon everyone did.

One after another, each speaker taught me about Audre Lorde. I didn't know of her years in Berlin, her many years with breast cancer, her mastectomy. Her daughter, not much older than me or Hank, spoke next. She was proud. This was when I learned that, like my mother, Audre Lorde died of her breast cancer. It was not insignificant, this way of dying, and not uncommon.

It was nearing sunset when we left the church and made our way down 110th to get the subway back uptown. It had been exhilarating, to lose myself in the experience of the ceremony, and now I felt the letdown, the move to melancholy. I couldn't speak to Hank, who sat next to me on the train. How awful, to have to return to the ward together. The most pathetic end to a date. We had to be back for the dinner trays. There was no goodbye kiss. It was just, go to your dorm, see you later, a dissolve back into the shame of the space we still needed. For a few hours we'd been normal.)

Blossom

Every three months, one doctor would leave and a new one would arrive. It was a teaching hospital. It worked for the state of New York, and it worked for the hospital's medical school. A curriculum; training ground. Yet we pretended otherwise. In thrall to the highly sophisticated and complicated rhetoric of Dr. Triel's unifying vision, we believed that it was all by design. We had to go with what Dr. Triel said—that this was good for us, that we would attach to a doctor and then say goodbye, every three months, over and over again until we were healed. This was how life worked, after all, so many hellos and goodbyes, this was training. If you could get attached then let go this way over and over again, you would be ready to do this for the rest of your life.

It was a training for death, too, I see now. Attach and let go. Training for my mother, my inability to let go of my mother, and, if not my mother—because it wasn't her anymore, my memories of her were fading—then training for anyone I would love and lose.

—//—

I'm sitting at a table in the dining room, listening to Hank read aloud from the newspaper—*boat people*, he reads, scornfully. It is 1994 and this is a euphemism for refugees, migrants trying to get out of poverty, to a place of possibility. The story of humanity. Dr. Triel calls me over. A woman stands behind him. She is much younger than Triel, she could be his daughter. She smiles with her mouth closed. She wears a white blouse, a bit snug, buttoned up to her neck. Her eyes bloodshot. The surprise of her face in that place.

Dr. B was pregnant, or just postpartum. Elena told me.

Elena and I may have been her first patients. In the small room of an office, which was not her office, she sat up straight with a notebook in her lap. She looked at me, nodding, taking notes. She took notes without looking at the paper. She asked for my story, why I was there, what happened. By then I had told my story many times, over and over, I was changing the story or I was finding new ways to tell it.

I don't know where the story was when we met. I thought back then that the content of the story mattered above all—that I needed to get it right. Getting it right would be the thing. She noticed my frustration one day—what was my story—and asked, or wondered out loud, do words matter here, what happens between us? It was a relief.

Still, when I read the medical records now, I am most grateful for Dr. B's notes, the way her handwriting, vivid still through the

Xerox, brings something back to life. She wrote every story I told her about my mother. I've forgotten many of these stories, and so the medical records offer my mother back to me. I had lost stories, details, without knowing it—and here they are. In the official records of the New York State Psychiatric Institute.

> *Patient's mother chased her with a spatula, spanking her—*
> *Her mother was fat, this bothered her—*
> *Her mother chastised her for sucking her thumb—*
> *Her mother was angry at her—*

Trivial things, mother-daughter things.

Telling these stories, I think now, was a way of not mourning. Remembering my mother in these moments of conflict or disappointment—this allowed me to keep our fights going. Fighting is a way to refuse to lose someone. If you keep the fight alive, you might never deal with the loss, the vulnerability of it, the deep sadness, the irrevocable and baffling fact of a total loss.

Nineteen eighty. I'm eight years old. I'll be nine in three days. A party. A birthday party at Happy Joe's—there will be balloons and pizza. My friends—Tricia and Carolyn. At school we talk about the party. Carolyn asks, Are you going to wear pants? I am going to wear pants. Carolyn has new pants. Why is it new, to have pants? Was this the long 1970s? I don't know but I am not allowed—I am not allowed to wear pants. I have pants. I must have new pants and I want to wear these pants. I have a pantsuit. I tell my mom. She is in bed, in her room. You are the birthday girl, she says, and you will wear a dress. How does she say this? She is alive enough to say this. She has a dress. No, she does not have a dress. Or she does, she knows

my closet, these are dresses she bought just months ago, she is dying, she was dying, she didn't know how soon it would be, that she'd have to say goodbye but still she bought me a dress. And I would wear that dress to my birthday party. To my ninth birthday party. No, I said. No. I went into her death room. Or I said this from the door outside. The room was always dark, the curtains closed. A king-size bed. Every day my brothers ran up there after school. Home from school, they climbed the stairs up to her room, to sit by her bed, a duty. One brother was eleven and the other brother twelve and how did they know to do that, to keep their duty? How did they know and why couldn't I do my duty? Because I could not, I would spend years, decades trying to make up for my lack.

I see Dr. B on Mondays, Tuesdays, and Fridays at 10:00 a.m. This gives my life on the ward a structure, a shape. Nothing happens in between and so I live for these meetings. Today I follow her down the hallway of the men's dorm. The first half of this hallway is full of offices. The second half toward the window are dorms. We are meant to avoid this hallway altogether, unless accompanied by a staff member. Dr. B uses her keys to open the first office door on the right. She stops abruptly—there is a doctor, a patient there already. I don't see them, but I see Blossom, her face flushed in red. I'm sorry, she says to me.

We try another door. Here we go! she declares with relief, turning on the lights. This will work, yes.

I had the sense that Dr. B was an outsider, like me. This had something to do with her age—she was only a decade older than me— and the small ways she didn't seem entirely comfortable in this place. I imagined that neither of us was meant for this system or it was not meant for us—and so, perhaps we could create something else in that space of non-belonging.

There is no window in this office. I'm sitting in the same chair. Dr. B asks about my childhood, my family, each family member. My siblings. Her interest and attention makes my life feel relevant. Consequential. That she asks, that she wants to know the answers. And so each time I answer a question, I wonder if I am getting it right. Is this the right answer? And I wonder if we are getting closer to the thing.

There was a psychiatric library in the building. If I behaved, I was allowed the privilege (as it is called in a mental hospital) of a visit. It was there I found the collected diaries and letters of Virginia Woolf. In one letter to her friend, the novelist Katherine Mansfield, Woolf describes her frustration with her doctor and her husband, both of whom make a study of her nervous illness. She and Mansfield share the status of writer and patient. Mansfield describes a recent appointment, writing, *Nothing does more to defeat one's sense of intellectual acuity than a visit with a doctor.* In her diary, Woolf writes of the delight of writing for women like Katherine. She links this to the delight she felt as a girl when her mother would read what she wrote. Though she wished to be considered as equal to the male writers of her generation, writing for a woman remained her greatest pleasure—to be *read* by a woman, she writes, *is like being a violin and being played upon.*

This must have been what it was for me as I told my story to Dr. B. I was not writing it yet, but this was the beginning of writing, or a kind of writing, this talking, this being understood, trying to use words to get at it. It was so unlike the feeling I had talking to Triel or any other doctor or nurse. It was attention and care. It was my sense that Dr. B understood—and what is madness if not the horror of being misunderstood, of being unable to make a self comprehensible to another?

A Friday, some weeks later. Dr. B begins our session by asking, How are you?

There is a softness to her, her hair held back with a clip, some pieces falling forward over her cheeks. Her voice has a quality—it is too obvious to say she reminds me of my mother, or she is the closest person to a mother, or that the transference was perfect, complete—but I could live in it.

It has worn me out, all this talk.

I had seen other girls on the ward who didn't speak at all. I often wondered if it was possible. If I had their strength. I'd begun to admire their commitment.

It seemed that the people who were good at talking, at speaking, who felt comfortable using the words available to express experience—they lived in another world.

I was so tired of saying, I feel X. Or, I feel Y.

In one of the required recreational groups, we were assigned tasks called "emotional identification." Each patient was given a turn to present an emotion—angry, sad, lonely, happy. The patient had to come up with examples, find literary references to the emotion, quotations by famous people (Winston Churchill, Helen Keller). We were required to discuss the emotion for an hour. I suppose the idea was that we did not understand our emotional experience. We did not understand what we were feeling, and understanding it would help us to heal.

But it didn't help me. Because everyone knows that emotions are not discrete, do not set themselves apart, so that you might never get ahold of one. After all, I read novels. I knew what emotions were. I knew nothing was one thing. I read to know about other people's emotions and so learned about my own— I learned that mine were not unusual at all. I loved how writers described feelings—I read that Emma Bovary

wanted both to die and to live in Paris—

and I came to know myself. In my notebook, I copied line after line from novels like Flaubert's—I was a collage artist creating a self.

We were asked to define our emotions and report back to the doctors, using the words of the place.

———

One identified and named feeling was *emptiness*. How many times I heard a patient say, I feel empty. And then how the rest of us found the sentence in our mouths, reported this, too, to our doctors, to the nurses. *I feel empty.* The feeling of emptiness was a designated symptom—it was in the *DSM* as criteria for a patient with borderline personality disorder: *chronic feelings of emptiness*. Many patients on our ward were diagnosed with borderline personality disorder. It was an expansive disease (if not a disease at all), allowing for a complicated narrative. Some took pride in this outlaw, ugly diagnosis. A few were prone to violent outbursts; others, like Stella, would take drugs, cocaine, heroin, whatever she could get her hands on. All of this connected, or so the story went, to their *chronic feelings of emptiness*.

Because this symptom (emptiness) was emphasized—and novel (before entering the hospital, I myself had never heard anyone describe this emotional state)—I believe many of us learned to use it as a descriptor of our inner state. Never mind that it was too vague to mean anything.

I think about that word floating around the hospital those days— becoming cliché—and I think, too, of another realm altogether, far from the medical diagnostic, it is the language of the seeker, the spiritual traveler. Poet Fanny Howe, a late convert to Catholicism, an "anatheist": she writes of Thomas Aquinas, of the "unknowable" elements of human nature. For Howe,

> *meditation, contemplation, prayer indicate that there is an emptiness already built into each body.*

Dr. B and I sat there for a long time in silence. She didn't push me to say anything, to my surprise. I was so used to the questions: What are you thinking? What's going on? By not asking, she was giving me permission not to answer—not to add meaning to the silence, which in those days seemed a diminishment, fixing the nothingness into language.

This is our medium, Dr. B said. It's what we have.

I could see I'd become a subject in this place, or my subject position had been shaped. I was the teller of a story and the story was determined by the terms of the place.

Dr. B nodded. I understand, she said.
    So we don't have to talk? I asked.
    Not if you don't want to.
    Will you still sit here with me? Will you stay?
    Yes, she said.
    We spent the hour that way, the first of many—me crying, Dr. B there, across the room, but near to me, with me.

After that Friday, our sessions went this way. Dr. B stopped asking questions. She sat across from me, holding her notepad. I saw her purse on the floor. A novel by a popular writer, tissues, lipstick. The light was soft, table lamps. There was a calm in there, in this space that was part of a century-old institution. Outside the door, a white noise machine. Some days I cried and she gave me tissues.

Other times I sat there across from her looking at the ground or closing my eyes. If she said, Do you want to talk about it? I just shook my head. I did not. That is what happened then, for weeks and months, we sat in that room of silence. It was the nearest I felt to—if not quite *stopping* time—*living in* time.

When Dr. B's rotation ended after three months, she arranged so that I would see her in the outpatient clinic, another area of the hospital. Three mornings a week, I was allowed to walk down to the first floor for my one-hour appointment. Eventually the story of the past pressed against the impossible story of my present—a present in which I was disabled, stuck, with no way out. Dr. B had moved on and I needed to. She made suggestions, ideas for what I could do. I was terrified at these suggestions, the discharge plan implied that I would be getting better and getting better meant losing this attention and care from Dr. B. I was terrified at the thought of living on my own.

I didn't know then how impossible it would be to take this relationship into my next life. It was not transferable, and for many years, I tried very hard to keep it going, to return to it, to bring the hospital back to me. It was a dead end, and when we eventually stopped seeing each other, rather abruptly, it was the best thing that ever happened to me.

The Spider's Web

> I am trying to address an abyss of sorrow, a
> noncommunicable grief that at times, and often on a long-
> term basis, lays claims upon us to the extent of having us
> lose all interest in words, actions, and even life itself.
> —Julia Kristeva, *Black Sun*

Some months after I left the hospital, I came across a book by
Julia Kristeva, *Black Sun*. A work of psychoanalytic literary theory, it spoke to me as if it were a self-help book. It offered a way
to understand my experience, my very sense of self, which had
nothing to do with being "sick" in psychiatric terms. In psychoanalytic terms, Kristeva argues that the loss of the mother to the
daughter (what Adrienne Rich calls the essential female tragedy)
is the noncommunicable trauma, and that the resulting sadness
is depression with specificity. Not an illness to be cured, but a
language to be understood—and the best way to understand is
through art. Art is the language, the communicable.

Kristeva wrote of *noncommunicable* grief—the *abyss of sor-
row*. Not mental illness. Not illness at all. Or if it was illness, it
was more than that. The illness had come about through grief.
The symptoms pointed to the illness, and the illness was a means

of reckoning with the black sun. In those days, I carried stigma around with me. I knew that I had been sick. I knew that I could not tell anyone, especially my new roommates, that I had spent the past years living in a mental hospital.

To Kristeva, grief wasn't something to get over. As such, it was the subject of great art and great literature. Grief is a fundamental and universal human experience. Grief is a word that does not stigmatize the one who is undone by it.

It was too expensive, this book from an academic press, still wrapped in plastic, but I paid for it with a credit card and brought it home to my apartment with the knowledge that it would explain myself to me. Unlike the identification I might feel with characters in a novel, Kristeva offered a way to know myself as a reader. She took seriously the link between reading and feeling. Identification. And not in a simple saccharine way, or a public service announcement way, where reading is unequivocally good. Rather, she acknowledged the risk and danger of it. Describing the experience of reading Marguerite Duras, she writes, *Death and pain are the spider's web of the text, and woe to the conniving readers who yield to its spell: they might remain there for good.*

The black sun becomes the guiding metaphor for Kristeva's reading of *The Lover. We now understand why Duras's books should not be put into the hands of oversensitive readers,* she goes on. Duras's books *bring us to the verge of madness,* in their representation of abject despair. Of a grief turned lethal, or at least personality defining.

When I had first read *The Lover,* four or five years earlier, I'd been untethering myself from all other connections. I'd lost interest in friendships, I found it increasingly difficult to connect with anyone, even those who loved me without judgment. In books, I found a replacement. Perhaps it would have been any book; there were other books, but I don't remember all of them. *The Lover* stayed with me, a book I've returned to over and over again.

Like Kristeva's fragile reader, I was oversensitive. I'd been told this my entire life. It was a liability, my sensitivity, but it was also a power when it came to reading, a hyperacuity. In my devouring of Duras, I'd located a self laid bare, a radical honesty, something possible only through death, through motherloss. I had devoured Duras and that was it exactly: I had no distance, no perspective. I was being formed, I was finding myself, trying on a self. Here was a self, a way to be, a place to live, in DurasSpace.

Duras wrote many of her books in the throes of her alcoholism. She would drink herself to near death, go into the hospital to be dried out, and then return to life, ever more fragile, writing her novels from the place of void, the nearness to madness, to disintegration. One writer referred to Duras's books as *death-saturated*. Her biographer Laure Adler described how Duras never really returned to health. She is "the dying-clairvoyant" kind of writer, as Clarice Lispector (another Kristevean subject) puts it. (Lispector's mother died when she was nine, just as mine did.) Kristeva describes Duras's books through this lens of a persistent death-love theme, and in this way explained for me what Duras meant at that specific point in my life. How I was hailed. Of the woman in *Hiroshima Mon Amour*, Kristeva writes,

> *To love, from her point of view, is to love a dead person. The body of her new lover merges with the corpse of her first love.*

—#—

Through Kristeva, I'd discovered a larger context for my sadness and its relationship to reading. Kristeva locates the meaninglessness of speech, the unspoken crisis that drives the form and content of her books. Kristeva reads this melancholia as a narcissistic space, a decision to identify fully with the loss of the maternal, an inconsolable loss. There is no alternative, no willingness to adapt, to adjust. Sadness had given me a sense of self, and reading Duras was one way to reify this identity. That is what made me a patient. My depression was a comfort: negative, yes, but protective, too. I stared at the black sun, the noncommunicable, and this was madness: I was too young, too inexperienced to know anything else. In DurasSpace, as Kristeva writes, there is no catharsis. I came to understand that my reading life and my actual life were not separate spheres. My reading life was not separate from my interiority, the very thing that had been so rigidly defined for me in the preceding years. The "medical model," as Erving Goffman described this imposed frame for self-knowledge.

Kristeva offered me insight—I was excited by her understanding, her linking of the meaning I'd found in literature and my own mindspace—but I didn't know what to do with it, caught as I was in my inchoate identity. I held on to it. One day it would help me—as a reader, as a teacher, as a writer—but back then it was only light, a call. Books were offering me the knowledge of another life, a larger and sustaining framework—life-affirming. I would not have put it that way back then, but I see now. These discoveries, the way I've carried that same copy of *Black Sun* with me for decades now, from city to city, from apartment to apartment, the nearly thirty times I've moved in my adult life, my life since the hospital—the book a bulwark against disintegration, against meaningless, against *noncommunicable grief.*

Grace

In this way, my reading in those days felt singular and possessive. To say, *I loved* The Lover or *Marguerite Duras is my favorite writer* or *This is my favorite book*—none of it would do. It was painful to use these sentences. When a friend or acquaintance told me that they loved the book, too—my friend Grace, for example—I chafed. I wanted Duras all to myself.

Grace was one of the only friends who ever visited me in the long-term hospital.

She came to visit those first weeks after my admission.

She brought my copy of *The Lover* with her on an early visit. I'd lent her the book years earlier, when we were in summer stock, where we met.

I loved this so much, she said.

It bothered me, I think, that someone else loved the book as I did. I felt possessive. Or my identity felt porous and fragile— I was the one who loved Duras desperately. She was *my* discovery (of course this was absurd, it was an international bestseller by the time I'd read it).

Grace and I went to see the film adaptation of *The Lover*, by Jean-Jacques Annaud—Duras worked with him on the film and then quit halfway, renouncing it, disgusted by the process. I remember the movie with moments of beauty, soft-core porn, but mostly how unlike it was to the experience of reading the book.

Grace was the only friend who tried to keep in touch with me through these years of madness. It did not occur to her to other me, to fear me. She was so full of love for me and now from this distance how I regret wasting that love. I was like Esther, unwilling to have women friends. It is silly to regret. But years later, I heard that Grace died in a car crash near Bard College, where her husband was on faculty. The last time we spoke she was dating the man who became her husband. We were both in Manhattan, she invited me to a party, she was gushing about this new love, Italian, intelligent. She was always this way, finding herself in love affairs. It bothered me, I think now, because we were alike this way. When she was hit, pulling out of a gas station onto a Hudson Valley highway, she was eight months pregnant. The doctors saved her baby, but Grace died. Thirty-eight years old.

Duras Now

The last time I taught *The Lover,* a student reacted to the situation of a fifteen-year-old girl in an affair with a twenty-seven-year-old man. In 2018 this seemed to be a very different fact of the matter than it had been when I read the book, or my experience of the book over the years. I had never read *The Lover* and thought about the so-called ethics of the situation, fictional or otherwise. This did not enter my mindspace, not once, while reading. In the same way I read *Lolita* and de Sade's *Justine* and many other books. It has always been the novelist's job to show how people experience their lives. My student wanted to be shown how people *should* experience their lives. She was losing so much, I couldn't help but think, by foregrounding her assessment of the morality of the situation.

The attention and focus on Duras has risen steadily over the years since I first read *The Lover,* increasing steeply over the past decade. There are many reasons for this, not least her profound body of work, her fascinating life, a career reflecting a monumental historical moment, the end of French rule of Indochina, the Holocaust, the atomic bomb.

But I think the attention in U.S. literary circles has something to do with the internet. The many photographs of Duras, like those of Susan Sontag, tell the story of her life. The story begins with the image that is the focus of *The Lover*, her own girlhood face—the *very-early-in-my-life-it-was-too-late* face. There are photos in between youth and old age, though these are less popular: Duras as a young woman, Duras at middle age. Duras with *the ravaged face*. Online, these photographs, captioned with social media–perfect lines from her books, promise to bring us closer to Duras. Or for many people, they are an introduction to Duras.

How different it was when I first read Duras in 1991. The only image I knew was the black-and-white cover image of a young girl's face. That image did a lot, but I don't think I had any idea what the author looked like in the moment of writing the book, at age seventy, or what she looked like at any other point in her life. The author image or images—the *paratext* that the internet provides in excess—was not part of my reading experience.

Then You Will Never Be Happy

A note in the medical charts: *Family dynamic marked by jealousy and competition.*

Dr. Triel wants to speak with me.

Get dressed, a nurse says.

I am wearing scrubs, a sweatshirt.

We don't want you stuck in these hospital clothes all day, no, that is not the way to get better.

But this is a hospital.

Even still, you need to get ready to go, to get out of here, get on with it. Not today perhaps but one day soon.

Also you're going out today on a pass, your family is here.

We go to Tavern on the Green. My father, stepmother, and three of my siblings. I order a plate of steamed vegetables. That's what a vegetarian did in the early '90s. My stepsister O is chatty, as usual, takes up all the oxygen in the room. She is in school to be a teacher. She has a new boyfriend, also a teacher. With a shrug, her own monologue continuing, she declares,

I know that I'm going to marry a teacher, I always date teachers.

Her mother can't repress her disappointment. She looks at O and scolds,

Then you will never be happy!

O's father was a high school teacher. We all knew what was happening, the way someone might reveal herself in ways she cannot understand. My stepmother was warning her daughter not to repeat her error. She read her early life as a mistake; this second marriage, this new family—it was meant to be her happily-ever-after, her do-over.

My mom had not been dead a year when we met our soon-to-be stepmom. She wore her hair in a wedge, curled under at the bottom—1980s Dorothy Hamill–style. Our dad had mentioned his new relationship a week or two earlier. We were having breakfast.

I'm going to go on a date this week, he said, awkwardly. Someone must have told him it was a good idea, to tell us.

Why? one of us asked.

Because I'm lonely, he said.

Who could argue with that? Not us.

I remember blue eye shadow, a guitar. It's a hot summer night, I am just back from the pool with my babysitter. My soon-to-be stepmom introduces herself and hugs me. Without meaning to, her hug pops a blister that's formed on my shoulder from a painful sunburn. I let her hug me and I don't flinch. This is the template for the relationship; the more alienated, the more afraid I felt of her, the further inward I turned. Like most children who are not taught, not asked, *How are you feeling?* I didn't have language to express my pain. My older brothers walk into the family room; they've been out with friends. They walk right by her. My dad says something, tries to make introductions; they refuse.

What did my dad think or do about this? We were kids. His sons rejected her before they knew her. It was never easy, in fact, it was full of conflict from the start. It was about them, not us. How did they think it would work, or did they just forge ahead, knowing it was impossible but also knowing it would be impossible for either of them to be alone, there was no going on otherwise, this is what you did as a Catholic, you got married, you moved on. You made a family out of what you had. The whole meant more than the parts. So: Instead of considering what is best for an individual child, the focus is on the larger nuclear family, which is what any child is supposed to need—to lack that would be the worst fate. We had lost that. Now we could have it again.

That must have been the idea.

Children who have a parent die before they are sixteen are at a much higher risk for adult depression and suicide. This is even higher in a mother-daughter relationship. In everything I read, the research around it, the key determinant of success or hope for the child is how the death is handled. What happens in the months and years after the death of the parent. I imagine it could have gone another way—there may have been the attention I needed, the support, a person who I trusted might have led me through it—but that's not what happened. I was on my own with my broken self. My grief, my terror, my terror that my life was broken with my mom gone, that no one would ever truly see me or know me again. There were too many of us kids, and so all the effort went into this new family configuration, the exhausting performance of that do-over.

Now this is our family therapy, for the family that didn't quite work. So Dr. Triel is trying to understand the family vacation we took a decade earlier, a year or two after this new family formation. Triel had asked my father when else I'd been hospitalized. I was born breech, feetfirst, it was traumatic—so that was the first time. Yes, my father tells them, an early hospitalization, just after she was born. A traumatic birth and then weeks in a hospital without us. Oh, does it mean something? The doctors imply it might mean something. But who can say? Everything might mean something. My father, a doctor, agrees that it could mean something.

(My dad told me that when he was in medical school, they—his friends, classmates—looked down on the doctors going into psychiatry. It was not a real field, the way that ophthalmology or hematology or cardiology were. It was *soft*, he said. Yet here, in the hospital, he respected what the doctors told him, he respected the course of treatment. He listened to what they said—he did not tell them they were wrong or this had become absurd or that there were other ways of helping me. Maybe he didn't know what those ways were. Or maybe when it came down to it, he did trust a medical establishment that had been the frame for his life's work.)

So then my father adds,

Oh, there was another time. A ski trip.

Before he can tell the story, the mere mention of it makes my stepmom angry. She nearly spits it out, this resentment she's nursed for a decade,

He left me on the mountain!

So here is what happened, as far as I can tell, after years of putting the pieces of this story together. It was the first day of our family ski trip. We were just over two years from our mother's death. In that brief time, my dad got remarried to my stepmom, who had two kids from her first marriage. Her daughters were the same age as my sister and I, nine and six. They married the year after my mom died. The next year, they had another baby. I was still in shock from my mom's death, a destabilizing grief, and now I had a new family, a compulsory arrangement, and a new house. Family photos pretending that we were like the blended families on *The Brady Bunch* or *Eight Is Enough*.

That first day, my father had taken my stepmom to a ski lesson. The baby was with a babysitter. Us six kids, all under fourteen, were somewhere else on the mountain. My stepmom had never skied before. So he took her to ski, just the two of them. And just as they began the lesson, the ski patrol came and found him— there had been an accident, his daughter was in the hospital. My dad left, went off with the ski patrol, and found his way to the hospital, to me.

What I remember: My sister and I flying down the mountain, laughing, racing and somehow I flipped, it was too fast, that second between thrill and losing control. Then a sharp pain, blinding, my sister confused, scared, and soon help comes and I'm in a hospital. When I wake up, my dad is there near the foot of the bed, telling me it'll be okay.

What I didn't understand for many years was my stepmom's anger. For her, the story was about how she'd been abandoned by her husband.

HE LEFT ME ON THE MOUNTAIN! she repeats to Dr. Triel, waiting for sympathy.

It occurred to me then why she is here for family therapy. This is about her. She wants to be the patient. She is *jealous* that I am the patient.

The doctor is confused.

My dad is frustrated, he rarely gets angry, he will not challenge her.

Suzy was in the hospital, he says.

The doctors want clarity. Dr. Triel goes over the story again,

Suzy broke her leg. She was eleven years old. She was skiing alone with her seven-year-old sister, fell, blacked out. They took her to the emergency room. She was put into a full leg cast.

And that made you angry? Dr. Triel asks my stepmom.

Well. He left me there.

To go to the hospital to see his daughter?

I try to imagine now what it must have been like for her, to marry a man with four unhappy children, their acute chronic grief a fact of the marriage from the start. Just as this one was meant to be on her own—off to college, first Los Angeles and now New York—she's sick. Now she's in a hospital, and her dad is going back and forth.

She wants to be a part of it. She comes along for family therapy. She tries to explain it to the doctors.

In her mind, I think, this was just another way of getting attention, being sick. She saw what was happening. The daughter was so good at suffering, and that's how it's always been. Moving on with life or trying to and there they were, all the kids screaming out in the middle of the night about this or that. But he had a new life. What about her? What about their daughter? She resented his attention to his past life.

This is family therapy.

Triel asks me, Did you feel you were neglected within the new family configuration?

I say nothing, so my stepmom tells the doctor,
She thinks I am the Wicked Witch of the West!

The three of us sit there, the doctor looking to each of us. *You know*, she adds, *he may be married to me, but she has his heart!*

I don't know this witch, or this fairy tale, I don't know which story *she* is stuck in, but I feel it deeply and there is not language for how these words move me, how I want more than anything to exit this room, to transport myself into a fairy-tale kingdom far, far away.

When they were first dating, not long after my mother died right there in her bed, my stepmom taught my father a game. Sometimes we were allowed to join in. I call it a game but it was more of an activity she directed while we were out to dinner. It involved selecting a person in the restaurant—any random diner or couple or group would do—and making up a story about the couple. It was often unkind, the story she'd project: "Oh, it's a first date! She's looking for a sugar daddy! Look how she's done up!" My father loved this game. Loved how she could tell a story or find a story where none existed. He was so impressed by my stepmom's imagination, her confidently judgmental worldview. I guess that for someone so confounded by his own interiority, her assurance was comforting. *It's nice to be with someone who knows everything,* a friend said not long ago, about a woman we both know. Even if that person is entirely misguided? I wondered. My stepmom's judgments masked a deep unhappiness. Her playfulness charmed me, too—in those first months. By the time they married and we lived together and their new baby was born—nine of us under one roof—the cutting nature of her judgments came to unnerve me, as they were juxtaposed with darkness and despair, as well as the moments when life seemed withdrawn from her; the buoyant air of personality released like helium. In those regular but unpredictable moments, no one could do a thing to engage her. It was here that she became terrifying to me, a girl looking for a model of who I might become.

I will tell the doctors: No more family therapy. And they will agree, though it isn't until the very end of my stay in the ward that a doctor will tell me something that is meant to help me move on: Ignore her. She doesn't want the best for you. She is jealous of you. It is called scapegoating. Designating a patient. Triangulation. Splitting. Language and language to describe dysfunctional families.

It may have been briefly satisfying, validating—but at the same time, I was the one in the hospital, I was unable to move on. There is a very large gap between understanding and change. Between analysis and creation. It would be nice to say that this awareness or insight helped me get better, but it was not so. If anything, it fed my resentment, my rage, my sense that the world had mistreated me. There was nowhere to go from *that* story.

I'd forgotten the ski story until a few years ago, when my son was about to go skiing. We were out to dinner, my son, my parents, his grandparents. My son was excited. My dad brings up our disastrous ski trip. I could see in his face, three decades later, that the memory pains him.

And somehow, as if on cue, my stepmother takes up her refrain.

He left me on the mountain, she sneers.

I'd forgotten.

Suzy was in the hospital, my dad says.

But now we are quiet. Things are different now, so many years later.

Roxane is sitting next to Bridget and Marion, having a cigarette. In between her exhales, she laughs, one or the other says something. Bridget and Marion were always laughing, there was no reason ever to take life so seriously. Roxane has softened now, when she sees me she seems less offended or put out. She is less skeptical. I may even be able to talk to her. I don't know what shifted—it was time, I think—I'd become part of the place now, she'd come to like me, especially in contrast to the new patients arriving, one more difficult than the last. Was that it? Or was it that she'd hazed me, that I'd passed some test.

Do you have time to talk? I ask her.

Bridget is still laughing, smiles at me.

Sure, Roxane says, after I give out the meds. I'll find you.

I watch her walk away and melt back into the comfort of Marion and Bridget's laughter. Now Bridget is teasing Marion for being a Jehovah's Witness, and Marion is talking about her father. Do you know what a sharecropper is? Tell me, I say. So he lived on someone else's land, though it was his land. He worked on the land his whole life. But it wasn't his. He gave those crops over, as rent. He paid rent on his own land. She laughed when she told me this story, always laughing.

I'd grown up in white-flight Chicago—my parents had left the city for the suburbs when many white people did—and so I grew up in that segregated world presented to me as neutral. What did I know then of the history that led me to that place of whiteness. Whatever we learned of racism, slavery, the Jim Crow South—it was all abstract, meaningless. Something that happened somewhere to someone else and most of all—or so this was the narrative of the 1980s—it was over. The past.

The majority of patients in the hospital were white, like me. That there were more white women in the hospital was a function of white supremacy, an implicit message that white women's suffering was more important than other suffering. This in contrast to the staff members, mostly Black, the low-paid staff, whose suffering wasn't recognized. Later, Hank and I went to see Anna Deavere Smith's play *Twilight: Los Angeles*, about the 1992 Los Angeles Uprising. Smith built her play from extensive interviews—with Rodney King himself, with a white police officer, with a Korean shop owner. She quotes Cornell West, who notes that white people have never felt the sadness of Black people, and that if they had to feel it, it would be too large, overwhelming, too much to bear.

In *Depression: A Public Feeling*, Ann Cvetkovich writes about racism and depression. Like the work of Lauren Berlant and other scholars of affect theory, Cvetkovich's book places depression in the context of the political. It is of course political that the most circulated literary narratives of depression, of madness, are those of white women. Affect theory was a revelation—the critical theory I read when I was in college in the 1990s didn't account for the role of emotion or feelings at all. So when I discovered affect theory years later, I couldn't help but wonder how shaped we might be, what parts of ourselves we consider possible, in response to the available discourses. Liberation from mental illness, or from the stigma around mental illness, requires a change in consciousness. The same is true, of course, with whiteness.

The narratives of Black madness, not only the novels of Toni Morrison, or Ntozake Shange's *for colored girls who have considered suicide / when the rainbow is enuf,* but also Gayl Jones, and Gloria Naylor's *Linden Hills*—it would be years before I discovered these stories, alternate narratives of what gets called mental illness—are linked to a culture of oppression, of disenfranchisement, of loss.

A few years after leaving the hospital for good, I read *Nervous Conditions*, a 1988 novel by Zimbabwean author Tsitsi Dangarembga. *Nervous conditions*—the same imprecise and evocative term used by Charlotte Perkins Gilman a century earlier. The novel follows the story of Tambu, growing up in Zimbabwe. It is a coming-of-age story, set against the backdrop of the postcolonial period of the 1960s and '70s. The narrative moves along a familiar female bildungsroman. Like *The Bell Jar*, it is a novel of a young woman's education, both formal and informal, an education full of tragic limitations. We first meet the protagonist through a stunner of an opening line: "I was not sad when my brother died." The voice of Tambu is vivid and compelling; we are eager to follow her journey.

As a woman in a poor family, Tambu must fight to receive the education her brother takes for granted. When he dies, Tambu has the opportunity to move in with her uncle, to attend his missionary school. There she grows close to her cousin Nyasha, who has received a British education. Nyasha fights for another sort of liberation, one Tambu hasn't yet considered. She is fighting to break free from her father's rule, and all the social limitations that come with his patriarchy—including a policing of female sexuality. Nyasha has no patience for her father's rules, nor the institutions of Christianity undergirding his power. After a series of violent fights with her father, Nyasha stops eating, a literal and figurative rejection of patriarchy. The book locates madness not in the women, but in the extremes of a patriarchal culture, the weight on the women who come of age within that female schizophrenia.

It took me years, decades, to realize how depoliticized our treatment on that ward had been. We had eating disorders, and yet this was never linked or discussed in terms of our culture of unforgiving beauty standards. We felt helpless, and yet this wasn't linked to the growing inequality and social isolation of the 1980s postwelfare state. The aggressive backlash against the gains of feminism and the civil rights movements of the sixties. We needed help and felt shame for asking. We had failed in some sense of an American individualist imperative. We had an obligation to recover. The narrative of progression. This was not only for the medical-pharmaceutical establishment which required our before and after stories, but also for a culture that locates mental illness in the self and not the society. If it doesn't quite work this way, there was no acknowledgment of that. There weren't stories of the ones who don't recover, or get better and worse over and over again.

Off the Couch

Dr. Tomlinson: Being sick is a cure for how bad you feel.

It's there on a page in my notebook, three years into my hospitalization. No context, one sentence between trivial concerns. Within an insignificant paragraph. It'd be easy to miss. The notebooks are often painful to read—the trivial, the insipid—and so this line stands out for being profound. Or at least interesting.

So much of what I wrote is uninteresting—who said what and how I felt about it, what this one did or didn't do, this feeling or that—I want to shake the girl, to say, Look outside of yourself—look up! What do you see? What is going on? *Self-involved,* if I were unkind I would describe her as self-involved. The girl writing in that notebook. That's her problem.

(That I could not look outside of myself is one way I know that I was ill. The narcissism of suffering.)

But who is Dr. Tomlinson? I remember the name but I can't picture a face. It is a not uncommon name. This is not the name of someone with whom I spent days or weeks in therapy.

He must have been a visitor.

———

The line is the most accurate and incisive I've found from those years. I wrote it down, I recognized the truth in it. What I could do with that truth, I don't know. Nothing, probably.

I was performing. Dr. Tomlinson was right. That was why I wrote the line there—because this doctor saw through the performance. Psychoanalyst D. W. Winnicott wrote about the desire to hide. Winnicott identifies the child developing a private self—one he can't communicate, and yet his hope to be magically understood. Adam Phillips calls this *a sophisticated game of hide-and-seek in which it is a joy to be hidden but disaster not to be found.*

On Google I find the name of a Dr. W. C. Tomlinson, associated with Columbia University medical school. The dates fit, so I do a Google image search and find a photo of a psychiatrist named Craig Tomlinson. I recognize him. He was there. He was visiting. He was not my doctor. He was a psychoanalyst. A consultation.

Perhaps that was why he could speak so bluntly—he was not my doctor, we were not involved in a power struggle. He did not work on that ward, was not one of the power brokers there to allow us to come and go, he was not anything to us.

He was not someone who would prescribe medication to me. That dynamic—asking for help for amorphous and complicated suffering and then receiving help in the form of a pill—determined the shape of the doctor-patient relationships on the ward.

Dr. Tomlinson's perspective as a psychoanalyst meant that he was not looking first for which medication would cure my symptoms, my illness.

Instead, he could point out that I'd found my own cure. And the cure was ruining my life.

So much of my treatment had become about transference, and the conversation between me and the doctors—was I sick or not?

How sick? Would I be allowed to stay? The hospitalization, as Erving Goffman pointed out, took over.

Cruel optimism—Lauren Berlant's perfect term to describe what it is to be alive today, where: *What you desire is actually an obstacle to your flourishing.*

This is how I see it now: that hospital as an exercise in cruel optimism.

The cruel optimism of my faith in that system.

I wonder at the initials, W. C.—odd, formal, alluding to the comedian—and then I make a discovery that might explain why Dr. Tomlinson is now known officially by his initials. The long life of Google. Not very far down in my search results I find a *New York Times* article, dated December 6, 1992, the same year I was admitted to the NYSPI. The long-form article seems to have been published in the Sunday magazine, with the title: "Off the Couch." Under this, a synopsis reads:

> On the front line of the psych wards, Freud is under siege and prescription drugs are gaining the upper hand.

The article documents the competing philosophies at stake on the ward, and at stake for the future of psychiatry as a profession. The biomedical and the psychoanalytic. The accompanying photo features two women, Dr. Alison Phillips and Dr. Susan C. Vaughan.

The writer is inside the NYSPI in 1992, the year I was admitted. But of course she is *not* inside—she is neither a patient nor a staff member—and if she were, this wouldn't be published. She is an outsider, a journalist who has been offered the rare insider view; as such, she offers a clarifying view of the historical moment within which I was caught.

The journalist does not chronicle the day and life of a mental patient—as, say, *Sybil* or Susanna Kaysen or many other now familiar narratives of madness. Instead, she follows the work of Vaughan and Phillips, among other residents, each entering their careers poised at the moment psychopharmacology has profoundly changed psychiatry. Just like the digital revolution to come, the pharmaceutical revolution dramatically shifted the field of psychiatry.

The accompanying photo features the two women in what looks like the dark narrow stairwell of the institute, one heading downward and one up, the grated tile of the stairwell between them. The caption reads: *Dr. Alison Phillips, left, and Dr. Susan Vaughan at the New York State Psychiatric Institute in Washington Heights.* The lattice-shaped metal in between the stairwells, another detail of asylum architecture. I recognize it from the times I was allowed to walk to the ninth floor, to visit the psychiatric library.

Dr. Vaughan is the main character in this *New York Times* article, and she is featured prominently in the photograph, in light. Dr. Phillips's face is obscured by shadow. Neither woman smiles; each looks soberly to the camera. Dr. Phillips looks especially unhappy, exhausted, or both.

If it were a photo of two men sitting in that dark stairway, would it have been remarkable? Would I see them as angry? Or merely appropriate. Could Freud's serious look be read as angry, or authoritative? No, no one would see Freud as angry. It was new back then, that women doctors would make up a large part of medical students. That there would be more women in medical school than men.

The article opens on the scene of a young man in the emergency room. The psychiatrists are considering how best to treat him; the question of whether the patient's problems are biological or psychological.

Another featured pull quote:

But new psychiatric drugs and new uses of existing drugs are changing how American psychiatry thinks about the causes of and cures for mental illness. . . . Freudian psychiatry—with its belief that mental illness starts in the mind and is curable by talk—is under serious siege.

The journalist has an angle—and it has as much to do with the ascendancy of pharmaceutical drugs in psychiatry as it does with the charisma of Susan Vaughan, a young doctor and third-year resident, who is learning to navigate a state psychiatric institute. She is the star of the article, working in high-stakes emergency situations. Dr. Tomlinson is the voice of skepticism.

The journalist is present for a luncheon sponsored by the pharmaceutical company Upjohn. The faculty and medical doctors in the ward are split, some favoring Freudian talk therapy, while others were excited by the new pharmaceutical options. The hospital was mired in this split, these opposing factions.

Reading this article so many years later validates my confusion over the nature of treatment all those years.

Dr. Tomlinson is not pictured in the accompanying photos yet his story features prominently. In the story, he is new on the scene. The two women doctors are a few years ahead of him. He is a first-year resident. He is trained in psychoanalysis, and yet he must learn to use medications. The doctor describes a lunch sponsored by Upjohn. The company is there to convince the psychiatrists that the "controversial sleeping pill" Halcion is safe, and to promote their popular drug Xanax.

Tomlinson is quoted saying that he wished the drug company wasn't there.

He becomes the voice of reason—the resistance to market forces.

How could I know the doctors who treated us were having lunch, just a few floors down, with representatives from pharmaceutical companies?

The article suggests that Tomlinson and the other residents are eventually swayed by pharmaceutical companies when it comes to treating patients.

I should not be reading this. There is an intended audience, but I am not part of it. It is the audience of *The New York Times*, and apparently they are not mental patients.

Not long after this revolution, mental patients became consumers. That neoliberal move—you, too, can buy your mental health care. And that means buying drugs exactly like the ones shilled here. Not long after, the marketing moved directly to the patients, through ubiquitous magazine and television advertising; patients began, as they still do, to ask doctors for medications by name.

The details in the article were not meant for me. The journalist describes the cartoons on the wall of the office. One cartoon makes a joke of sedating patients. Another jokes about suicide. Gallows humor—and yet, who is in the gallows? Surely not the doctors.

The journalist doesn't speak to a single patient.

I remember Dr. Triel racing about, commenting on his work of saving lives—often adding: No good deed goes unpunished. He is saving lives and unappreciated for his trouble. For his good work. He didn't save my life, that was clear early on, but in those years I observed him from a distance, and I learned something from him, a stable presence in a shifting place. His dedication. His complete immersion and belief in a system of knowledge. His kindness. I also learned something about myself, my need for a hero, a leader, a guru. *It's nice to think someone is in charge.*

Part Three

MIRROR CITY

It was September 1996 when I decided that I was not going to kill myself. I remember it as a deliberate choice, like quitting drugs or alcohol. I'd become addicted to the idea that I could get out of this.

It was the end of a Belief System that had been guiding my life, allowing me to believe both in Suicide (death/despair) and Psychiatry (life/hope).

I woke up one day and realized that all the drugs I'd been taking, the long and expensive and unresolved conversations I'd been having with doctors—was a waste of time. I no longer believed in it.

I could identify this moment years later, that I made this choice to live. It was one of those decisions you make only to yourself, quietly, the kind of New Year's resolution you aren't sure you'll keep. I could only claim it as a choice years later, after it became part of me. It wasn't triumphant or bold; I was fragile and terrified. But I saw my life as the dead end it was. I had wasted too many years. Living the rest of my life as a career patient scared me, but so did the fate of the women in my college, reading *The Wall Street Journal*, getting internships or going to graduate school.

It felt like a betrayal. I mourned my illness, the hospital. I grieved the years I spent in that system. It was something like being in a relationship—and then realizing that it was false or full of holes. There was nothing more to do. Once you saw through it, you had to leave. Either that, or accept the lack.

Which is not to say I had another life to believe in. I did not. I wanted to write, but I was a lousy writer. I wanted to act, and I could get a part in an Off-Off Broadway play here or there. This did nothing to help my emotional stability; I'd fall into a deep depression after closing night. I wanted equanimity, but did not know how to achieve it. I wanted a Belief System that might sustain me; one that would take into account—or hold space for—my extremes of feeling.

My overwhelming sense of an unstable self. This had to do with my mother's death and how I was raised, but also with my sense that a stable self did not exist. This was one problem with psychiatry, I began to see, the belief in a fixed self. We are always changing, that no identity is stable, and especially not through adolescence and early adulthood. If we have a fantasy of the individual self in American culture, we are relational, we define ourselves through another. My mother's death meant the loss of the self I was in her eyes, an untethering, a loss of the person I knew through her knowing of me.

Toward a Theory of My Illness (II)

1. One friend clarifies it this way—the depression of his mother, regularly declaring she was DEE-pressed, which meant her life was generally disappointing, or she was bored. The Emma Bovary depression.

2. Another friend distinguishes lowercase-d depression from uppercase-D Depression.

3. The word is used so broadly it begins to mean nothing at all. In the past week, I have heard about many crazy people. A friend described her sister-in-law as crazy. Someone else I know referred to two family members as crazy. Over breakfast, a writer referred to three other writers as crazy. In each case, the meaning was clear and contextually indisputable.

4. My uppercase Illness: I wanted to die but not enough to actually kill myself but enough to sign myself into a hospital where I'd remain for years. Sick enough to believe that this place, these doctors, the institution itself, could help me. Give me instructions. Sick enough to stay so long without objection so that I couldn't imagine leaving so that I'd never really become a normal person again. Never really get that feeling of *illness* out of my system.

5.   After all, it's not about getting it out; it's about living with it. One nurse, early on, casually let it slip, *There's no cure for what you have.*

6.   *How does that make you feel?* A psychiatrist asked me, upon hearing of this accidental disclosure. I wasn't sure. It is strange now to say that I never thought of myself as disabled—given that I spent years in a psychiatric institution and have been on psychiatric medications most of my life—but it's true. I was trying it out, testing the limits of it. That's what I told myself. That I was in control.

7.   I came to believe that *something* was in my system. Maybe it ran in my family. There were no diagnoses or psych meds when my grandparents and great-grandparents were growing up in Ireland. It would be nearly impossible to know if any of them suffered as I did, if it was in their systems. My guess is they did, and it was.

8.   Not long ago, in *The Irish Times*, there was a report that Ireland has one of the highest rates of mental illness in Europe, ranking number three out of thirty-six countries; 18.5 percent of the population.

9.   The fraught term *chemical imbalance*. Which chemicals? There are genetic markers for schizophrenia, but none for other mental illnesses. Scientists study predisposition for suicide, which clearly runs in families, but again, it's not known what exactly is biological. For decades, people have repeated the idea that depression is caused by a "chemical imbalance" and that SSRIs fix the imbalance. SSRIs help a lot of people—by increasing levels of serotonin, a feel-good chemical—but that doesn't mean they are correcting a chemical imbalance. Low serotonin does not cause depression. The theory of chemical imbalance has been debunked over and over again, most recently

in a British study that concluded: *There is no support for the hypothesis that depression is caused by lowered serotonin activity or concentrations.*

10.   So the drugs can lift your mood, but that doesn't mean an imbalance caused your depression. This does not mean that the drugs are not helpful; it does mean that the narrative (likely pushed by pharmaceutical companies, and especially so when I was in the hospital) is reductive.

The Notebooks

I have a stack of notebooks. Each a different color, each dated. They go back as early as 1990, just before I lost my mind, and continue on to the present day. At some point in the late '90s or early 2000s I shifted these notebooks to the computer; I still wrote in paper notebooks, but they became slimmer. Around the same time—and certainly after my son was born—I no longer felt the need to write so insistently about my daily concerns. I began to focus on fiction and essay and critical writing.

So this stack symbolizes not only a record of these years, my mental patient career, but also a material object, marking time—the before of the analog, just before the culture turned toward the digital. I was thirty-two when I first had a cellphone. My generation will be the last generation to know fully two ways of being—living within the predigital revolution and the post-.

As I began to write this book, I sorted my notebooks first into years and then by color. I had a vague sense of this book as a sort of *The Golden Notebook,* I would use Doris Lessing's organization as a guide. I'd read Lessing's novel while in the hospital, and it taught me something about how women's experiences—intimate, ugly, shameful, complicated—could find form in a book. The mess of it. That a notebook was a book.

But when I returned to my notebooks in my forties, I could hardly get through them. There was no way to use that writing in a book like this. To read was to meet the delusion and myopia of my younger self, page after page. At times, I wanted to help her; how I wished to be her mother; other times, I thought she was crazy, insufferable, impossible.

And yet, every once in a while, I came across a note or a sentence or a passage that offered something larger: the return of memory. Validation, surprise. A clue.

For example, on one page, I write about a man who regularly visited the ward one summer. I remember it as a summer that seemed endless (what that says about age! How brief summers seem to me now), a time when doctors were out of town, when residents had to fill in, when the mood was very much one of just, Hold on, we'll get back to you. Of being put on hold. And so we lingered on that ward that summer, each summer, with staff and nurses who wanted to be at the beach. We waited. Nothing happened. No one gets better in the summer.

On one of those long summer days I wrote about the man, the visitor:

[from The Purple Notebook]

The man comes to visit his wife at the mental hospital where she is undergoing electro-shock treatments for what the doctors call a "severe depression." Her name is Diane. She is frail. She stopped talking. She began staring at walls. She began staring out windows. Not seeing anything. He comes to see her every day. He tells us, the other patients here, that his wife, Diane, used to make a delicious spice cake. He says something about how pretty the young depressed patients are. He tells us about his wife. How she used to love to cook and clean all day long.

He speaks of her in the third person though she is there, right there at the table. He weighs himself on the hospital scale. It is dull to be a patient but it is not especially fun to be a visitor, either. Today he comes from the beach, a George Hamilton tan. An expensive silk shirt. Today he can't stop talking. He loves his wife. I hear him speaking to a social worker, there is little privacy here. You might be surprised. Somehow we know so much of each other's fate. He tells the social worker that he is afraid to be here, to visit every day. He tells her that he is starting to feel like a patient, too. He laughs, as if he is not serious, but he is serious. It is a serious laugh. He tells her that after he leaves he has to go out with friends. He has to have a good time, to assure himself that he is not going mad, too.

The next day he is calm. He had a good night. He knows that he is not a mental patient after all. His wife is a mental patient. He comes to visit, and again, because his wife won't speak, he talks to us, the other patients. On and on he talks. His tan. His fun. It is a holiday weekend, after all, you don't know that in here, do you? It's a shame. A real shame.

July 3rd, 1994 1:20 p.m., NYSPI

Last Days of the Long-Term Ward

Roxane has been so busy: something had changed. More patients were admitted. Many for short-term treatments: rounds of ECT. Adolescents, too: part of a new study of antidepressants on children. Fewer patients like me, or Hank, or Elena, or Molly—no one was admitted for long-term care anymore. Roxane told me the ideas around this whole thing had changed. You shouldn't be in here so long, you have to find a way out. It's not good for you, and anyway, she said, the state was no longer going to pay for it. The long-term ward was being defunded, she said.

Or she didn't say this all at once, but here and there. We saw what was happening: Tilda was the first to go; to get her out was complicated. We all knew she would never live a normal life; no one could imagine her living on her own. It had been seven years.

By the midnineties, the long-term ward closed for good.

Tell me about your family therapy session, Roxane asked. How was it?

Awful.

I mean, it's never fun.

We both laughed at the truth of this. Something had shifted between us. Her blue eyes brighten as she considers something, and takes her time figuring it out. What I've said, and, too, what she'd read in my chart. The notes. She wasn't a doctor, so there wasn't the same sense of distance. It was a relief now.

You have to make therapy work for you, you know?

I guess so.

No, really, she said, 80 percent of therapy—if not more—is you. The patient. Stop focusing on these doctors so much. They don't have anything to give you. You don't need a perfect doctor. They're human, flawed like the rest of us. You have to figure it out for yourself.

I nodded, surprised by her candor.

You have to tell your own story, and if you don't, they will tell it for you. Not just the doctors but your family, too.

She crossed her legs, her left hand leaning on the sofa, moving into me. She was taking her time. We didn't have much left. If it all seemed simple, her advice, it didn't matter. I never forgot it.

Now I was getting ready to go, the idea was in the air, I knew it had to happen and so I fell apart, over and over again. I didn't know what would happen to me now, if there would ever be a place for me in this world.

But I had to leave, that was clear. So many new patients coming and going. Get over it, I wanted to say to them; now that I *had* to get over it, I didn't want to witness this bathos.

A year before this, I was required to meet with a psychiatrist provided by my college. It was an assessment. I didn't quite understand that. I assumed it was a formality. All I wanted was to take one class again, I would stay in the hospital, go back and forth to campus, one day a week.

The doctor reported to the administration, and then to my doctors. I was not ready, they said, I had decompensated severely since my original admission, and they did not trust that I was well enough to return to campus.

And so, six months later, when I had to meet with another doctor provided by the college, about provisional readmission, I was prepared. I had *healed*, I said, the years of therapy, both analysis and drug therapy, had been *healing*, and here I was now, my studies would mean more to me than they ever had, given my experience. I looked forward to returning to college.

This time, I spoke clearly, I didn't mumble, I made eye contact. I wore a feminine blouse and painted my nails for the occasion. I would pass, I knew how to do it now.

The doctor was impressed. I was allowed to return to campus that fall, the first time since that dark winter of my arrival. I would report to Dean Silverman about my progress, in weekly meetings, and she would continue to assess my fitness for enrollment. It was provisional, they reminded me. I could take one class. I would stay away from Amsterdam Avenue, where I'd lived back then, preferring the brightness and business of the Broadway campus, the newly constructed dormitories with views of the Twin Towers.

Hank told me the news. It was around the time of the shift change. Elsie's gone, he said. I was just back from campus. What did *gone* mean? I don't know, he said, but apparently she doesn't work here anymore. She quit? Maybe quit, maybe fired. I noticed Roxane in the nurses' station with a nurse I'd never seen before.

A few weeks later, Roxane, too, was gone, only she still worked in the New York State Psychiatric Institute, they'd just moved her to the fourth floor. Schizophrenics.

Neither Triel nor Prince nor anyone else explained these sudden changes. In the early days of the ward, this would have been cause for great complication, conversation, community meetings and individual therapy sessions would center around the loss. But not anymore. Tilda and Elena later told me that they'd been reported, Elsie and Roxane. That an angry parent of a patient noticed the intensity of Elsie's relationship with Molly, as well as Roxane's with a newer patient named Claudia. There was a review and both nurses were let go. Later I heard that Elsie and Molly moved in together, to an apartment in Inwood, not so far from the hospital.

Sometimes I would see Roxane, coming or going, though she never showed me warmth again. The kind of intimacy we shared, years of my life there, the four or five days each week with her, and now it was over. Her nod or brief hello reified the hierarchy of the institution—something I thought we'd dismantled. I never knew the whole story, and eventually I stopped coming and going. That was it.

Not so many years ago, I was in the lobby of the Minetta Lane Theater, about to see a Caryl Churchill play (*Love and Information*), when I saw Dr. Prince, standing near me with a woman I took to be his wife. We exchanged glances, he surely recognized me, or at least knew me as a once-patient. That was all, of course, we didn't speak or make some feigned connection. How silly small talk would be in this context. And yet how uncanny in the middle of this life, to encounter that one.

I often find myself walking around New York, looking for Roxane. In a museum, at a crosswalk, in a crowd. There is no one else I'd like to see, no one else to whom I can imagine saying, Hello, let's get a drink, can we talk?

All of Us Vanishing

Forever Overhead

Today, like every day in this place, I walk by Freud. It loomed there, the nine-by-fourteen image of Sigmund Freud as we walked by, back and forth over and over again. You had to walk by Freud to get to the women's dorm, and you had to walk by again to get to the dining room, the kitchen. You saw him again while lined up for medications three times a day. Nurses and doctors chatting, laughing. Freud overhead. Nurses not bothering to notice us until they must, time for meds, time to open the top door to the right. Freud with one hand on his hip, opening his jacket, his three-piece suit, the vest, the watch chain. Line up now, the nurses say. In his other hand, a rolled cigar. He looks to the camera, his right eye squinting, his left eye open, he is balding, he has a beard. A photographic portrait, 1932. Was it a gift? A reminder? We never knew. We line up. This is our job. We will do our job. One at a time. Here is your cup full of pills, cup of water, I will cross it out now. Let me see that cup, let me see your tongue, open wide now. Did you swallow or what nonsense?

There was always someone tonguing—I learned the term a day or two in, learned it from a fellow patient—this is how you do it. You save the pills under your tongue. Save for when you need them. Or you flush them down the toilet because you don't need them. They are poisonous. It is an early pattern, a strategy within *the system of betrayal*—Goffman's term for the antagonistic relationship between patient and staff. We rarely left the fifth floor. We became overweight from drugs, from lack of exercise. These were very specific ways to begin looking like a mental patient. Another was to turn inward, to stop acting normal, to indulge all of what you've been told is wrong with you.

Airless Spaces

In her 1997 book *Airless Spaces*, the once-radical feminist Shulamith Firestone describes various women in a New York City psychiatric hospital: *From this time on Corinne began to look like a mental patient, not an attractive woman who just happened to be thrown into a mental hospital. Airless Spaces* tells the stories of women's lives in and out of psychiatric hospitals, and was part of Semiotext(e)'s Native Agents series, which featured stories of underrepresented female subjectivity. (Semiotext(e) was founded by Chris Kraus, author of *I Love Dick*, the iconic novel exploring the debasement and abjection of women.)

Goffman's analysis of the generic "mental patient" is purely descriptive, nothing personal. Which is why it felt so personal when I first encountered it. Goffman has no stake in his relation to the patient—or at least he doesn't mention it, which is a relief.

He is not here to evaluate or offer a moral judgment: *The category "mental patient" itself will be underscored in one strictly sociological sense. In this perspective the psychiatric view of a person becomes significant only insofar as this view itself alters his social fate—an alteration which seems to become fundamental in our society when, and only when, the person is put through the process of hospitalization.*

The women of *Airless Spaces* can be understood through Goffman's lens: the category of "mental patient" has altered their *social fate*. It is the process of hospitalization (in the late-twentieth-century era of defunding mental health services) that secures the alteration. As critic Sianne Ngai put it, the book demonstrates the *somewhat oppressive, institutionalized services for the mentally ill and poor which since the late 1970s have . . . been cut, in decades of escalating attacks on the welfare state.*

Airless Spaces traces the trajectory of Firestone's stage two, the inpatient stage. Goffman does not spend much time on the ex-patient phase; what is more important to him is the way the inpatient phase can create a self. And how many get stuck in that moment of definition. So that Allen Ginsberg's very real experience of the mental hospital—that you bring that view of yourself back out into the world with you, that he walked the streets of New York wondering, Am I crazy? Or were the doctors wrong?—is a key to an ex-patient life trajectory. Often, the patient believes the doctors and never moves beyond the inpatient stage. Firestone's pre-patient stage is alluded to on the back jacket copy: *Refusing the career as a professional feminist, Shulamith Firestone found herself in an "airless space"—approximately since the publication of her first book* The Dialectic of Sex.

The Dialectic

Shulamith Firestone moved to New York City in 1967 from Chicago, where she'd been a student at the School of the Art Institute. In 1966, she and Jo Freeman had organized the first women's liberation group, Westside. That next year, her first in New York, she co-founded the New York Radical Women, the first women's liberation group in New York.

Firestone's arrival in New York took place within a specific moment, during the rise of what I would study in my women's studies courses: the second wave. Consciousness-raising groups. By the time I was in college, her work was considered too radical to be assimilable. (In one of my women's studies classes, we read Susan Faludi's *Backlash*, a book tracing the cultural rejection and diminishment of feminism's gains.) Firestone had argued for the elimination of childbirth and the abolition of sex roles tied to pregnancy and biology. It was quickly dismissed, absorbed into a larger culture. Feminism, by the late eighties, or so the very effective backlash had taught me, was the cause of ugly, man-hating lesbians. This was how I grew up—we made fun of "lesbos" and "dykes." When I announced that I was moving out east to attend a woman's college, a family friend warned me: *Watch out for the lesbians.*

(Of course I did watch out for the lesbians, if not in the way she implied.)

I had not read Shulamith Firestone before entering the hospital, though I'd heard about her 1970 manifesto for feminist revolution, *The Dialectic of Sex*. In this book she challenges the pervasive influence of Freud, writing: *Freudianism has become, with its confessionals and penance, its proselytes and converts, with the millions spent on its upkeep, our modern Church. We attack* it only uneasily, for you never know, on the day of final judgment, whether they might be right. Who can be sure that he is as healthy as he can get? Who is functioning at his highest capacity? And who not scared out of his wits? Who doesn't hate his mother and father? Who doesn't compete with his brother? What girl at some time did not wish she were a boy? Who told me this book was too difficult, inaccessible, and most of all impractical? For many years, this is what I believed. It was only recently that I actually read the book, a text so bold, daring, and forthright that I thought my head would explode. In ten chapters, Firestone offers up a theory of radical feminism, building on the work of Engels and Marx, as well as her hero, Simone de Beauvoir. She criticizes the culture of romance—the way women's desires are shaped by society. This was something I could not understand as a young woman; it has taken years for me to understand it. Or perhaps it is aging—the brainwashing of young women is so effective in part because when you are young and pretty you are valuable to patriarchy, you can convince yourself that there's something to be gained, that you enjoy the role you've been assigned. Years later, you become the hag, unuseful to capitalist production, and you can see it. The water you were swimming in. This was Firestone's argument. She had a stunning grasp of history, extending this philosophy into the intransigent sexism of the midtwentieth century.

Firestone was twenty-five when she wrote the manifesto, and to read it is to hear the brilliant young woman, the smartest and most assured—the bravest of all. Everyone is drawn to her. We know she will change the world.

And she did. But somehow, by the 1990s, she was barely remembered. She had withdrawn, returned to the solitude she'd lost after the publication of *Dialectic*. There was a shifting sense of political urgency. Ann Snitow later described *The Dialectic of Sex* as one of feminism's *demon texts—books demonized, apologized for, endlessly quoted out of context to prove that radical feminism in the early '70s was strangely blind . . . it was patriarchy which Firestone wanted to smash, not mothers.* Firestone was to be admired as part of the past, a moment of excitement and possibility, but ultimately impractical—and frankly offensive. Offensive most of all to the women of the '80s and '90s who *wanted* to be mothers, to have children. The backlash was in full force through the Reaganite 1980s, demonstrated by the '90s fetish of competitive child-rearing. The novelist Joy Williams nailed this emergent era in her own satiric manifesto, "The Case Against Babies": the Cabbage Patch dolls, Anne Geddes's wildly popular *Babies* calendars. Everyone wanted a baby and no one wanted to hear Firestone's declaration that "pregnancy was barbaric" or that child-rearing was the "heart of women's oppression."

August 2012. I read every obituary. Hers was the worst sort of New York City death, any death—alone, dead for days before being found by a super, alone in a small tenement apartment on the Lower East Side. *Alerted by neighbors, who had smelled an odor from her apartment, her superintendent peered in through a window from the fire escape and saw her body on the floor.* She'd paid rent with her disability checks or money lent by friends and family. Indigency and social isolation within the thriving late-capitalist machine of New York City. *What happens to people?* Now we know what happened to Firestone, who suffered for years from mental illness and then suffered from the treatments for her illness. The details from the obituaries were grisly. A *curious building manager* found her. Her landlord spoke to the press. In some obituaries, her death symbolized feminism's failures. The failure of a sustaining framework of sisterhood. Or the failure of mental health care, the failure of the state to care for the most vulnerable.

Her death the unsurprising if horrible culmination of debilitating mental illness. As Kraus put it: *Sixty-seven is a ripe old age within the indigent, mentally ill population.*

Six months after Firestone's death, Susan Faludi published a *New Yorker* article about Firestone. Faludi reported that after Shulie's death, there was a push to make her rent-controlled East Village apartment into a protected space for women writers. A place for a young feminist, a retreat of sorts. There was a petition—you can still find it online at Change.org with only sixty-four signatures, put forward by a group of feminists. It didn't happen that way. As has long been the case, New York City is defined by real estate, not social services. The property owners cleaned up the apartment and relisted it for a higher rent, with plenty of eager tenants ready to pay. Another example of what Sarah Schulman has called *the gentrification of the mind.* Of course, a young visionary like Firestone would not be able to move to that neighborhood today. The ideals of feminism erased and reshaped by the market. Do the new tenants—and how much do you think they pay for the pleasure of the tiny bleak apartment?—do they have any idea that Shulamith Firestone lived there? If they knew, would they care? Just another day, another erasure of history. Of women. Of feminism. And as I write this, ten years after her death, *Roe v. Wade* is overturned.

Should This Occur

Goffman: *The career of the mental patient falls popularly and naturalistically into three main phases: the period prior to entering the hospital, which I shall call the pre-patient phase; the period in the hospital, the inpatient phase; the period after discharge from the hospital, should this occur, namely, the ex-patient phase.* It is many years later now and I am walking in the neighborhood where Firestone lived and died alone. I try to imagine her here. I try to remember myself, visiting Henry, who lived around the corner from Firestone, in something called transitional housing. I remember Tilda lived nearby, too, in a halfway house. Tilda was not halfway to anywhere, but Hank was—or so I hope, twenty years now since we met, and nearly that many since we've spoken. I pass the building where Tilda spent the last decades of her life. I stop at a café, I sit outside and check my phone. A friend has texted me with news of Lauren Berlant's death. I gasp, I didn't know. I search on my phone for more information—this modern ritual in response to death—but as I do, I notice a man approach my table. He is strung-out, homeless, psychotic—it is hard to say which—he walks up to me too close, screams out—*bang bang bang*—startling all of us. The café owner lets me in, locks the door. It was not a gun, it was his finger, it is someone suffering—and there is no support for such suffering, there is less support now than there ever was.

So many like Firestone—the paranoid, the deluded, the once famous—just one more of many such encounters. This neighborhood where many artists lived, alongside the mentally ill and disenfranchised. This neighborhood, however homogenized, expensive, white it had become through decades of gentrification, was still the site of supportive housing and Section 8 vouchers. Holdovers from the 1960s and '70s lived there in rent-control apartments, many living (like Firestone) on Social Security disability checks.

This had been *the social fate* of my fellow mental patients. No one got discharged back into life. One of Tilda's roommates started a fire in her apartment, I found out years later, leaving

Tilda permanently injured. Hank's apartment, the few times I visited, depressed me. The scene of his altered fate. His roommates: overmedicated and mute. Our years together in the hospital seemed idyllic by comparison. I don't know why—we'd lived with plenty of mute and overmedicated people—but here it felt final. All promise of hope and cure gone. Hank left a few months before I did and it had been, he told me, extremely difficult. On one of my first visits he seemed especially distraught. He missed the hospital terribly. This was the way it worked, the way the social fate was determined—you had been a mental patient, in a hospital, and now you were a mental patient in your mind.

How could Hank live like this? I wondered. I stopped visiting. I wanted to distance myself from the hospital, from everyone I knew on the inside. The fate of my friends terrified me. Or my own fate was terrifying. Hank and Tilda were at least a decade older than me.

It was clear to me that, though they'd been discharged from one hospital, they would never move beyond phase two—or that phase three was no better than phase two.

I wanted another life, though I wouldn't admit it. Admitting it would mean risking the care I received.

So this might have been my fate, but there were differences between us. The fact that I could return to college now, that the hospital, encouraged by Dr. Blossom, was considering letting me move back into a dorm room on campus, pending the approval of a lawyer and the college dean. This trajectory would set me apart from my fellow patients, allow me a pathway to another social fate. Or so I hoped, in my desperation, that the books that had led me into this place would now lead me out, into another life.

Henry could not move into a dorm. He had finished college, I think, and Tilda had graduated a decade earlier. To go to college now was to resituate myself. I had time on my side, as they say, that profound stroke of brief luck, what you don't recognize until it is behind you, until you are on the other side. And so my education saved me, but even then, it was only the beginning of the true lifelong education that would save me—becoming a writer and an artist.

Dr. B was helping me. It wasn't through language or analysis, or anything at all. It had something to do with sitting there with her, in a room, across from her, this beautiful woman. Three days a week to sit in that space with her. I began to see these compulsions—and suicide was the thing—as a choice. Hours and hours of sitting in the room with her, and then no longer the room or her, but something happened in me, something shifted, and I didn't need her or the room. I could see myself as she saw me; and I could see my choice. I could live or I could die.

On the Beach 1969

Shulamith on the beach reading The Second Sex *by Simone de Beauvoir, 1969,* included in the program for the 2012 memorial service in honor of Shulamith Firestone. An ekphrasis: In the photograph she sits on a beach, a small towel and endless sand. She tilts her face to the left, sunglasses atop her head, maybe she's taken them off for the photo. The sun is too bright in her face, so when she looks at the camera she must squint her eyes, tilting her face toward the sun, she is not smiling but she is looking, forthright, as in every photo from the early days to the late, she looks into the camera. One of the most famous lines from *The Dialectic of Sex*: *The revolution will begin when women stop smiling.* She wears a long necklace and a bikini of the era, with the V-neck plunge. Her legs folded, her left arm rests on one leg and her right supports her, she leans toward the book next to her right hand. It is as if she has been reading and someone said, Hey, Shulie, smile! or, Look over here, I'm taking a picture!

It wasn't like now, you couldn't take one hundred pictures at once, you took one or two, later you developed the film, maybe one or two or three were worth saving.

Her hair is long and dark and thick.

Next to her, the thick paperback, Simone de Beauvoir's *The Second Sex*, near her right hand.

It is as if she has just closed the book, for the picture, but in some deliberate or fortuitous framing, the title is legible. It is an edition I've never seen, a paperback. *The Second Sex* was published in 1949, four years after Shulie's birth. In the photo, it is 1969. The year everything changed, the year women decided it was not enough to be a second-class citizen. The year of the revolution.

The shadow of the summer sun falls to her left. It is late in the day, July or August. Her arms are muscular, toned. This is the body of a young woman, with the lost "figure" she refers to later—her hair before it went gray, her face before it fell, shifted into middle age. I think of Maggie Nelson quoting Edgar Allan Poe—about the most tragic death—or the most beautiful—the death of the young woman. Often looking at the photo of a powerful woman in her youth, I think of that death. Aging was not death, but loss, and, too, the opening into a moment, the death of an unknown potential. A brilliant mind shaping itself while living in the temporary shape of youth.

I came to read my mother's death this way—that she died in her youth. But she wasn't young, not exactly. She was going gray. She was too young to die, at forty-one years old. Was that young?

Well, of course I didn't think so, not for many years. Not until I was forty, forty-one, forty-two, the years coming on fast.

The photos I love most of my mother are something like this photo of Firestone, where she remains forever young and beautiful, an unknown future ahead.

Susan Sontag: *Photography is the inventory of mortality. Photographs state the innocence, the vulnerability of lives heading toward their own destruction, and this link between photography and death haunts all photographs of people.*

This photo of Shulie, a memento mori, not just the lost youth and beauty so resonant in her later writing, but the death of the firebrand—the brilliant feminist—this young beautiful woman who was willing to channel her intellect and passion into a cause— the women's liberation movement. I see the punctum—the squint in her right eye, not unlike Freud's eye—and the authority, the restlessness, the body and mind ready to pounce.

Anne Koedt: *And if Shulie had not started the women's liberation movement, it would all be like how it was in the 1950s which I still remember. We were second-class citizens in every way. Revolutions are more than about rights gained, they are about revolutions in consciousness, too.*

Firestone grew up in a large midwestern religious family. Her Orthodox Jewish background, laden as it was with sexism, was not unlike my own Catholic background; the expectations for women, even twenty years after the radical feminist movement, had barely evolved from the 1950s. My mother was born in 1939, seven years after Sylvia Plath, and six years before Shulamith Firestone. My mother worked as a nurse until she got married;

she then followed her husband for his career, the more important career of the doctor. She'd chosen—happily, I think, but what do I know—to be a housewife and a mother, as her own immigrant mother had been. My Irish grandmother's marriage certificate—ten years after she moved to this country—listed "Housewife" in the space for Occupation. My mother did not have anything like Plath's education or rigorous artistic training, and she did not have Firestone's rebellious independent drive. Still, I imagine she knew herself to be a second-class citizen in every way.

The Story of the Story Is This

Firestone's privacy was shattered after the publication of *The Dialectic of Sex*, her provocative manifesto, which was met with both great praise and serious criticism, including from her own family. In *Airless Spaces*, the narrator describes her father's hostile response to the manifesto, and her own fear that the book's publicity and critical attention somehow led to her brother's early death.

Airless Spaces refuses redemption. This is an academic way to read it, the truth of the book the urgency of it is in the form—fractured, underdeveloped, immediate—that will not redeem itself, a book with a nearness to life. I read her stories and recognized moments of my own, some I'd even written about in my first book: a banana, a woman who wears inky patches for her wrinkles. The odd touches of vanity among the women recovering from failed suicide attempts. Best of all, what *Airless Spaces* recalled was the strange intimacy of mental patients and the abject reality of Shulie's life, which I knew well. The dead-end desolation, the impossible relationships. So many books about these places or these experiences lack the awareness of the inside, the view from the altered social fate.

In the final chapter, Firestone tells the story of her brother, Danny, one year older and her best friend. *We were almost like twins,* she writes. She remembers her childhood with Danny, playing in the house in St. Louis, enjoying the storms, sliding down the laundry chute, going to the store to buy penny candy. In a brief chapter, the essay moves dizzyingly and vividly through their relationship, without sentiment, including a detail about her brother torturing stray kittens. The two siblings grow apart, but live somewhat parallel lives. After an Orthodox Jewish childhood, educated in the yeshiva, each becomes secular, reading passionately, developing as autodidacts, and becoming intellectuals. By 1974, Shulie was in New York, her brother had moved to Ithaca, living in a Zen center. She has not spoken to him for a decade. One day in 1974, Shulie, already famous for her groundbreaking *The Dialectic of Sex,* receives a call from her sister, telling her that Danny had died in a car crash. When she returns home to St. Louis for the funeral, her father admits that Danny had killed himself—he was found with a bullet hole in the chest. The rest of the story moves from various theories and investigations Shulie pursued into the details of her brother's death. The chapter moves from the obvious—she even goes to his home in Ithaca, and reads the journal where he wrote and planned his suicide—to her growing belief that Danny had been murdered by a government agent. Shulie does not comment on her theories, but reports the reality of her madness as a natural and understandable response to trauma.

It is telling that Firestone or her editor saved "Danny" for the very last in the book. This story is so large that it swallows up the earlier story. Which is the pre-patient story. *In the end, theories about his death, whether murder or suicide, afterlife or no, contributed to my own growing madness—which led to my hospitalization, medication, and a shattering nervous breakdown.*

What I love about *Airless Spaces:* Not once does Firestone's narrator say: I have a chemical imbalance. I am schizophrenic. I am X label or Y diagnosis. What is clear in Firestone's case, in the case of these characters, is what was clear to Hermione Lee, who wrote of Virginia Woolf,

> *It is nearly impossible to separate Woolf's condition from the effects of the treatments she received.*

Firestone alludes to symptoms—the reader knows she has been diagnosed ten times over—and yet in the book she remains a person irreducible to illness. This has so long been my fear. I became a writer because I believe in that part of me who is not limited by age or gender or time or disability—yet still I am afraid to say it. Yes, I was ill. Yes, I am writing about Shulamith Firestone because she was ill. I am writing about her because I think I am her—I think I was as crazy as she was—or I am writing about her because she was crazier—and more brilliant—than I'll ever be.

Toward a Theory of My Illness (III)

1.   There are many things scientists don't understand about the way medications work. Monoamine oxidase inhibitors, for example, were discovered by accident. A drug ineffective in treating tuberculosis turned out to be an effective treatment for depression.

2.   Poet Jane Kenyon, writing about her own uppercase-D Depression, invokes Chekhov: *If many remedies are prescribed for an illness, you may be certain that the illness has no cure* (*The Cherry Orchard*).

3.   Not long after my son was born, in New York with my then-husband, a poet who was giving a talk downtown, I visited Dr. B. I asked her why I was in the hospital so long. She nodded and said, vaguely, It was the best option we had at the time.

4.   I thought about that for a while. If you were a psychiatrist, it was the best option, is what she meant to say.

5.   That's one way to define my illness: The part of me that didn't want to die agreed that that hospital was the best option I had at the time.

6.   So maybe that is my illness or was my illness. But if I'm
being totally honest about it I think, it's been hard for me for a
long time to talk about it or to mention a diagnosis not because
there isn't truth in them, but because it's just part of me and I've
had to work for years to untangle the identity that was formed
around that hospitalization—remove myself from the part of me
that still gets depressed, can be paralyzed, stopped, overwhelmed
by life, can't function, takes psych medications, doesn't sleep, or
sleeps and wakes up in a panic.

7.   Goffman describes the way a mental patient accustomed
herself to the institution, shifting into a career patient, whose
identity shifts in response to how she is treated. Fitting myself
into the category of patient was something like fitting myself
into a diagnostic category. The patient's presence in the hospital
is taken as prima facie evidence that he is mentally ill, since the
hospitalization of these persons is what the institution is for.
It took years of returning and leaving treatment, over and over
again, before I finally and completely could believe myself sane,
could believe that I was capable of taking care of myself, of not
being a mental patient.

8.   I've learned of a growing movement in the UK to do away
with diagnostic categories altogether—the pathology and stigma
attached to anything related to mental illness is so great. It
makes me wonder: What if, instead of being diagnosed—being
called mentally ill—what if I had been able to receive care for its
own sake. To be in distress, to ask for care, to receive it. What if
there were space in this world for *care*.

Good Old Nardil

After leaving the state psychiatric hospital, I spent the next two years in and out of hospitals, for longer or shorter periods of time. For a time, I attended a day hospital. These subsequent hospitalizations were a result of the regression that comes from living in a hospital for so long—a well-known and documented result of institutionalization.

When Tilda eloped from the hospital and arrived at Dr. Prince's building, when she spoke to the doorman, she told him she was there to see Richard, as she called him, as if he were an old friend. He's expecting me. She wore exaggerated makeup, a low-cut blouse. When I picture her now, the makeup, the bizarre outfits, the glassy eyes and slur, the way she would stand too close to me, or anyone, moving in, too much eye contact, staring. When I picture her, I think, Well, she was crazy. If I saw her on the street: She's insane, I would say. I hope she gets help.

Is that what people said of me? For different reasons, I'd guess. In the years following my hospitalization, I was haunted by Tilda's look. I didn't want to read as crazy, and so I tried to pass. Every time I went out, for years, I was trying to pass, though some days

I would walk down the street in tears, or I'd stop and sit some-where—on a bench, in a park, on the subway platform—and be unable to move. I'd stay there for hours, paralyzed.

And then there were the days when I was so unable to pass, to even attempt it, the days I'd stay in my room in my apartment, the doors closed, ignoring my roommates, my room a mess, dirty clothes piled up. I could lie there for hours staring at the wall. I'd cry and I'd call my doctor. I could not live, I would say. I am out of the hospital and yet I can't live. What should I do? I would cry. Dr. B, my love, she would listen, she would suggest something, anything. She would say, Do we need to put you back into a hospital? You know you can't go back there, don't you? You know that is not a home, it doesn't exist anymore. I know, I would cry. You have to go out, she said. Go to a movie. Call a friend. I didn't have any friends. Or my friends were mental patients. Or my friends made it worse, the inability to connect. The gaps, I was so aware of them. In the hospital, it had been clear to anyone I spoke to, my suffering, my disability had been clear. But here in life, if that's what this was, I was treated as if I was fine, was okay, a normal person who could get out of bed in the morning, keep a job, main-tain a friendship.

Nineteen ninety-six. I was in the hospital again, on and off. It was more difficult to be out. This is to be expected after many years inside, this is why it is ill-advised, or so they soon allowed, that it wasn't ever good to keep anyone in that long, that a person would become irrevocably ill-equipped for life outside. Dr. B consulted her superiors, who suggested Nardil, a rarely prescribed MAOI. It was meant for resistant cases.

> *We move on to the monoamine / oxidase inhibitors. Day and night / I feel as if I had drunk six cups / of coffee, but the pain stops / abruptly. With the wonder / and bitterness of someone pardoned / for a crime she did not commit / I come back to marriage and friends, / to pink-fringed hollyhocks; come back / to my desk, books, and chair.*

This is from Jane Kenyon's poem "Having It Out with Melancholy." Until I read David Foster Wallace, Kenyon was the only writer I knew to reference Nardil.

Fifteen years later, after a string of miscarriages, I became depressed. It was not the same as it had been—it would never be that bad. I returned to Kenyon's poem, finding it on my bookshelf. I read it aloud to my then-husband. What do you think? I asked. It's okay, he said. Do you like Jane Kenyon? I said. Not really, he said. Why not? She's a boring poet, he said.

Often, I agreed with my then-husband. There are so many boring poets! But in this case, his assessment stung.

But only for a moment, because I needed this poem, and others, and so if I am in the school of boring poets, so be it. Jane Kenyon brought me back to Nardil. She describes exactly how it felt: the list of bottles, the years of attempts to find a drug that would work, the last-ditch try at an MAOI.

> *Pharmaceutical wonders are at work / but I believe only in*
> *this moment / of well-being. Unholy ghost, / you are certain*
> *to come again.*

I never thought of it this way, because I don't believe in cures, but writing this now, it may appear obvious: I began taking Nardil in 1995 and my last hospitalization was in 1996. That part of my life was over.

> *High on Nardil and June light / I wake at four, / waiting*
> *greedily for the first / notes of the wood thrush. Easeful air /*
> *presses through the screen / with the wild, complex song / of*
> *the bird, and I am overcome. . . .*

If I am required to recover—if I am obligated to tell my story with a before and after trajectory—well, then, Nardil is part of the story. Never mind that I didn't take Nardil forever, or that there were many other factors in my before/after story. Time, aging, writing. Love.

I left New York in 1998 and moved to a small town in central Illinois to study with David Foster Wallace, who wrote about the reality of depression like no contemporary author I'd read before. He wrote about the reality of being drugged and diagnosed and hospitalized over and over again. What did I think he could tell me, or teach me? How to write about it, I guess. This turned out to be something like asking the doctors to tell me what was wrong with me. In one of our first conversations he revealed to me that he also took Nardil. It was unusual even among my fellow mental patients to meet someone who also took Nardil. But he had been hospitalized on the East Coast and, like me, prescribed Nardil while hospitalized, as a last resort, a resistant depression, etc.

I learned later that for a time it had been an East Coast psychiatric trend, especially in the 1980s and '90s. Everywhere else, including Chicago, MAOIs were considered an unusual and ill-advised treatment.

A year or two later I started dating the man who became my husband and that was when I became ashamed of taking Nardil. My then-husband came from a family and a culture that appreciated wine and cheese, long meals. It was a way of enjoying life and I was attracted to it. I was searching for other ways to be alive, to work the trap (Judith Butler). We are all here in the trap of a limited world, defined by capitalist production, shaped by the specific historical moment and social conditions of our lives—and yet, we find ways to be a self.

Soon enough, this became a problem—wine and cheese are at the top of the list of foods/drinks you cannot have when you are taking an MAOI. I had occasionally had other foods from the forbidden list—chocolate or coffee—but wine was another story. I would drink one glass and my heart would beat so heavily and intensely, I'd be up all night with blinding headaches and dizziness, terrified that I was going to kill myself with the Nardil and wine.

To make matters worse, I was too afraid to tell my husband of this reaction, or to tell his family, because to tell them would be to tell them of the severity of my illness (disability), which was something I couldn't imagine doing. I was sure that if my then-husband knew this about me, he would leave me. I was sure, too, that his family—full of doctors—would view me differently.

But I loved my then-husband and his family and I wanted to enjoy life in the way that they did so I stopped taking Nardil.

Around this time something happened that I never could get full information about, or clarification, because by this time I did not have good health insurance. I was on Medicaid, which was assigned to me upon leaving the hospital. This meant that I could go to public clinics, see doctors who knew nothing or cared little or had no time for my history.

What happened was that the manufacturer—Pfizer—changed the formulation of Nardil. Or it became generic and, as a result, changed. Or it was sold to another manufacturer. There was no official change—the compounds were the same—but my experience of the medication changed drastically. And I was not the only patient to report this. I began going on various message boards where people spoke of their psych meds, and a number of people reported getting "brain zaps" on the new Nardil. That was what I had experienced—brain zaps—only I hadn't had the words. A zap was a sudden headache, followed by a dizziness. A sense of confusion. It could last a few moments or more. I would close my eyes and recover quickly, or I would be in bed for hours. I became even more convinced that this new formulation of the medication was not worth staying on.

I google it now—did the formulation of Nardil change? And there it is,

> Nardil was changed in late 2003, due to a complete
> reformulation by Pfizer, who removed many of the excipient
> ingredients, including the hard coating. It is possible that the
> current version is not surviving the stomach acid content and
> therefore not as much is being absorbed into the bloodstream.

It is painful to discover this on Google now, so clearly, so matter-of-fact, and so many years later. Why was it such a mystery at the time? Why couldn't anyone tell me that what I was going through was real, and there were reasons for it? Scrolling down, I see a Change.org petition: "Old Nardil pre-2003" detailing exactly what happened, suggesting that many patients noticed the change, that Nardil stopped working, that the pharmaceutical company did this to save costs, and so on. The petition is sad in the same way that the failed petition to make Shulamith Firestone's former apartment into a feminist residency was sad. In the case of old Nardil, there were fifteen signers; we know who won. In the comments, a man named Charles Leslie writes of the old Nardil,

> Worked wonders for me from 1981–2003. Now, housebound.

By then I had some sense that I was going to have a baby with my then-husband and I knew that there was no way you could take Nardil during pregnancy or even while you were trying to conceive—you would certainly conceive a baby with three heads—and so I took myself off Nardil and it was very dark for a few weeks and I couldn't exactly tell my then-husband about it because there was something about him—or about us—that didn't allow for the revelation. Later he said that he wouldn't have judged me at all, that I should've trusted him. We moved to Istanbul for two years; from the year we left, through my subsequent pregnancy and breastfeeding, I was off Nardil. I didn't take anything. I sometimes thought that the pregnancy and the breastfeeding did something akin to an antidepressant. It was the longest stretch of my adult life that I did not take any medication. I was happy in those years, not all the time, but often there was a deep, meaningful joy. The happiness of having a baby—for me it was the greatest feeling, his body, his baby body against mine, and nursing him. In that same visit, Dr. B told me that oxytocin is released in breastfeeding, a feel-good hormone, and for over a year this was it. Occasionally, I would say it to myself, quietly, I would whisper: I am happy. This is the happiest I have ever been. I would leave, for work or life, and I would miss him and when I came home to his baby body I was so happy, all over again. It makes me cry to think of it now, to write it, because it is gone, it's always going, it won't be again, like everything in life, and it doesn't matter how many times people say "enjoy every minute," because you can't enjoy every moment, or even if you do it still ends, leaves you—but at least this is true, I did know it, I did say to myself, I am happy. This is joy.

The Shadow Story

There is a shadow story to this story.

Patrick was my best friend in high school. We were in plays together. We spent our weekends together. I was a pom-pom girl and though boys could not be on the pom squad in those days, Patrick learned every routine I choreographed. He especially loved the hitch kick. He could sing, songs from *Oliver*, *Annie*, *Joseph and the Technicolor Dreamcoat*, *Damn Yankees*. He played Fagan, Joseph, the Devil.

It was clear to everyone that Patrick was gay, and so he was taunted, called *fag* and *homo*, this throughout the years of high school. Patrick wrote a long essay senior year of high school about growing up Catholic, attending a boys' Catholic military high school, about being gay. Or being called gay even though he was not gay. He was gay but it would be years before he could call himself that. And how dare they, how dare anyone.

In the years that I went mad, Patrick left home. He graduated from Northwestern University, where he'd majored in theater. It was there in his theater training at Northwestern, from 1989 to

1993, that he was told by his favorite professor that he needed to learn to act *straight*. He had to get rid of his gay mannerisms or he'd never be cast in anything. He adored this professor, and he took this advice to heart. He would tell me of his attempts, how he'd study the straight men in his life. On occasion, he performed *straight* for me: how to walk, how to hold your hands, how to stand.

In these years, I entered the hospital, began my own mental patient career, and we lost touch. Or I lost touch—I stopped responding to anyone, no matter how close our friendships had been. Once or twice, Patrick reached out to me, sent a letter, called the hospital payphone. He wasn't so much concerned as he was interested in my sudden and surprising trajectory. He noted something in what was happening to me—that it had something to do with acting. With playing a role. That it was not wholly unlike our experiences as theater kids.

From time to time my sister would fill me in on what was going on with Patrick. After college, he moved to L.A. He got a low-level industry job in Hollywood. He began writing screenplays. He had his first sexual encounter, his first love affair. He wrote a letter to his parents and told them that he was gay. His father wrote back to him. His father was clear, *in no uncertain terms*, he told Patrick that this was unacceptable. That if he, Patrick, *made this choice— chose this lifestyle*—he would be disowned. They would cut him off, financially and practically. And so his father made it clear: His love for Patrick was conditional.

Patrick had few defenses. He loathed his father but didn't know himself beyond the shape of his family, the configuration of himself in that family. He valued what they valued: grades, achievement, high SAT scores. Patrick disappeared, quit his job, ran away. The family traced him by his credit card. He was in Colorado, he was manic. They cut him off, bought him a one-way ticket home. At home, he tried to kill himself and was put in a psych ward. Or he went mad. Here is where I lost track. For years, I didn't speak to Patrick. I would hear about him, his own surprising trajectory—that he was back in our hometown working as a cashier at the mall. He was heavily medicated with antipsychotics. He had gained fifty pounds. His speech was slurred, he could no longer look anyone in the eye.

After some years, too, I learned that Patrick had moved to New York. I heard he hitchhiked all the way there, had no money. He ended up in the hospital, again, or the ER. He asked to be put in the hospital where I had been.

By then I was long gone and the hospital no longer existed. The program had been defunded.

Was he trying to find me? To follow me? I'll never know.

(The awful punch line: a month ago, after I'd finished this book, I got the news of Patrick's death, in Queens, age fifty-one.)

In *The Bell Jar*, Esther is hospitalized after a suicide attempt. After some weeks in the hospital, Joan Gilling arrives as a patient. Joan becomes a double for Esther, as many characters in the novel function as doubles to Esther. Esther knew Joan from her hometown. They'd attended the same church, and later Joan dated Buddy Willard, the same boy Esther will date. Esther is both repelled by and envious of Joan, who is a lesbian. It is clear to Esther that Joan has followed her to this place. That Joan admired Esther's own trajectory into the space of not-quite-oblivion, the space of madness. Joan took it as an example, wanted to move there, too. Esther resists Joan's arrival, her intrusion; she then resents her for being cured. Later, Joan returns to the hospital and dies by suicide.

When Patrick arrived in New York, I was out of the hospital—but I was not cured. If I were cured, I could have told Patrick it wasn't worth it. I would've told him that this escape—the going mad—the madness—all these madnesses, as Janet Frame or Virginia Woolf described their own protective strategies—was a trap.

I may have said: It is the perfect escape, isn't it? To lose your mind. To go mad. To fall apart, go crazy, all of it. To become a patient. To need help and to receive help. To be cared for.

I would have added: The perfect escape becomes a trap. You learn this soon enough. You escape and then you begin to play the part. And once you are playing the part, people respond to you that way, to the role you are in. And there you are, trapped. It might become your life.

I wish I could've told Patrick this, what I learned, and I wish it would've made a difference.

For years, he was in and out of hospitals, state hospitals, Kings County Hospital in Brooklyn.

For years, I would read the Christmas cards Patrick's father would send to a wide group of friends and acquaintances, including my parents. In the two-plus-pages-long letters, his father would include paragraphs bragging about his eldest son, a genius who went to Harvard and now was a professor of economics at the University of Chicago. On and on he went about the eldest brother (who later worked in the Trump administration).

Patrick's father would include a paragraph or three about his daughter and her husband, the heir to a wealthy oil-rich Texas family. He might include a paragraph about his wife, their travels, the time spent at their second home.

And then, only sometimes, a sentence or two about Patrick: *Patrick is still sick,* or *Patrick is stable for now,* or *Patrick won't join our family gatherings. We try to include Patrick but he won't comply.* This is the message: *how difficult it is for us to have a mentally ill family member.* The letter might include an address for Patrick, always the address of an institution, or a supportive housing facility. *Much as we've tried, Patrick won't use email. We can't get him on Facebook.*

His father also mentions that his wife, Patrick's mother, spent years working with NAMI. NAMI is the National Alliance on Mental Illness. This is an organization primarily set up to help *the families* of the mentally ill.

It wasn't long after Patrick began his mental patient career that his mother became involved in this organization.

In this way, the family narrative became one of concern and suffering.

And so his family won the narrative, or so it seemed to me. From then on the story was Patrick's Mental Illness; Patrick-Is-Sick; Patrick, who won't take his meds; and so on.

The narrative would never be the story of Patrick as he was meant to be, living as an openly gay man, a fulfilled life, despite the devastating rejection by his family.

The family narrative, Patrick's father's Christmas cards, will never mention this—the family's threats and betrayals, the choice they gave Patrick: to be himself or to be nothing.

This is the shadow story to my story. The escape that becomes the trap. The way that the family can win—and how narratives around mental illness or madness help them win. Patrick's family will never have to say that he was gay or that they hate people who are gay—they will never have to change their views or to accept their part in his madness.

This is not just Patrick's story, it was not just my story; there are so many of us. There is so much shame attached to stories of mental illness, and I myself have internalized the self-loathing that at times can make me feel ashamed to be writing this book. But I also believe that, as my heroes have shown me, this is where a writer must go.

If I don't tell this story, they win.

I know Patrick read and wrote intensely but I don't know what he wrote. It's too late for me to ask him. Maybe he tried to write himself out of the received knowledge of mental patients, of illness, of the class of indigent mentally ill of which he was a member. Or maybe he wrote himself into madness, which is another kind of commitment. Commit to your bit, as it were. Either way, I don't see myself as a winner, I'm Patrick as much as anyone. Life is ongoing and we are shaped by what we go through, and it all makes us who we are at any moment. I don't want to pretend that I have access to some transcendence that he was denied. Perhaps he had it, too, in that other truth of madness.

Still, what I hate about Patrick's story and the way it will be told is that it allows the teller to situate him- or herself in the camp of the Not-Sick, the Well, the Sane. In *Madness and Civilization*, French theorist and philosopher Michel Foucault wrote about this need to separate the mad from the sane as a feature of modern life. After the Renaissance, moving into the Age of Reason, the mad were put in asylums, separated out to be observed. It was necessary for the reasonable citizen to see the madmen; it was a way to define yourself against disintegration. In contemporary society, we still have this desire to separate the sane from the insane. We do it ourselves. Maybe you are reading this book and you situate yourself there, on the side of the sane, and so you want to know about how I live on the other side. Or how I did, and how I came back. Maybe you are quite sure that you are not the mad one, you are not sick. Not mentally ill.

So maybe I am the freak, the weirdo, and there is something sensational for you in this story: the how did this happen? or, I can't believe she was a mental patient or, I could never imagine that, being there.

But I suppose I am writing for the ones who read this and think: This could be me. Just as I read Patrick's story and think, This is me. I am not the post-sick while Patrick is sick. Every time I sit down to write I'm reminded of it, of the fact of this, what I don't believe, in the sick and the post-sick, I think we are all sick, I think of what Kathy Acker, who had breast cancer, told my friend, also with cancer: I'm a survivor, too, he said, and she said, *Oh honey, none of us survive.* We are all mortal, and we are all fragile. We are all one moment away from disintegration.

And grief, like madness, is not something that resolves, or climaxes, etc. You just learn to live with it, and get used to it, or not. The point of Didion's vortex is that it will come back without notice, it's not resolved. It's part of who I am.

For me it was a decision not to suicide—it was sharp and clear and that's it. A decision not to consider suicide. It wasn't therapy—Dr. B stopped helping me at a certain point. Leaving her, leaving New York helped me, as did making other banal life decisions—having relationships, having sex, having a baby. Getting older, which isn't a decision so much as inevitable, if you stick around to find out. This isn't transcendence but it is committing to life and sticking with it. It's far more tedious than climactic.

Patrick did it, too. He stuck to it. You're reading my book, but you could be reading his. You could be reading Hank's book or Elena's book or Tilda's book. I'm not special, I've not moved into

a post-sick realm where I can say, Oh, look at that, those people. No, I'm as sick as the rest, and that's why I'll never situate
myself with the so-called normal people, will never set myself
apart from the weirdos. If this hospital taught me anything, it's
that.

Angry Women

I was eighteen when I decided to become a feminist—two years before I landed in a mental hospital. Back then I needed a structure to support my plan, so I enrolled in a women's studies class. My dad found it amusing, that such a department existed. Women's studies! He rolled his eyes. My teacher, a graduate student named Belinda Edmundson, assigned us to read Audre Lorde. I was back in Chicago that summer, and I'd just discovered literary readings. I didn't know that authors went to bookstores and read aloud from their books. It was thrilling. Sometimes they read aloud in universities. That is how I heard Toni Morrison read from *Beloved* in a lecture hall in downtown Chicago. I discovered a bookstore called Women & Children First in a neighborhood called Andersonville. The city might as well have been another country compared to where I'd grown up forty miles west in Aurora.

Chicago was the first site of my transformation, a coming alive to literature and art. I'd been spending time in Wicker Park with a group of actors and artists. That's how I met an actor named Tim. He took me to see a play about the Chicago Eight, at the now long-defunct Remains Theatre. I didn't know who Abbie Hoffman was, or the story of the trial, which had only occurred around twenty years earlier. Wicker Park was full of artists and writers, but not yet gentrified. (Shulamith Firestone lived in the neighborhood before she moved to New York.)

Like many adolescents who are shaping an identity, I needed to mention regularly that I was becoming a feminist. I may have also added that I was becoming an intellectual, and an autodidact. Tim was annoyed by the feminist part. As were other men I met. I remember one actor declaring—this was 1991: *Women libbers get everything they want and they still aren't happy.* (I wrote this in my notebook.)

I don't think people wholly understand this, now that feminism is corporatized and mainstream. In 2002, when I began teaching, I had students complain that I only taught "feminist books." (I found this, too, in a notebook, otherwise I wouldn't have believed it.)

I often wrote about Tim. On the one hand, Tim admired me, my willed transformation; on the other, he didn't want to hear about it so much. One day at lunch with a group of his actor friends, he told me that becoming a feminist would get in the way of my relationships with men.

We went out a few more times after that, until one tense dinner, where Tim accused me of not really being a feminist because I was obviously starving myself, I had become rail thin, I wouldn't eat anything in restaurants.

In ways I couldn't explain, being thin felt connected to my transformation. I agree with Rachel Aviv, who linked her own early anorexia to, perhaps, a spiritual search—in *Strangers to Ourselves*, she quotes René Girard: *No one wants to be a saint, but they want to look like one.*

And: *In our destruction of religion, we create new religions.*

In Andersonville, I bought a thin rayon tight black turtleneck at a shop down the street from Women & Children First. I was learning that clothes could look good on me, and be part of shaping a new identity. I was used to being ugly, but now I was figuring something out: You didn't have to be beautiful. I wore the black turtleneck to hear Adrienne Rich read at Women & Children First. She was reading from a book called *Diving into the Wreck*. She was tiny. The small feminist bookstore was full to bursting. She must have been in her sixties, but seemed elderly to me. I was enchanted, alone, I didn't speak to anyone, but I didn't feel lonely. I had begun pulling away from most people, I was on a journey few could understand. Some months later, a doctor, many doctors and nurses, would tell me this was part of my illness. But now I think that my trap saved me, because I saw Adrienne Rich read and, on the table in the bookstore, I saw an anthology called *Angry Women*, a title and cover image hailing me. It was in *Angry Women* that I learned about Annie Sprinkle and bell hooks and Karen Finley and Kathy Acker and Holly Hughes, who would one day become my teacher.

Adrienne Rich spoke, too, of Audre Lorde. Belinda Edmondson assigned us to read Audre Lorde's essay "Poetry Is Not a Luxury" and her poems "Recreation" and "From the House of Yemanjá." I knew nothing about Lorde, but from her I learned what poetry could do. How it could be both prayer and divination. I copied her poems in my notebook, and spoke them aloud, soon from memory:

> My mother had two faces and a frying pot
> where she cooked up her daughters
> into girls
> before she fixed our dinner.

Later in my official English major education, I was not assigned to read Audre Lorde. When I read her again, it was on my own. I read *The Cancer Journals*, a collection of diaries and essays she wrote throughout her long struggle with cancer. It was uncanny to read as her experiences so mirrored my own mother's. Through women writers like Lorde and Kathy Acker, who died of breast cancer at age fifty, I became aware that my mother's illness and death was not extraordinary, she was among a cadre of women. As Lorde wrote,

> Breast cancer and mastectomy are not unique experiences, but ones shared by thousands of American women.

I was not assigned to read Adrienne Rich's poetry again, except for one class at Barnard, a junior seminar on critical writing. *The Norton Anthology* assigned for that class contained the work of two women poets: Marianne Moore ("Poetry") and Adrienne Rich ("Aunt Jennifer's Tigers"). "Aunt Jennifer's Tigers" was one of Rich's most traditional early poems—one she would later claim as marked by her desire to be an obedient girl, to write in a way that men would respect. I recall only that there was nothing exciting about that poem by Rich, it was so dull and repressed compared to the electric free verse of *Diving into the Wreck*. Despite the many thrills of my official education, I was reminded over and over again that to be a real artist, a real intellectual, meant a lifelong autodidactism, the drive to follow your passion as a reader and a writer. Of course, I was lucky to have the liberal arts education I had, if only as a surface against which I could shape and sharpen my own intellect and artistry.

My English major was generally speaking a canon of male writers. Milton and Faulkner and Shakespeare and T. S. Eliot and Spenser. Petrarch and Montaigne and Pascal. Keats and Yeats and Auden. Machiavelli and Marlowe. I wanted a real education, and this was how I would get it. While I loved my classes, I was learning implicitly that Audre Lorde was less important than T. S. Eliot.

But it was Lorde who'd reached through to my bones, who remained there, even if it took me decades to understand her— *Your silence will not protect you.* The emotion in Lorde's poetry moved toward extremities, as in Plath's poetry; yet Lorde was committed to survival, to radical love, joy, and community. This was the other side of hunger, of longing, without the death drive of Plath or Anne Sexton.

Your silence will not protect you was both warning and prophecy, as it turned out. I was silent when Dr. Triel dismissed "feminist rhetoric." Silent when I was prescribed to take each new and trending drug, one after another. Silent even as I wondered—I must have wondered—if each was pushed through by a rapidly expanding and influential pharmaceutical lobby. On and off drug after drug in some attempt at an elusive cure—until a decade of my life was completely muddled by a psychopharmaceutical fog. There are entire years, events I can't recall because I was on heavy doses of antipsychotics.

Silent in my passivity, believing what I was told, that I'd never be better, that I'd be disabled in some capacity for the rest of my life. SSI disability checks, Section 8 and day programs. It was a life right there, ready for me, and if I stayed silent, that story would become my story.

> *My mother had two faces*
> *and a broken pot*
> *where she hid out a perfect daughter*
> *who was not me*
> *I am the sun and moon and forever hungry*
> *for her eyes.*

I am the sun and moon and forever hungry—I've repeated Lorde's line over and over again and shall for the rest of my life, the poem that will live inside of me, this line the *excess*—the *too much* of maternal need. The *too much* of the mother-daughter love. (Adrienne Rich: *The loss of the mother to the daughter, the daughter to the mother is the essential female tragedy.*) On the page and in my mouth, Lorde's line extends—the length reaches beyond the other lines, and in that way I felt the speaker's need reaching beyond the acceptable into the need of a daughter.

Reading saved me. It can sound ridiculous, embarrassing to say this—you may be accused of being grandiose, romantic, or worse. But it can be true, we all know this, and it was true for me. What if I hadn't gone to that bookstore that night, hadn't heard Adrienne Rich, hadn't read *Angry Women*—what if I hadn't read Audre Lorde? She wasn't celebrated or known in a mainstream way back then. What if I hadn't found this other world?

Lorde was also telling me something about my own need, the forever need never to be fulfilled, that this need and impossibility had a place, too. Extreme emotion, overflowing need. There was a place for it here, in poetry.

> *I bear two women upon my back*
> *one dark and rich and hidden*
> *in the ivory hungers of the other*
> *mother*
> *pale as a witch*
> *yet steady and familiar*

The mother is frightening, inaccessible, and still desired. This was how I felt for every woman in those years and, in the hospital, it was the women who held the mystery, the space of home. And so I fell in love: with Roxane, who came to see me, to care for me, and there was an erotic charge to it, and with Dr. B, the first woman doctor who saw me.

For many years, it seemed to me that my reading life was not separate from my mental illness life; these grew side by side, the one heading me into a life of literature, which is a life of reading and writing, the other heading me toward a dead end, the silence that would not protect me. My forever hungry. Of course, I did get better, in many large and small ways, and it is the reading and the writing that sustained me, gave me another life. It is my life. For a long time I didn't think I deserved it, that I wasn't good enough to make it my whole life. I thought I should be more connected to real life, not thinking about writing, writers or books all the time. But by the time I was in my late thirties or early forties, I realized how lucky I was. All this thinking about books had made me into a person, an artist. This was real life, and I'd worked so long to make it real, more real than any diagnosis had ever been.

The sun and moon and forever hungry—

To be forever hungry, this excess of desire, this wouldn't ever be held by a medical-pharmaceutical model of illness, but it would be held by a life dedicated to reading, writing, to art.

It would have to do in those years, the language living in my body, I could not yet, as Lorde wrote, transform silence into language and action. Starving myself was a manifestation of my invisible emotional starvation. Like suicide, it was a way to express the inexpressible.

Lorde offered me an example of how to tell your own story in the face of a dominant medical model story of illness and recovery. To live outside of normalcy was possible—in this way, the grief (the forever hungry) is a part of you, not an obstacle to life, but rather something that made you who you are.

Lorde's rebellious artistic spirit was present, too, in her writing of the breast cancer that eventually killed her. But long before it did, she wrote vividly of the experience of illness and medical treatment and her return to life—forever altered, bravely marked by illness, not hiding it, a battle wound. A rebellious body. This is how I want to be, this is how I want to write. I don't want to do what Dr. Triel and the college dean suggested—put it behind you, don't talk about it—or I do, but I also want to speak about what it gave me, my battle wounds, how I live with it, how I don't have to hide it, be shamed by it, despite constant insistent societal forces that would prefer that.

In Lorde's *Cancer Journals*, I heard the voice of my mother, what I wished my mother had been able to tell me about her own experience with cancer. I believe she was ashamed, that this was why she wore the prosthetic breast and the wig. My mother was a child of first-generation Irish immigrants, her parents grew up in the violence of Northern Ireland, made it to Chicago with a trauma always close to the surface. My mother came of age in the 1950s, she loved beauty pageants and the ballet, it must have been devastating for her, this specific illness that destroyed her beauty, her overvalued femininity.

If it was possible to be this honest, this bold about the body's decay—it was necessary, too. Had my mother found language? How had she met her disaster? When I finally read *The Cancer Journals*, years later, it came as revelation. Why had it taken me so long to find this book? I felt like a detective who'd been trying to solve a mystery, that is, the mystery of my mother's death. Here was Audre Lorde, the same writer who, years earlier, taught me what a poem could do. *Mother I need* could reveal something of my forever longing, the horror I couldn't articulate. What Lorde did in that poem was let me know it wasn't just me. Now, in the story of her own cancer, she would provide evidence related to my own mother's disappearance. Testimony. She would tell me the story that my mother could not tell me.

———

In Lorde's essay, "Breast Cancer: Power vs. Prosthesis," she speaks back to the establishment of the American Cancer Society whose response to breast cancer focused on the cosmetic over prevention: Why hasn't the American Cancer Society, she asks, *publicized the connections between animal fat and breast cancer for our daughters the way it has publicized the connection between cigarette smoke and lung cancer? These links between animal fat, hormone production and breast cancer are not secret,* she writes, and cites her sources. She calls out a country that doesn't value women's health, and especially doesn't value the health or survival of Black women.

At the same time, Lorde's essay affirms her post-mastectomy power, as she rewrites the narrative of lost femininity: *For me,* she declares, *my scars are an honorable reminder that I may be a casualty in the cosmic war against radiation, animal fat, air pollution, McDonald's hamburgers and Red Dye No. 2, but the fight is still going on, and I am still a part of it.*

Reading Audre Lorde, I learned to see my mother as a warrior. My mother was not brave in the way that Lorde had been; she was neither an intellectual nor an artist, she did not meet her tragedy with defiance and leadership. Most women do not. Lorde was exceptional; my mother was typical. Yet because she helped me understand my mother, Lorde helped me to forgive her. Like many children who've lost a parent, I was full of rage. Angry at my mother's failure, that she couldn't stay alive for me.

Anne Carson: *Why does tragedy exist? Because you are full of rage. Why are you full of rage? Because you are full of grief.*

If my mother could not show me how to die, then Lorde would, with her words, her example, her wisdom, she showed me how to die and how to live.

Audre Lorde rejected the prosthesis, affirming her transformation into a one-breasted woman. When I first read her description of herself as one-breasted, I returned to a long-held memory, but with new eyes. It was a memory that always seemed out of place. A memory that had come back to me often over and over again of being in my mother's room as she was getting ready for a fancy ball, a fundraiser for the hospital.

What I didn't know and what no one would tell me was that my mother had been sick for most of my life. Terminally ill. Her cancer had first appeared just after my sister was born, when I was just barely three years old. That was likely when she had her first surgery. At some point—again, no one has told me and it's too difficult to speak of these things—the cancer went into remission.

That's when I saw that my mother was one-breasted. She hadn't ever told me that so I didn't know what to make of it and when she got dressed, she put a squishy plastic thing in the space where the other breast had been. I didn't know that it was unusual, that other women had two real breasts. I didn't know there was something wrong. That this signified illness and death.

> *After a mastectomy, for many women including myself, there is a feeling of wanting to go back, of not wanting to persevere through this experience to whatever enlightenment might be at the core of it.*

Only now am I putting together the timeline. This moment in her bedroom was long before I knew she had cancer, before I knew she was going to die. Though of course I never did know that. In my memory, she was healthy. Now I know she'd had this cancer all along. She had the surgery, the mastectomy. As with Audre Lorde, it went into remission for a while. That *while* was my entire life with her. Another bit of evidence, a puzzle piece: I had never known her without a terminal illness, without the reality of death present in her, without the missing breast.

> *And it is this feeling, this nostalgia, which is encouraged by most of the post-surgical counseling for women with breast cancer. This regressive tie to the past is emphasized by the concentration upon breast cancer as a cosmetic problem, one which can be solved by a prosthetic pretense.*

Lorde writes of the Reach to Recovery program from the American Cancer Society, meant to help women after surgery. She describes the women coming to her hospital room just after the mastectomy. They were well-meaning, but insisted that she be fitted for the prosthetic. They gave her a little lamb's wool piece to put in the space of the missing breast. She refuses it. They tell her she should stay attractive for her husband. They reassure her that she could still be a beautiful woman, as if anticipating her worry. They imply this is important in a collective sense—to keep up morale. What would happen if so many women went around with one breast?

Here I stop myself from comparing my mother to Audre Lorde. I am drawn to Lorde for reasons that had nothing to do with my mother. I knew that there was something magnificent and inspiring about her that had nothing to do with where I'd come from, so beyond the world of my mother.

I thought of my mom and how attractive she looked to me that night dressed up in her gown. And I thought of her later, the weeks before her death, how there was something desperate attached to her beauty. It wasn't just the plastic thing in her left bra, it was the wig, the one she put on that Easter, determined to have one final family photograph, the six of us dressed up, my sister and I in bonnets. And how it fell apart, how she needed my dad to take her immediately up to her room, the dress and the wig meant nothing. These were superficial attempts, gestures. The pain of the cancer was too deep, obliterating prescribed femininity.

Lorde writes: *According to the American Cancer Society stats, only 50 percent of women with cancer are alive after three years. This drops to 30 if you are black, or poor, of otherwise disenfranchised.*

When I think of my mom in 1979, who didn't know Audre Lorde, I end up thinking of who she did know, her favorites: Tammy Wynette singing "Stand by Your Man" and Debby Boone singing "You Light Up My Life." Erma Bombeck.

What if she'd read what Lorde wrote after her mastectomy, what she wrote as she was dying? Am I trying to give my mom another life? Am I trying to give her another death? I want *her* to teach me how to die. In that space of silence, I return to Lorde:

> *I am talking here about the need for every woman to live a considered life. The necessity for that consideration grows and deepens as one faces directly one's own mortality and death. Self-scrutiny and an evaluation of our lives, while painful, can be rewarding and strengthen journeys toward a deeper self. For as we open ourselves more and more to the genuine conditions of our lives, women become less and less willing to tolerate those conditions unaltered, or to passively accept external and destructive controls over our lives and identities. Any short circuiting of this quest for self-definition and power must be seen as damaging, for it keeps the post-mastectomy woman in a position of perpetual and secret insufficiency, infantilized and dependent for her identity upon an external definition by appearance.*

On Recovery (I)

Near the end of my stay, I was selected to be the subject of a case conference. I would be the subject of a meeting of doctors, nurses, and students. Nearly a hundred people gathered in an auditorium. Dr. Triel interviewed me. He asked me if I thought I was better now. Was I ready to enter the world again, as a civilian? He asked me if I would date. He asked me about those I had fallen in love with on the ward. When did you start being attracted to women? he asked. Have you always been attracted to women? He asked me if I'd masturbated. This was healthy, he said. What about Roxane, your feelings for Roxane? What was I to say? I knew Roxane was there, too, on a vinyl sofa to my right. That I loved her? That I would miss her. That I did masturbate and when I came, it was always her face I saw, standing over me, penetrating me.

I sat silent, looking at the ground. I understood then that this was the end of my story, or a story they wanted. I loved women. I loved men and women. I desired men and women. This was the insight of those years, or so it was for Dr. Triel. There it is in the records: PT coming to terms with her bisexuality.

—#—

I met Tommy during a relapse hospital stay. This was 1996. The year of Charles and Diana's Royal Separation. This hospital felt populated, lively. I'd become a regular. This must have been when they put me on Nardil.

Let's try you on Nardil; Dr. B was upbeat.

A last-case scenario. I could do it but I couldn't eat cheese. Or drink wine.

You don't eat meat so that's good, they said. Other fermented foods are out.

Okay, yes, I'll take it.

For days I didn't notice Tommy, until one day, sitting at the table, he introduced himself. His last name was Heinz, like the ketchup, he said. He had a great smile, and everything was a joke. He had, as he put it, unipolar depression, and he took Parnate, another MAOI. He told me not to worry about the side effects—he ate hot dogs, a restricted food, but there was some drug you could take to reverse the effect.

One day he pulled me into his hospital room and kissed me. A nurse walked in on us. Before he was discharged, he gave me his number. We made a plan to meet. Some days later, when I was discharged, a nurse warned me: *Just remember. He is very sick.*

I took the train to visit Tommy on Long Island. This was my first time on Long Island. He picked me up and we drove back to his parents' house. I don't know what he is doing there, what his life is like. I know very little. He invited me to spend the evening, and I said yes. We watched *Clerks.* We made out. We went to his childhood bedroom and had sex. It was my first time having sex with someone since 1990, and so it was my second time ever having sex. All I remember is thinking, Okay, this is what you need to be doing from now on. I could see it clearly: This is how you get better. And still that nurse,

Just remember. He is very sick.

Soon enough I realized that I was too sick to date most people but too healthy to date the other mental patients I knew. I saw Tommy only a few times after that. Months later he called me, asked me to visit him at his new apartment on the Upper East Side. He was into investing now, he said, financial planning. He gave me his card.

I began seeing a woman I met in a day program. Eve. She was a folk singer and she made mixtapes for me. The very first song on the mixtape was Leonard Cohen's "Suzanne." She said that she often noticed me eating oranges and drinking tea and it was just like the song. She lived in a single room in a Section 8 housing building on Central Park. Often she came to the apartment where I lived with two roommates. I had never had sex with a woman before. I told her that I didn't know what to do. I can't write this without coming apart, it was like nothing I'd ever felt in my body, that love, the intensity of it, of Eve inside of me, it was a merging that annihilated all else. I wish I could reach this, any of this, of sex, of her, that time in my life, that love, which wasn't love but it was sex, and I'd never had sex before, now I knew. I can't get there with language but there is pleasure in writing it, trying to reach it, that place.

In place of it, I'll return to Clarissa Dalloway's orgasm, which I now understood:

Only for a moment; but it was enough. It was a sudden
revelation, a tinge like a blush which one tried to check and
then, as it spread, one yielded to its expansion, and rushed
to the farthest verge and there quivered and felt the world
come closer, swollen with some astonishing significance, some
pressure of rapture, which split its thin skin and gushed and
poured with an extraordinary alleviation over the cracks and
sores! Then, for that moment, she had seen an illumination;
a match burning in a crocus; an inner meaning almost
expressed.

I must have internalized the idea that I could sleep with women
but I should date a man. I desired men, too. Or I desired a man
who was not sick, not pathetic like me or Hank or Tommy. The
next man I fell in love with was not sick, though he found it interesting that I was sick, or had been sick. He found it interesting
and frightening. I told him half the story of where I had been. He
was the Japanese architect of Duras's *Hiroshima Mon Amour*—
with one key difference—we never had sex. Then he moved. I
started dating an actor, twenty years older than me. That might
have been the first time I actually had good sex with a man, at age
twenty-seven.

Perhaps that is how it all ended—the madnesses, all the rest.
That was what I needed. Not sex, or not always sex, but the awareness of possibility, the opening to another life. Later I understood
how unlovable I felt for so long, and how I held that in my body.
To make love was to lose the self and to give over the self was the
way to heal. The erotic as cure.

The Homelessness of Self

Many writers are mad in the way Janet Frame was mad. Outsiders. Always or necessarily outside. Shy or ill-equipped for society, easily depressed, occasionally or chronically suicidal, stuck in stories of the past, of trauma or loss or simply befuddlement—trying to be understood, writing the past over and over again, each time now an attempt to get it right, to figure it out. The writing itself becomes the way to make sense of the failure of living, the failure to be normal. Which is something you stop wanting to be, if you ever did. As César Aira put it, *I write to compensate for my inability to live.*

Janet Frame is a hero, or she is my hero. She is the exemplary ex-patient, saved from her mental patient career (then going on seven years) by the great luck of timing, and nearly destroyed by the bad luck of it, too. See her there, Janet Frame, six years a patient at the infamous Seacliff Lunatic Asylum in New Zealand. The year is 1951. She is twenty-seven years old. She has lived her adult life in psychiatric hospitals. There is a promising new treatment and so Janet Frame is scheduled for a lobotomy.

The lobotomy—a brain surgery that includes cutting into the frontal lobe to sever neural connections—was brought to the United States in the 1940s by the Portuguese doctor António

Egas Moniz, who invented the procedure and won the Nobel Prize for it. By the 1940s in the United States, it was considered an effective treatment for mental illness. Between 1949 and 1951, at least fifty thousand Americans underwent the surgery, children and adults. The news and popularity of the treatment spread to the psychiatrists in New Zealand, and the treatment was recommended for long-term mental patients like Frame.

The story, as it is told, as I heard it, couldn't be more dramatic: her debut book, a collection of short stories, wins a national award. A doctor hears about the award. He suggests that maybe she isn't so sick after all. Maybe not the lobotomy? It is not an exaggeration to say that Frame was saved by her writing—this is demonstrably true in a way it is not for most writers who make the same claim. She was reassessed and released. You are not schizophrenic, after all, the doctors told her. It was a false diagnosis, though she'd spend several years in mental hospitals. Some say it was four or five years. Others say eight years and that she was subjected to two hundred electroshock therapy treatments. Her literary executor states, *Between 1945 and 1955 she spent a total of four and a half years in several New Zealand mental hospitals.*

The canceled lobotomy wasn't the end of her mental patient career, but it was the beginning of the other life, the career that would bridge out from the other. She wasn't cured, sent away. In fact the story that is rarely told, the story that Jane Campion didn't tell in her film about the author, was the story of Frame's repeated admittance to psychiatric hospitals, often voluntarily, even after the award, and the rescinded diagnosis. She'd become used to it, or she'd realized she was mentally ill, at least a little bit. Or she couldn't quite get the knack of what was supposed to come next. This ex-patient life. In her biography, she described the lost comfort of her diagnosis, her status as mental patient, and how she would "put on my schizophrenias" when she needed care, or relief from outside demands.

It is not a clear before and after story—but then few stories of illness and recovery ever are. Regardless, Janet Frame is the success story we needed—the patron saint of writers once institutionalized, the long-institutionalized, the young women everywhere told they were hopeless, what would become of them now, defined by the places where they lived. The young women with a lot to say but no ability to translate that meaning into legible personhood. The cripplingly shy. The ones who fall in love with their doctors. The ones who don't know how to be.

She is like Allen Ginsberg in this way—the one whose early hospitalization led to a great literary career—she is the rare woman with this trajectory—the only woman. And yet she is nothing like Ginsberg, or so her writing makes clear, the enormous body of work she put out after those years in asylum—over a dozen books, novels, stories, poetry. Ginsberg's work was community, informed by the communal—he was a member of the Beat Generation, his work of collaboration spread widely. Life was never this way for Frame. She had friends, but her disability was present for the rest of her life, manifest as a difficulty being with people, being in relationships. The trauma of her siblings drowning, her grief—the grief that led to her paralysis, inability to be an adult, the grief that made her a writer, or became the power of her writing—*if I can't feel it, I can't write it*—it was this way with Janet Frame and that is the transmission reading her—how Etgar Keret described her work—*Janet Frame writes as if she wants to figure out what this world is about and what she is all about. She needs to write to survive. She is writing so that she can feel less strange to herself.*

In one obituary, Janet Frame is described as "a writer who explored madness." It's true, of course, but it is so imprecise. She explored madness because she lived in an asylum for many years. She explored madness because she had lived it, or lived near to it. But what was it? The madness of being shy. The madness of not getting over your siblings' death by drowning when you were a girl. The madness of that loss, and every loss to follow. The madness of a family, full of love, and a father's violence, too. This is what she explored. Her books are described as being about isolation and alienation. So that is another way of putting it. Madness as the untethering from connection, the too far out. The isolation of the hospital and of the self, too.

She is Lispector's dying clairvoyant, she writes into a Kristevean spiderweb. She is the weirdo writing for the weirdos, like me, the weirdos who didn't know we could write ourselves into being.

Perhaps she is most like the famed Japanese artist Yayoi Kusama, who has lived for decades in a psychiatric hospital, walking distance from her artist's studio, the only way she says she's been able to survive and thrive as an artist. The art is the only way she can express her suffering, and like Janet Frame, it is a suffering that does not go away, a daily struggle. In this way, the idea of the hero madwoman must be revised. Goffman's story of the sublime or stunted ex-patient must be transformed into a story of coping. Of living with disease. Of making art as one way to make sense of an ongoing daily struggle.

Owls Do Cry was the first novel Frame published after leaving the hospital. The novel revolves around three siblings after the death of the eldest sister. Daphne, who ends up in an asylum, is most linked to Frame herself. Daphne's madness stems from her endless return to the early trauma, how this became the thing to define her, and to stop her, to keep her from life. That moment of childhood will be the last, the end of any sense of a secure self, the sudden loss of her sister will echo throughout her life. Here madness means grief and loss and longing. A homelessness of self. The plot of the novel plays out the "what if?" of Frame's life, the near miss; at the end of the book, Daphne is lobotomized.

Responding to the death of her daughter, Daphne's mother prays, says *Have faith*, and I think of what I was told when my mother died—that she was with me, up in heaven looking over me, at peace now—these bromides became for me another violence, led me into madness, which was a desire to speak back to the emptiness of language, impossible to refute as a child.

Many of Frame's characters, as with Daphne, have extreme personality traits—extreme reactions to loss. Extreme terror over death. Extreme despair. *You think you're the only one who suffers?* No, no, not that at all. Extreme paralysis. Extreme inability to form a self around this loss, no place for it. It is not only the official mental patient in Frame's novel who experiences isolation and alienation, but Daphne's mother, too, who is haunted by her past, by the sense of always being outside. Frame taps into a universal non-belonging.

In one scene, Frame focuses on a tiny square of a red velvet tablecloth. Amy Withers, Daphne's mother, thinks about this square while recalling a moment from her youth. She was working for a magistrate, and had been given the night off, while he hosted a party. Amy walked through the town that evening but, with nowhere to go, she returned early, to the home of her employer, where she lived. Reaching the house, she could see through a small window into the party. The view was obscured, so she saw only a square of the red velvet tablecloth. That red square seemed to mark the limits of her life. That night, she cries herself to sleep with loneliness and disappointment. With non-belonging. And here it is again, one Christmas so many decades later, the small red square appears to her, and she cries herself to sleep.

When I read about Amy Withers, I think of Woolf's Clarissa Dalloway, planning her party, overcome with the knowledge that she has not been invited to a luncheon party at Lady Bruton's house. Frame admired Woolf and in many ways her characters are linked. Like Clarissa Dalloway, Amy, like Daphne, is overwhelmed by her sense of being outside—of a self, of a life. A stranger to herself. Extreme sensitivity. *She always had the feeling that it was very, very dangerous to live even one day.*

She was not meant to feel so deeply—there was no space for it in this world. Like Woolf's, Frame's genius lies in making space in literature for this depth of feeling—a sensitivity that can be a liability in daily life, and yet the power of her artistry. How seen and comforted I have felt reading these writers who wrote the interiority of characters so alive, hypervigilant, teetering on the edge of disequilibrium. Nerves on fire, able to feel both beauty and terror, dread and awe.

Jane Campion was in film school in New Zealand when she asked Janet Frame if she could make a television movie about her. It would be her first movie. Campion had just read the first in the trilogy of Frame's autobiographies. Frame put her off, said no, she wasn't done writing her autobiography, which would contain three volumes. She wanted the young Campion to go away. She didn't believe that this young woman would honor her book. Frame continued to write and then published the second and the third volumes. Campion did not go away, and eventually Frame agreed.

Campion's 1990 *An Angel at My Table* introduced Janet Frame to an international audience, and to me, too, who saw the film when I was just out of the hospital, stunned by the awareness of this life, this true story, again how my story was not unique, but also the hope of Frame's story, I think, that she had reshaped her story—that she claimed her story—that unlike the fictional nar-

rators of *The Yellow Wallpaper* or *The Bell Jar*, she had not suc-
cumbed to the narrative of the institution and instead wrote her
own stories, found her own way to tell it, from within. Frame's
story—which Campion revealed—was not about being mad, was
not dominated by the received knowledge of the mental hospital. Like Gilman's story, though, hers was a horror story, or a near
horror story—in believing the doctors, in trusting their authority, in placing her life under this authority, she had nearly been
lobotomized—she had come so near to it that she would spend
the rest of her life writing as if to ward off that barely missed fate.
She was, in many ways, as sick as Shulamith Firestone, and yet
she had been able to create with a constancy and productivity
that Firestone had not. It was thrilling to discover Janet Frame,
and when I saw Campion's movie, in the 1990s, Frame was still
alive, somewhere in New Zealand, still writing books. Her books
tell the story of madness as variable and complicated, nothing simple about it, and it is never far from what it means to be
human. That is, alone, afraid, and other. Or as King Lear puts it—
unaccommodated. Shakespeare's linking of the human condition
with homelessness—man as little more than a *poor, bare, fork'd
animal*.

What we call mental illness is so rarely portrayed with any depth
or complexity; on the contrary, every day I encounter an offensive
media representation. What makes Jane Campion's film so brilliant is the refusal to reduce Frame's story.

A haunting scene from Campion's film: A young woman stands
at the chalkboard. She has just left home. It is her first year
away from the familiarity of family. Two sisters dead now, both
drowned. Her father's rage at her brother, who is ill, epileptic, who

would never really have his own life. Only three surviving siblings and now the youngest has left to be married. Janet feels every loss, one the echo of another, a blinding rearview mirror; she is looking for what was once otherwise, and it doesn't exist, of course. This is life now. She has become a teacher. She must put her terror, her fragility, aside. She will stand in front of these rows of children, dressed up in their tidy uniforms. Sitting at desks. Looking at her. Today a senior teacher arrives to observe. A class visit. She stands at the chalkboard, and turns to write her lesson.

Kerry Fox played Janet Frame in *An Angel at My Table*, a performance subtle and wholly embodied—her glance to the children and the man in glasses, sitting at a desk now. She sees them and something—*barely perceptible*—shifts. She's frozen. She holds the chalk, makes a mark or two. Her face flushes and now she is mute, paralyzed. She will cry but not here. She drops the chalk, runs out of the classroom and out of the school, into the woods, the forest. She cannot go back, she will never go back. We have a sense that she is running in order to save herself. Through Kerry Fox, we see and feel Frame's vulnerability. The awkwardness of her dress. The gauziness. Her face flooded with blood, like mine, women like me—Irish, red-haired, we bleed more, or so a midwife commented to me as I was giving birth. *You wonder how we survived at all*, she laughs.

There are so few films about writers that come near to animating what it is to be that artist who created that body of work. The reason is obvious—we become viewers, we see the artist as object: This is Nicole Kidman playing Virginia Woolf; Jane March as Marguerite Duras; Gwyneth Paltrow as Sylvia Plath. We see actress-as-writer and we lose the voice on the page. We lose the experience a reader has with a book, the intimate transmission. Most of these attempts are failures and end up revealing the truth that what brings a writer to life is the medium of her art. Which is why *An Angel at My Table* is remarkable. Rather than a spectacle, the film is a translation of Frame's autobiography, in conversation with Frame's work, a complementary revelation.

Through Fox, I feel Janet's shame, fear, humiliation. The film is an immersion and each time I watch I am there with Janet, in her childhood, I feel the horror of her sisters' death, the way it leads to more losses, her inability to live a normal life, her fall into madness, into an institution, the "putting on of" her schizophrenias, as a way to receive care. How this led her to the non-space of the asylum, the beginning of her mental patient career. Whatever got you there might be minor compared to what will keep you there. Like mine, Frame's suicide attempt was half-hearted. Before long, that didn't matter. The logic of the institution took over. Describing these years in her autobiography, Frame wrote, *I behaved as others around me behaved. I who had learned the language, spoke and acted that language. I felt utterly alone. There was no one to talk to. As in other mental hospitals, you were locked up, you did as you were told or else, and that was that.*

It wasn't just the experience of institutionalization, it was the way that experience extended into our lives long after we were discharged: *My burning sense of loss and grief, my aloneness, and now, with another sister, June, soon to be lost in a marriage, I felt as if there were no place on earth for me. I wanted to leave Sunnyside, but where could I go? I grieved for everything lost—my career as a teacher, my past, my home, where I knew I could never stay more than a few weeks, my sisters, my friends, my teeth, that is, myself as a person.*

No one else has described for me so precisely and honestly what it was to be a mental patient. That awareness that you have entered another zone of what it is to be human, that you will be permanently considered other. The impossibility of truly connecting, of meaningful relationships. And the knowledge that there is nowhere else you could be. The sense of doom. To feel the limits of your life through this place, where it is another autumn Sunday, and the doctors have gone home, and you are here with nothing to do. The doctors you now love and need, as Frame did, have other lives, and no one would want your life. To know there may not be a way out. After her discharge, Frame was free and yet she was never free, it was too late to be free, Goffman's moral career is a forever career. You are a mental patient once and if it's long enough, if it takes, it's hard to shake. I must *put on my schizophrenias* when I like—she wrote. She was good at it now, accustomed to the role. It provided something. As my brother said at some point, when it had all gone on too long: *Suzy likes being in a hospital.* For Frame, there was good reason to put it on. What does an artist want but to run away, to find an alternative way to live? If not madness, because no, that wouldn't have worked, she was after all about to be lobotomized, it was something else. The thirdspace. The hope of that, the reach toward something else. In the final volume of her autobiographies, Frame called this thirdspace Mirror City. This was her entrance into the world of literature. This was her true home, her true diagnosis—*a writer*—and there she would live.

Towards Another Summer was Frame's last novel, published posthumously in 2007; she felt it was too personal to be published in her lifetime. The concerns of the book are familiar from her earlier work—this sense of being far out. Far away. The aura of self-protection she'd cultivated in asylum—a refuge that has now become a trap. Frame's narrator is a migratory bird, never quite here, never at home, a permanent alienation.

The novel is based on a weekend Frame spent as a houseguest at the home of a New Zealand couple, also living in England. Frame called it her most autobiographical book; it is among the most vivid descriptions of loneliness I've ever read. The book considers the awkwardness of that familiar position—the houseguest. The narrator is so utterly unable to live in a world of social convention; she struggles to live in the present tense. Every encounter or conversation or moment returns her to a moment from her past. Her hosts are kind and generous, but she is a "migratory bird" who will never be comfortable. The couple will say this or that and she will find herself pulled swiftly back into her own childhood, a moment with her mother or father or sister. What is felt most deeply is her long early life as a mental patient, and her many years as a writer, one who spends a lot of time alone. Because she is so sensitive, every conversation feels dangerous, high stakes. Her failure to connect is heartbreaking, a daily failure, rendering her more deeply and completely apart. Here, as elsewhere in Frame's work, madness is the inability to use language, a distrust of it, a constant awareness of the gaps in meaning and intent.

What I love about the book, which I read some years after her death, was the honesty of it. However successful and accomplished she was as a writer at this point in her life, she was still ill at ease, she did not fit. She lived as if she'd accommodated to this life, but in her work she revealed her true unaccommodated self, she was as we all are, a *poor, bare, fork'd animal.*

The Carceral

Only in retrospect might I say I loved it there. I didn't love it. It became familiar. I got used to it. I became dependent upon it. This is not love. But you can get used to many circumstances, no matter how awful they seem from outside: used to the comings and goings of doctors and the nurses; the rhythm of the days; the way at night after sunset, after the doctors and the day shift left, after the dinner trays were collected—dinner was at 5:00 p.m., so all was cleared by 6:00 or 6:30—the way it all moved, was structured, something to count on. And then the huge gap of time between dinner and bedtime. Those long summer months.

But then love is not the right word, and I'm suspicious of nostalgia. Can you love a life in a carceral space, a space of surveillance? It was only in the past ten years that I began to hear this language. I did not have that language back then. You can become used to care and attention. You can get used to anything, I suppose, that is what I am trying to say. I got used to it.

Q&A

(Unanswerable Questions: Did it help you in any way? If you had not been hospitalized, do you think you would be where you are now? In a society where you can't rest, or where no one is supposed to rest, or where rest is undervalued, considered laziness, where productivity is the measure of success—wasn't it a gift to be able to rest? And were you chosen then to be healed or helped or cared for because you had promise, and so wasn't it unfair, when so many others were not chosen, will never be chosen? Those of us chosen were chosen because we already had something, because the doctors—Triel and Prince and Blossom and Tomlinson—could identify with us on some level; they could talk to us, to me, about Thomas Merton and W. H. Auden and about *reading Proust in the original French*—and I could understand, and so then it wasn't really so simple, was it, that I got help, care, that I got to rest?

So, yes.)

Skepticism and Affirmation

My return to campus that semester felt uncanny: I was a foreigner, impostor, a fraud soon enough revealed. At the same time, I judged my classmates as fraudulent—carrying on lives, or so I told myself, with ease and disregard for my asylum compatriots. There was no way for me to tell my college classmates of my other life, my experiences in asylum; though it is not fair to assume they would have judged or ridiculed me, had they known; many of them would, to be sure, but some would not. Regardless, it was impossible for me to share these facts of my life.

My days spent traveling into the sanctioned, so-called real world (of the subway, on campus) and then out again (toward asylum) inspired various cyclical mind states. I felt relief from the absurdity and grotesquerie of the ward; riding the subway downtown, being on campus again provided the distance with which I could convince myself of temporal stability; the belief that I might become as functional as the women around me; awareness that I was not as bad off as these others. I'd feel relieved to be away from certain sights: the particularities of one patient's arrival, another's deterioration. How pathetic and intolerable it all became: the contained, complete asylum world—from the vantage of my college. I might remark to myself on this awareness and still wait for the moment, invariably arriving, of the reminder that I did not belong on a college campus.

I *needed to be institutionalized.* I *was not safe.*

And so the return became a relief and respite. I recall preparing myself, as I neared the door to the institute, before walking up the stairs that led into the building. The impulse to not return—to elope—occasionally came over me, yet remained a passing urge. A way to remind myself of a lost autonomy. The urge was disingenuous. However humiliated I was by the situation, it was also true that I had, early on, lost my ability to imagine *not* being there. It seems simple now to classify it as feeling or thought or mood—but to say otherwise would be to diminish its power. That, linked to a belief or understanding of myself, gave this feeling power beyond what is commonly ascribed to feeling. It was a willingness, too, to hold on to the moment of suffering, to believe there was something vital there, something necessary: I would devote my life to understanding it.

In the morning of a class day, I'd meet one of the day nurses at the station, passing other patients on my way, pajamas and cigarettes marking status. Some days, I got up early to ride the stationary bike in the television room, looking to the Hudson River. I was reframing and reigniting the program, in preparation for exit. The nurse would dispense my morning medication and include various prescriptions in a plastic cup intended to be used for urine specimens, I zipped it into a pocket of my backpack: Klonopin or Mellaril or Ativan PRN. Drugs as transitional objects.

With my official temporary release pass, I was allowed on the elevator. I'd switched out my hospital gown for ripped jeans and Doc Martens; my hair fell in my face, marked by pimples and redness. In the elevator, I might meet another doctor or resident on his way to see patients on other floors: the schizophrenics on four, the eating disordered on six, the adolescents on three, the

ECT patients on seven. When the doors closed, I became a peer, within proximity of a person who, in our only other known contexts, would have institutional authority over me. I walked out onto 168th Street and became part of the bustle and mess of helping professionals, patients, families, students, and vagrants. I was young. To be aware so precisely of my youth was painful.

At the same time, that I would one day be as old as any of the doctors or nurses I met each day did not seem real; if you had asked me, I'd have said I wouldn't live to see those years.

But the more difficult truth, I think now, was that I *would* live to see these years, with all the necessary cruel loss to mark time's passing.

The other difficult truth I might not have acknowledged back then was that I still sought a life situated somewhere between campus and the hospital, each of which, in some very real sense, offered an alternative, resistant narrative to those imposed by the rest of the world—my family, my church, my Catholic education.

On campus, we nurtured what our college president called our intellectual identity, something I had never before been asked to value; in hospital, we nurtured the identity of illness: the part of me that wished to die, that knew this world was impossible, that felt unable to live.

That this was not true did not matter; what mattered was that there was a figurehead there, the imprimatur of medical authority, to inscribe our death wish into something real.

Campus and asylum, and the distance between the two; this was my third option. This was where I hoped to find a space of true asylum, both within and beyond the so-called real world.

The closest I came to knowing the depth of this feeling again occurred years later, in the time just after a terrible breakup. I found myself dialing the number of a suicide hotline. *I need someone to tell me that I must continue to live,* I said into the receiver. I don't remember what the voice said in reply; I know that next I hung up and, some minutes later, a police officer rang my doorbell. After some discussion, I convinced the officer that I didn't need help, that I wouldn't harm myself. I wore a blue nightshirt. I needed to hear someone's voice on the other end of the phone line (I didn't say). Someone who cared, or performed care; it didn't matter which.

These moments of remaining alone in my apartment, of not going to asylum, were minor victories, even if the thought of keeping myself alive was worse than the thought of death.

My return to the ward marked the shift from a free person, a college student, into a very ill, sick inpatient.

On campus, I learned that madness persists as a dominant theme throughout literature because there is truth in annihilation. We need the voice of madness to remind us of all that is unexpressed in polite society, or even among friends. As Susan Sontag wrote of Simone Weil—*we need her voice of unreason.* There is truth in insanity, and while no parent would wish for her child to be Weil, she was a truth teller. Sanity, to Sontag, could be compromise, a lie.

After all the years, the truth is that there was nothing practically liberating about my madness—even if it did, at times, bring me closer to a sense of truth, to personal authenticity. There is no such thing as stopping time. And it only goes in one direction.

While I was in the hospital, Susanna Kaysen's memoir *Girl, Interrupted* was published, an account of her 1967 eighteen-month-long stay in McLean Hospital in Belmont, Massachusetts. It was an instant bestseller. It also became a joke, one more in a canon of white women mental illness memoirs, like *Prozac Nation*, all of which could be read as attempts to add status to melancholy.

Dr. Triel had "heard about" Kaysen's book, he said, dismissing it. *His* patients didn't need to write a book like that, he said. *My patients are so successful they'd moved on to do real work*—now that they've recovered—*and thanks to me*, was always the implication.

In one of our biweekly meetings, Dean Silverman, too, dismissed Kaysen's memoir. I read it in a few hours, she said, a gesture with her hand, a shrug.

The brevity more evidence of insignificance.

Serious women wouldn't bother writing about their lives, about the past. A real writer—a real *Barnard student*—would move on, look to the future.

Dean Silverman intimidated me, and yet she, like Roxane, was the most forthright anyone had been with me. She was not interested in my so-called illness. That was for the doctors to work out; it was their game. She wouldn't discuss it directly, but she did say to me, They are holding you back in there. You do realize that? This is *changing the course of your life*.

Goffman: The institution is *the forcing house for changing persons— a natural experiment on what can be done to the self.*

Like *Prozac Nation*, *Girl, Interrupted* fit somewhere between *The Bell Jar* and *Airless Spaces*. But somehow Kaysen's and Wurtzel's stories were not tragic in the way that *The Bell Jar* and *Airless Spaces* were, because Kaysen was alive and well, as far as we knew.

Kaysen has said more than once that a memoir is a construction, full of delusions and omissions. Memory is a fiction. She leaves so much out in her memoir, and this adds to the lasting power of the book. She doesn't say anything about how it was to leave, to return to real life. What that transition was for her. I once heard Kaysen read from the memoir at a bookstore event. Someone in the audience asked her about leaving, and what it was like afterward, and she said, *Well, it was very difficult. That's why I didn't write about it.*

The social worker set me up to receive Social Security disability checks, explaining this was protocol for anyone institutionalized that long. This confirmed my altered status in the world, how far I had fallen. However small, and aside from the fact that my dad paid my college tuition, these exit payments stated that I was disabled, that it didn't end after I left. That I was a mental patient. This, too, a self-fulfilling prophecy, one more thing that helped me and hurt me, that supported my belief, lasting many years, still arising from time to time, that I was stuck in the story of my loss, my despair, my utter incompetence.

For years, I lived in and out of the hospital on this thin line. I moved back and forth to either side. The closer I got to thirty, the more Dr. Triel's words haunted me. What if I was still a fuckup at thirty? What then? What was supposed to happen, even if I was alive? Would I always be this way? What if I hadn't or could no longer balance myself on the correct side of that line. The *going sane* side of things. What then?

Even if you do make it there alive, nothing stops when you turn thirty, there is no magic, and for years I was awash in it, the fear and overwhelm. Dr. Triel also alluded to the fact that women mental patients were less likely to marry. I didn't necessarily want to get married, I could hardly imagine it, though many I knew from childhood, my sisters and high school friends, were thinking about it. It was a marker of some success, some idea that you can fit in, move on with normal life. I had internalized this midwestern idea of normality, and yet I saw the mistake of it. I needed to imagine another life.

On Recovery (II)

So after I decided I would not kill myself and, just as importantly, would not try to kill myself and so not be a career patient, I began observing people I knew well or not well at all, in an attempt to figure out how to live.

For example, I had for many years been opposed to coffee. This was part of my purification routine.

One day, not long after I was out, I called Dr. B. I was lying in bed in the fifth-floor walkup I shared with a singer-songwriter named Linda, who had a day job as a software engineer at Linux. I would stay in my loft bed until I heard Linda leave. And then I would get up, walk down the hall, use the bathroom, and return to our apartment. Some days, I would step up into the shower in the kitchen, and then get dressed. I had a job as a temp.

But on this day, I went back to bed. I knew I wouldn't be able to leave the apartment.

This morning I was crying. It would begin as a kind of relief and then grow into something all its own.

Dr. B was calm, but concerned. This was not the first time. I'd been out of the hospital a few months. She wanted me to attend a day program, as it was called, and that seemed a fate worse than death.

She reminded me that I usually felt better once I got to work.

It was true.

She had to go, she became impatient. Will you just go get a cup of coffee, Suzy?

I don't drink coffee.

Do you know I can't get out of bed without coffee?

I imagine it now from her perspective, a mom with young kids, with babies, or pregnant, a demanding job, a new fellowship, a commute, all of it—listening to this twenty-five-year-old baby whining from her bed about a stupid little temp job, which was all she had to do in life. And take a class. One or two classes. This was her drama. I'd be impatient, too.

You know, she said, calmer now, I just read about a new study in *The New York Times*, a study out of Harvard, a study of nurses.

Pause.

Well, they followed nurses who drank coffee and those who didn't drink coffee, and the nurses who drank coffee were less likely to kill themselves than the nurses who didn't drink coffee.

Pause.

Well, it's more complicated than that. But you get the idea? You're not the only one who has trouble getting out of bed.

So that was when I started drinking coffee. The first Starbucks had opened in Manhattan a year or two earlier. Dr. B was a fan.

Go get a latte! I have to go now.

I could hear the noises of traffic around her, before she hung up. She was the first person I knew to have a car phone.

Another person I observed, on and off, mostly from a distance, was my old friend Leo. After all, he had been as suicidal as I had, but somehow I had ended up in a mental hospital for years, while he hadn't. Instead, he'd moved to Berlin for a while. Now he was back in New York, in analysis. He had a Lacanian analyst, and would tell me of their sadomasochist relationship.

It took me a long time to realize that though Leo spoke of suicide regularly, and still does, that he wants to drop dead, or kill me now, etc., it was a very different experience of it, of the idea or depression than it was for me. Since 1996, I have never once said, *Kill me now.* Or, *I want to drop dead.* I've had to be deliberate about it; for a while I would just repress the feeling, not put it into language, but over time it became true. And when my baby was born, I knew I would never ever kill myself, which would be the very same thing as killing him. Even to imagine it became impossible.

I do not want to say that having a baby healed me, because that seems retrograde and embarrassing and obviously is not the case for many women, but it did show me another way to be alive. To become like Dr. B. Too busy to fall into despair, and at the same time, more aware of life's brevity.

I know the true philosophical question, Camus's question, my once-husband's question, which he put in a poem—"the true test is how to get through life without killing yourself blah blah blah"—a line that surprised me when I first read it in his poem, since he was far better at getting through life than I had ever been—I understand that. But the question becomes less interesting the older you get, the closer you get to dying anyway, so what's the rush? You'll be dead soon enough.

Plus, I love many people and most of all my son and I can't really imagine saying goodbye to him, even when he no longer needs me. I know it has to happen, and will happen, but it is the saddest thing in the world.

My once-husband had ways of talking about things that helped me, back when we were first dating. *You can do anything for twelve weeks,* he would say, when I became terrified of teaching—or the little ways he would coach me into faking self-confidence, and then the way his Chilean family enjoyed life, the long meals, the wine and cheese, the walks together, the regular phone calls just to say hi. I was not good at any of that, but I admired it, again, saw this as another way to live.

I would observe my friends, acquaintances. Strangers. One day I read an interview with Meryl Streep, who said she would prefer to do nothing if she could. That moved me. Even this person with the best life imaginable, the most fame and fortune, would prefer to do nothing. To stay in bed.

Mostly I read, always looking for lessons. I read a biography of Clare Boothe Luce, who said she never left the house without putting on lipstick. I tried that, and it helped. I'd shunned makeup altogether, all through my years in college and after, it was toxic, impure, and unfeminist, I'd decided. But I began to see that it could help.

I signed up for an acting class. There were many women there worth observing. Some like me had day jobs. But there were others, such as an actress who had been in *Cats* for nine years. A famous model who was taking the class so that she could be in a movie. I was assigned to do a scene with the famous model.

One day on my way to class, I called Dr. B from a phone booth in Times Square. I was aware of the theatrics of my situation. And yet. I was unhappy, as a Chekhovian character might declare. More than anything, I needed Dr. B to know how much I suffered. I had made it out of the house, I had my Starbucks, but I was not well. I needed her to know this.

This must have been part of my illness, I think now. Why did I refuse to let her know any single positive thing, why did I have to exaggerate all the horrible things, or every little dark feeling? I needed her to know all of it. It was transferential, of course, she was my mother, I would not mourn, I would not let her forget about me. I needed her to *worry* about me.

What are you going to do? she asked me on the payphone.
    Now?
    Yes.

Well, I might walk into traffic, I said, considering it, looking around.

There was a long pause.

Or I might go to class.

Suzy. If you are going to walk into traffic you need to get in a taxi and get to the ER right now.

Pause.

Are you going to do that? she asked, calmly now.

No.

Okay.

Okay.

Have a good class.

I feel terrible.

That's fine.

I want to die.

But you won't.

The class was taught by a woman named Sande Shurin. She had her own self-published book with the rules of acting. Like every acting teacher, she fashioned herself a guru. She spoke as if she was the Dalai Lama of acting technique. That was the structure and power dynamic of every acting class I ever took. What bell hooks would identify as the toxic banking system of education—we are passive learners and here is the leader to worship on the pedestal, the sage on the stage.

bell hooks experienced this in her undergraduate classes at Stanford, but for me it was in acting class.

So that's how I met Shalom.

There were about eight of us in the class, mostly men, and three women: me, Shalom, and the woman from *Cats*. The *Cats* actress would tell us how bored she was of *Cats*, how tiring it became to do the same thing over and over eight shows a week, but also how impossible to quit, since it was such a steady job in a city where few actors had steady jobs. The *Cats* actress had a husband, which seemed strange to me at twenty-five, why or how one would have a husband. I was too focused on my therapist to have a husband.

Shalom had terrible acne and did not wear makeup. She was kind to me, her gentle voice cozying up to me in a way some women do so easily with other women. This was another way of being that interested me, it still does, a quality I admire, am drawn to. I am not made this way, this easy intimacy, perhaps that was my illness, too.

In those days we did not have ready access to the internet or Google and so it was only later, or that evening, when I talked to Leo on the phone and told him about this model in my acting class named Shalom and he screamed, OH MY GOD, YOU KNOW SHALOM? that I realized she was a supermodel, whatever. Internationally famous, huge, he explained, he had a poster on his wall of ICM models and Shalom was one of the models.

Shalom may not have been the best actress, but she was so comfortable to be a human being moving through the world. She leaned in to whisper, held my hand. You remind me so much of my best girlhood friend, she would say, which made me feel so loved I couldn't stand it.

On break, one of the men in the class asked me about Shalom. Do you know why she's here? I did not. She's going to be in a movie with some famous actors. But she doesn't know how to act. At all. Can't you tell? He laughed. Also, why is she named Shalom? he asked, but I didn't know. Is she Jewish?

The next week I did not go to class. Again, I had told my therapist that I was going to die, and was committed to a mental hospital for a week. The day after I got out, I returned to acting class. Shalom and I were scheduled to do our scene that day, from a Beth Henley play, but she, too, had been out of town. When I arrived, she was there on the sofa in the waiting room with her friend Amber. I had never seen someone as beautiful as Amber in real life. Later, Leo explained that Amber, too, was a supermodel, perhaps more famous than Shalom.

While we were going over our lines, I decided I would tell Shalom where I had been. I thought this might make us closer. I was still figuring out intimacy. But then Shalom told me that she and Amber had just come back from working in Paris.

It was so *hot* in Paris, she whined. I really *hate* Paris. You would *not believe* how hot it gets there in the summer, worse than New York.

And, she added, they are *so* old-fashioned there, they don't have air-conditioning.

That sounds awful, I said, shaking my head, sympathetic.

But then it was our turn. Shalom grabbed my hand, and together we walked into the studio.

How interesting life could be, with people like Shalom and Amber and Sande Shurin and the *Cats* actress, too. I was beginning to see it, to see out of it, that you could look elsewhere, beyond yourself you could look to the others and see yourself, too. I would never be Shalom, but in moments like these I could live in her world. And then I could go home and I could write about living in her world, seeing myself through her eyes. And I would live it again.

Over and over, the rest of my life. It was often moving to be inside of life, so full with the banal right next to the profound, but it was at least as moving, I realized now, to be a writer, to experience life again.

It was not long after this that I decided to leave New York, quit acting, and become a writer.

You Seem So Normal

Chicago. Twenty years later and I am sitting in another room, waiting for a new doctor. Now the doctors are younger than I am. This room is on the second floor of a shitty public access hospital, a behavioral health center, the catchment for people of all ages, children who are too young to be here, in another world no child would ever be here, to the poor, the homeless, the disenfranchised. I have shitty health insurance now, and I'm lucky to have it. There were years I didn't have any, years on Medicaid, years I couldn't keep a job and even then the jobs didn't come with health insurance.

You seem so normal, a poet had said to me some months earlier at a dinner party.

We were admitting our psych histories to each other, his severe bipolar disorder, he's heavily medicated and must ride his bike many miles each day. Otherwise, it's over, he said. The bike, the writing, the medication—it's how I stay out of a hospital, he explains. It's an instant connection we make, I tell him my story, my life.

There was a group of us talking and now it's just me and him.

I felt pleased when he said it—you seem so normal. Not because I am, but because he knows now that I'm like him, not normal. It is a relief, like I was hiding something and what a relief to say it. It doesn't have to be everything about me, but it is not nothing, it never was.

He stares at me, looking for the seams, and I don't mind because I've noticed his, the near melting, glossy eyes and the stiff rigidity that comes from years on antipsychotics. His halting speech, a discomfort speaking aloud, finishing a sentence, so distinct from the fluency, elegance, and electricity of his voice on the page (I have read his poems).

Though he sometimes writes about his mental illness in his poetry, the truth of it can never appear on the internet, he explains. He has a google alert set up and he will email blogs, other poets, anyone who posts his writing about his mental illness, or shares it on social media. He will ask them to take it down.

I could lose my job, he says.

(I wonder what jobs I have lost—or never got—because of my writing about mental illness—information available with a quick Google search—it feels paranoid to think so, and yet . . .)

I haven't had real mental health care since I left New York, and that was only because I was in a state hospital. Still, I know it's better this way. There are people in Manhattan who pay hundreds of dollars for forty-five-minute sessions. That is how psychiatric care looks now—the rich can afford the best doctors, the specialized care, long-term analysis—and the poor, indigent mentally ill are in and out of group clinics, hospitals, never healed, managed. Or not. Homeless, dead. This was how it was when I left the hospital, and the extremes have gotten worse. Tracing the last twenty-plus years, from my institutionalization to the end of it, it was a few years later that the state defunded the program altogether, these decades marked the end of an era, the gradual and radical diminishment of mental health funding, a governmental process that began with Reagan and continued steadily through the coming decades. It was not enough, it is never enough—but it was much better back then than it is now.

That would never be me—I couldn't afford to see Dr. B or Dr. Triel or Dr. Smith privately—and I think that's a good thing. I'm lucky I left when I did.

The largest psychiatric hospital in the United States is here in Chicago, within the Cook County Jail. The other two largest mental health centers in the United States are also in jails: L.A. County Jail, and New York City's Rikers Island. I know this because I'm meeting with a new doctor at the clinic where I get my medication. I have a ten-to-fifteen-minute conversation and leave with my prescription.

She is young, she works here two days a week, and two days in the women's section of the Cook County Jail. She is still in training.

(Not long ago, I was invited to lead a book group here in Chicago, society women, who told me that they went on a tour of the women's jail and saw the psych ward. I didn't understand. A tour? Yes, they said, and then: *We know someone, she got us in. It's a terrible thing, but worth seeing,* another woman tells me, before returning to *Americanah*, the novel under discussion. One of the women is annoyed by the depiction of rich white people. *Why should I have to feel guilty?* she complains. *I'm just reading a book, I want to enjoy it.*)

This public clinic reminds me of the halfway houses, the day programs, the supportive housing where I spent time and visited my friends from the hospital. If I'm going to be back in a room like this, I prefer that it's here in this sad waiting room full of sad people.

This young doctor is passing through. She will go elsewhere soon, to study depression in pregnancy. A new center, a new initiative at the University of Illinois Chicago.

When it is my turn, I sense the doctor's unsmiling guardedness. A professional detachment. (At the time, I was teaching Tolstoy's *The Death of Ivan Ilyich*, and so was reminded of how Ilyich, himself a detached high-court magistrate, falls ill and finds himself asking detached doctors for help. Now that he has become vulnerable to their care, or lack of care, he understands how spiritually empty his life had been. He had lived in a superficial way, social climbing. His relationships with people were transactional; the opposite of what Martin Buber called the I-Thou relationship, where two people recognize each other in all their humanity.)

Why are you here? she asks. I tell her: I had a baby, I'd managed to be off medication for a few years, the only time in my adult life, just before getting pregnant, during my pregnancy and the year of breastfeeding. And then I became pregnant again and again, three times in a row, all miscarriages.

It destabilized you.

Maybe. Here I was again, after so long, back in a room asking someone I didn't know to help me.

She looks through my chart, my medical history, now on a computer.

It says here that you were an inpatient for two years?

A bit longer than that, but yes.

Really?

Yes.

This is very unusual.

I know.

They don't keep patients in hospitals that long. It makes things worse.

Well, they did.

Is your family very wealthy? she asked.

No. It wasn't that kind of hospital. It was a state hospital.

I don't understand.

It doesn't exist anymore. This was the '90s. (You were probably in high school, I don't say.) Things were different. It was all defunded a year or two after I got out.

Wow.

She looked uncomfortable. I wasn't going to make her comfortable. But this is a response I'm used to—what happens when I tell someone my story, how they look at me, how a face turns to sadness, pity—how, like grief, the response mirrored back to me heightens my shame, or makes me feel that I need to reassure the person, No, no, it wasn't so bad! This is so often the problem with communicating our struggles, our sorrows. It is why Simone Weil's question matters—*What are you going through?* (This is also the title of Sigrid Nunez's recent novel.) How much can we ask of each other, really? How much can we hold, without shrinking?

What was it like? she asked. I was surprised how little she knew, or could imagine of it.

It was partly a research hospital. They tried things out on us.

They tried medications?

Yes. And different therapeutic approaches, strategies. Of the era, I say, leaving it at that.

(I don't say, Honestly, the hardest part was getting over it, moving on, after having been labeled, considered sick. I never felt normal again. I couldn't get it together, not for a long time.)

The doctor looked surprised and curious, I imagined she was scanning me—where was the madness, what part of me retained this, was it in my face?

She was doing her job, fitting me into something called illness, this medical history, a set of symptoms.

It's a very unusual experience, she said, looking at the computer. Yeah.

I wanted to tell her to read the books; there are books about the hospital, the floor, books written by the men who created the ward, full of data and case studies and charts about patients, indicating which factors make a given patient most likely to survive.

I didn't say any of this. We weren't getting to know each other, after all. She was doing her job and I was a curiosity.

Still, I wished she wasn't surprised. Why was this recent history such a secret, even among psychiatrists? I wish she had been assigned to read these books in medical school, to read critically—and to read Ntozake Shange or Virginia Woolf or Audre Lorde or Charlotte Perkins Gillman's *The Yellow Wallpaper.*

What is lost when the humanities are so separated from modern medicine? Back then, a psychiatry resident had to add an additional year of training in psychoanalysis. This was not part of medical residency, but it is clear that those, like Dr. Triel or Dr. Prince, with psychoanalytic training, were also the most literary and intellectual.

I may have needed it all, once, and I may have been saved by that place, but it would never offer me a way to understand my experience, as books have, as reading has.

William Carlos Williams—

It is difficult to get the news from poems yet men die miserably every day for lack of what is found there.

(You can't get a diagnosis from poetry, but I would have died if I hadn't found my way there.)

Did they think you were schizophrenic?

For a time, I think, yes.

As she said this, I thought about how my relationship to diagnosis had changed. How I once believed in what now I see as so vague and imprecise. I know that in many cases, for many people, a diagnosis can help locate and treat real experiences of pain, but there are many ways for us to find comfort in the preexisting condition of being human, which is always inexplicable, on some level. This is why we read books. This is why I needed the stories of these other women. Why I wish this doctor knew them, too.

I think we should talk about your reproductive capabilities.

What do you mean?

I think you should consult someone.

Consult?

A fertility specialist. If you want to have more children.

I'm okay if I can't have more children.

Well, if you do want to, you should see someone now.

Right.

After all, you're forty years old.

I'm not forty years old.

She nodded, condescending.

I'm thirty-seven.

Yes, and in childbearing terms, that is close enough to forty.

Well, I'm also close enough to thirty-five.

She didn't seem to find this funny. She wasn't going to laugh with a patient. My fifteen minutes was up. She prescribed two new medications and assured me that while I might have once needed such treatment—those years, she said, whatever that was—you don't now. You aren't schizophrenic, she said, as if completing her medical report, and answering a question I didn't ask. I really can't imagine why you were institutionalized for so long, she said.

Acknowledgments

Parts of this book appeared, in different forms, in *Granta* and *Make Magazine*. I am grateful to the editors: Sigrid Rausing, Luke Neima, and Jessica Anne. The idea of DurasSpace is inspired by Dodie Bellamy's conception of Sexspace in her *Academonia*. Kate Zambreno first suggested I read *Airless Spaces*. The ideas of "universal non-belonging" and the "obligation to recover" come from a talk given by Stephen Harper, as part of the Media and Mental Health Symposium at Northwestern University. My reference to the "poor, bare, fork'd animal" in *King Lear* comes from Laurie Shannon. The "loneliness that can be rocked" is from Toni Morrison's *Beloved*. Thanks to the Virginia Center for the Creative Arts, the Ragdale Foundation, and Cathy Stocker (The Snug) for essential gifts of time and space.

Endless thanks to my editor, Ellie Pritchett, who made this book so much more than it would have been, and to my agent, Sarah Levitt, who believed in this book before it was a book. I'm lucky to have these two on my side.

Special thanks to Sarah Schulman and Natasha Trethewey, for encouragement and inspiration.

This book would not be what it is without the many readers and thinkers whose notes, conversation, correspondence, and/or enthusiasms helped to shape and sharpen my ideas: Chris Lombardo, Matthew Richardson, James Hodge, Kira Tucker, Katana Smith, Ryan Nhu, Samantha English, Christopher Lane, Laura Joyce-Hubbard, Becky Payne, Surya Milner, Jackson McGrath, George Abraham, Lydia Abadeen, May Dugas, and Nicole Schnitzler. I would also like to thank Chris Abani, who helped make this work, Reg Gibbons, Shauna Seliy, Juan Martinez, Laurie Shannon, the Litowitz family, and everyone at Northwestern—especially Nathan Mead, for help with the printer and much else.

I am grateful to the women of my writing community, near and far, spiritually and truly: Amanda Goldblatt, Anne Yoder, Kate Zambreno, Amina Cain, Azareen Van der Vliet Oloomi, Danielle Dutton (and all the Dorothies), whose words and ideas I think about when I write, always my dream readers. I'm forever grateful to Danielle and Martin Riker, who believed in this story enough to publish me that first time. Thank you to my family, especially Erin, and to my friends, especially David Adjmi, Dawn Tefft, Meg Simonton, Kris Alegria, Amy O'Rourke, Shirley Reese, Dika Lam, Erin Teegarden, Kelly Dwyer, Juliet Patterson, and Sarah Saffian.

In loving memory of Quinn Mulligan (1971–2023). I wish we had more time, and another world.

Endless gratitude and love for my son, Lorenzo Borzutzky, who gave me life; and my dearest, Joe Bass. You two make it all worth it (and so much fun).

Bibliography

Acker, Kathy. *Don Quixote (which was a dream)*. New York: Grove Press, 1986.

Adler, Laure, and Victor Gallancz. *Marguerite Duras: A Life*. Chicago: University of Chicago Press, 2000.

Aviv, Rachel. *Strangers to Ourselves*. New York: Farrar, Straus & Giroux, 2022.

Bellamy, Dodie. *Academonia*. San Francisco: Krupskaya Books, 2006.

Bergman, Ingmar, director. *Fanny and Alexander*. Sweden: Sandrew Film and Teater, 1982.

Berlant, Lauren. *Cruel Optimism*. Durham, NC: Duke University Press, 2011.

Campion, Jane, director. *An Angel at My Table*. Artificial Eye, 1990.

Clark, Heather. *Red Comet: The Short Life and Blazing Art of Sylvia Plath*. New York: Knopf Doubleday Publishing Group, 2020.

Crispin, Jessa. "Made to Disorder." *The Smart Set*, Oct. 28, 2011.

Cvetkovich, Anne. *Depression: A Public Feeling*. Durham, NC: Duke University Press, 2012.

Dangarembga, Tsitsi. *Nervous Conditions*. Seattle: Seal Press, 1988.

Davidman, Lynn. *Motherloss*. Berkeley, CA: University of California Press, 2002.

Didion, Joan. "On Keeping a Notebook." *Slouching Towards Bethlehem*. New York: Farrar, Straus and Giroux, 1968.

———. *The Year of Magical Thinking*. New York: Knopf, 2005.

Duras, Marguerite, and Barbara Bray. *The Lover*. New York: Pantheon Books, 1985.

Duras, Marguerite, and Richard Seaver. *Hiroshima Mon Amour*. New York: Grove Press, 1961.

Faludi, Susan. "Death of a Revolutionary." *The New Yorker*, 2013.

Firestone, Shulamith. *Airless Spaces*. Cambridge, MA: MIT Press, 1998.

———. *The Dialectic of Sex: The Case for Feminist Revolution*. New York: Bantam Books, 1970.

Foucault, Michel. *Madness and Civilization: A History of Insanity in the Age of Reason*. New York: Random House, 1965.

Frame, Janet. *An Autobiography*. New York: George Braziller, 1990.

———. *Faces in the Water*. New York: George Braziller, 1982

———. *Owls Do Cry: A Novel*. New York: Counterpoint, 1957.

———. *Towards Another Summer*. United Kingdom: Virago, 2008.

Gilman, Charlotte Perkins. "Why I Wrote the Yellow Wallpaper." *The Forerunner*, October 1913, https://www.nlm.nih.gov /exhibition/theliteratureofprescription/education/materials /WhyIWroteYellowWall Paper.pdf.

———. *The Yellow Wallpaper, Herland, and Selected Writings*. New York: Penguin, 2009.

Goffman, Erving. *Asylums: Essays on the Condition of the Social Situation of Mental Patients and Other Inmates*. New York: Anchor Books, 1961.

Hacking, Ian. "Making Up People." *London Review of Books*, vol. 28, no. 16, 2006.

Hardwick, Elizabeth. "On Sylvia Plath." *The New York Review*, 1971.

hooks, bell. *Teaching to Transgress*. New York: Routledge/Taylor & Francis, 2014.

Ionesco, Eugène, and Horovitz, Israel. *Man with Bags: A Play*. New York: Grove Press, 1977.

Kaysen, Susanna. *Girl, Interrupted*. New York: Turtle Bay Books, 1993.

Kenyon, Jane. *Otherwise: New and Selected Poems*. St. Paul, MN: Graywolf, 1996.

King, Michael. *Wrestling with the Angel*. London: Penguin Books Limited, 2001.

Kraus, Chris. "Continuity." *Feminaissance*. Los Angeles: Les Figues Press, 2010.

Kristeva, Julia. *Black Sun: Depression and Melancholia*. New York: Columbia University Press, 1989.

Lane, Christopher. *Shyness: How Normal Behavior Became a Sickness*. New Haven, CT: Yale University Press, 2008.

Lee, Hermione. *Virginia Woolf.* New York: Vintage, 1997.

Lorde, Audre. *The Cancer Journals.* New York: Penguin Classics, 2020.

———. *The Collected Poems of Audre Lorde.* New York: Norton, 2000.

Marcus, Jane. *Art & Anger: Reading Like a Woman.* Columbus, OH: Miami University, 1988.

Millett, Kate. *The Loony Bin Trip.* Urbana and Chicago: University of Illinois Press, 1990.

Morrison, Toni. *Beloved.* New York: Vintage, 1987.

Nathan, Debbie. *Sybil Exposed: The Extraordinary Story Behind the Famous Multiple Personality Case.* New York: Free Press, 2011.

Ngai, Sianne. "Shulamith Firestone's Airless Spaces." *Berfrois,* 2012.

O'Connor, Sinéad. "Famine." *Universal Mother,* Chrysalis, 1995.

Phillips, Adam. *Going Sane.* New York: HarperCollins, 2009.

———. *On Kissing, Tickling, and Being Bored: Psychoanalytic Essays on the Unexamined Life.* Cambridge, MA: Harvard University Press, 1994.

———. *Terrors and Experts.* Cambridge, MA: Harvard University Press, 1997.

Plath, Sylvia. *The Bell Jar.* New York: HarperPerennial Modern Classics. 1971.

———. *The Unabridged Journals.* New York: Anchor Books, 2000.

Russ, Joanna. *How to Suppress Women's Writing.* Austin, TX: University of Texas Press, 1983.

Saadawi, Nawal El. *Woman at Point Zero.* London: Zed Books, 1983.

Schulman, Sarah. *Gentrification of the Mind: Witness to a Lost Imagination.* Berkeley, CA: University of California Press, 2013.

Shange, Ntozake. *for colored girls who have considered suicide/when the rainbow is enuf.* New York: Scribner, 1975.

Sontag, Susan. "Simone Weil." *New York Review of Books,* 1963.

Stone, Elizabeth. "Off the Couch." *The New York Times,* Dec. 6, 1992.

Stone, Michael. *The Fate of Borderline Patients.* New York: Guilford Publications, 1990.

Tortorici, Dayna, and Stryker, Beth, co-editors. Shulamith Firestone Memorial Pamphlet, 2012.

Vale, V. *Angry Women.* San Francisco: RE/Search Publications, 1991.

Woolf, Virginia. *Mrs. Dalloway.* New York: Harcourt Brace Jovanovich, 1925.

———. *A Room of One's Own.* New York: Harcourt Brace Jovanovich, 1929.

———. *The Waves.* New York: Harcourt Brace Jovanovich, 1931.

If you or someone you know is
in crisis and needs help:

Suicide and Crisis Lifeline: 988

National Suicide Prevention Lifeline:
800-273-8255